What Survives?

A NEW
CONSCIOUSNESS
READER

This *New Consciousness Reader*
is part of a new series of original
and classic writing by renowned experts on
leading-edge concepts in personal development,
psychology, spiritual growth, and healing.

Other books in this series include:

Dreamtime and Dreamwork
EDITED BY STANLEY KRIPPNER, PH.D.

Healers on Healing
EDITED BY RICHARD CARLSON, PH.D., AND BENJAMIN SHIELD

Reclaiming the Inner Child
EDITED BY JEREMIAH ABRAMS

Spiritual Emergency
EDITED BY STANISLAV GROF, M.D., AND CHRISTINA GROF

To Be a Woman
EDITED BY CONNIE ZWEIG

What Survives?

*Contemporary Explorations
of Life after Death*

EDITED BY
GARY DOORE, PH.D.

JEREMY P. TARCHER, INC.
Los Angeles

Library of Congress Cataloging-in-Publication Data

What survives? : contemporary explorations of life after death / edited by
Gary Doore.
    p.   cm.
    Includes bibliographical references.
    ISBN 0-87477-583-3
    1. Future life.   2. Death   3. Materialism.   I. Doore, Gary.
    BL535.W46   1990   90-35084
    129—dc20   CIP

The author wishes to acknowledge the following: Poem by Kabir in the
article by Kenneth Ring is from *The Kabir Book* by Robert Bly, copyright
1971, 1977 by Robert Bly. Reprinted by permission of Beacon Press. "Can
Our Memories Survive the Death of Our Brains?" by Rupert Sheldrake is
reprinted from *Consciousness and Survival: An Interdisciplinary Inquiry into
the Possibility of Life beyond Biological Death,* edited by John S. Spong
(Sausalito, Calif.: Institute of Noetic Sciences, 1987). Reprinted by
permission of the Institute of Noetic Sciences.

Jeremy P. Tarcher, Inc.
5858 Wilshire Blvd., Suite 200
Los Angeles, CA 90036

Distributed by St. Martin's Press, New York

Manufactured in the United States of America
10 9 8 7 6 5 4 3 2 1

First Edition

Contents

Acknowledgments

I would like to thank the many people and organizations, too numerous to name individually, who helped in the preparation of this book. Special thanks go to the contributors for their insights and willingness to participate; to the Institute of Noetic Sciences for permission to reprint "Can Our Memories Survive the Death of Our Brains?" by Rupert Sheldrake; to Patricia Jones of the Center for Advanced Technology in Education at the University of Oregon in Eugene for technical assistance; to Bob Plantz for practical advice and encouragement; and to Jeremy Tarcher, Connie Zweig, Dianne Woo, and Paul Murphy at Jeremy P. Tarcher, Inc., for making it possible to bring the information in this book to those seeking more light on the shadowy topic of death and beyond.

Introduction

What is it like to die? One woman describes the experience in this way:

> Lying in the hospital bed, I began to have a very severe pain in my chest. I pushed the button beside the bed to call for the nurses, and they came in and started working on me. I was quite uncomfortable lying on my back so I turned over, and as I did I quit breathing and my heart stopped beating. Just then, I heard the nurses shout, "Code pink! Code pink!" As they were saying this, I could feel myself moving out of my body and sliding down between the mattress and the rail on the side of the bed—actually it seemed as if I went *through* the rail—on down to the floor. Then, I started rising upward, slowly. On my way up, I saw more nurses come running into the room—there must have been a dozen of them. . . . I drifted on up past the light fixture—I saw it from the side and very distinctly—and then I stopped, floating right below the ceiling, looking down. I felt almost as though I were a piece of paper that someone had blown up to the ceiling.[1]

Others who have undergone similar near-death experiences (NDEs) report even more bizarre phenomona, including the sensation of passing down a long, dark tunnel and encountering a brilliant light or a "being of light" at the end of the tunnel, or of emerging into another world inhabited by the spirits of deceased relatives and friends.

Do such experiences tell us anything about the fate of human consciousness after death? Or are they nothing but hallucinations induced in the dying brain by the trauma of physical death—mere figments of the imagination indicating nothing about a possible afterlife?

From long before the dawn of recorded history, humankind has been fascinated by the question, What survives the death of the body? And during the ages, virtually every possible answer has been proposed. Generally, these answers fall into two broad categories: First there is *dualism*, which says that the "soul," or spiritual aspect of a person, which is distinct from and independent of the body, survives after the death of the merely physical aspects of our being; second, there is *materialism*, which says in effect that *nothing* survives after death because consciousness is merely a by-product of the physical brain and is therefore incapable of surviving the demise of that organ.

Historically, dualism seems to have been the first answer to appear. Thus, in virtually all tribal societies that still adhere to shamanism—a magico-religious healing and divination system dating back at least thirty thousand years[2]—the belief in a "land of the dead" inhabited by the spirits of deceased persons is ubiquitous. Traditionally, the shaman, or "master of death," was a person who had explored this spiritual realm while making shamanic "journeys," or excursions into altered states of consciousness, and was therefore qualified to act as a psychopomp, a conductor of the souls of the deceased to their suitable resting places in the afterworld. Another function of the shaman was to visit the spirit world in order to rescue, or bring back, the souls of critically ill people who had gotten "lost" there before it was their natural time to die. Obviously, this kind of shamanic activity and belief presupposes that the soul or spirit of a person is something quite capable of existing independently of the physical body.

In the West, the belief that the human soul is independent of the body and goes to another existence after death is found in various forms and guises, usually associated with a religion, from Greek Platonism and Neoplatonism to the later teachings of Christianity, Judaism, and Islam. In the East, the same belief is found in the Hindu and Buddhist doctrines of reincarnation, which presuppose that consciousness can transmigrate from one body to another. True, the Buddha denied that human beings have a permanent soul; but virtually all Buddhists believe that the human ego, in the form of a *relatively permanent* collection of conscious states, takes rebirth again and again until final liberation, or enlightenment, is realized.

Opposing this "survivalistic" strand of thought in both the East and West is the school of materialism, which denies that consciousness can survive bodily death. From the time of the Greek atomism of Democritus and Lucretius to today's scientific materialists, it has seemed self-evident to the members of this school that a person's death represents his or her absolute and final annihilation and that all beliefs to the contrary are simply evidence of wishful thinking, self-delusion, or gross superstition.

For most of recorded history, the materialists have been in the minority while the vast majority of people believed that human beings have a soul that survives after death. With the spectacular rise of modern Western science from around the sixteenth century, however, the materialistic worldview has gradually gained ascendancy, until today it commands enormous influence, primarily through the power and success of the technology it has made possible. Thus scientific materialism and materialistic explanations of conscious processes, near-death experiences, out-of-body phenomena, and other alleged evidence for survival after death offer a serious challenge to anyone who believes that physical death does not represent the final annihilation of human consciousness.

Nonetheless, the heyday of materialism seems to be waning. During the 1950s and 1960s, virtually all reputable scientists and philosophers subscribed to a strictly materialistic worldview. To profess a serious belief in the possibility of survival after death was, in effect, a form of heresy, a straying from the official dogma, and automatically relegated one to the status of crank—or, worse yet, made one subject to blacklisting as "unscientific" or "irrational." In the last decade, however, new evidence and developments from parapsychology, near-death studies, and consciousness research, as well as recent developments in "new paradigm" biology and physics, have made the flaws in the materialistic worldview more evident and have strengthened the case for the hypothesis that human consciousness does indeed survive death.

In this book, we will examine some of these new developments as seen through the eyes of various scholars and researchers. In Part One, "The Evidence for Survival," we will look at recent data that seems to support the hypothesis of survival, including information from modern consciousness research, parapsychology, and near-death studies. In Part Two, "The Challenge of Materialism," we will explore the implications of the evidence for materialism and see whether the materialist's denial of the possibility of survival holds up. To put the question of survival in a broader perspective, we will investigate in Part Three, "Death and Beyond in the Perennial Philosophy," the teachings of the world's great mystical traditions, finding further evidence that supports a survivalistic worldview and corroborates some of the modern evidence examined in Part One. And in Part Four, "The Transcendence of Death," we will see how one's attitude toward death and a life beyond death can influence the quality of one's present life and one's relationships to other people and the world. With the exception of Rupert Sheldrake's contribution, "Can Our Memories Survive the Death of Our Brains?", all the articles here have never before been published and represent the latest thinking of their authors.

Obviously, the jury is still out on the question of survival—and probably will be for a long time, judging by history. Yet the fate of our soul after death—or, indeed, whether we even have a soul—is a topic worthy of serious reflection, because what we believe about death and beyond can have an enormous impact on how we live in the here and now. To put it succinctly: If the pessimist is less happy than the optimist, it behooves us to find evidence for optimism, if it indeed exists. Accordingly, I hope the material presented here will help the reader arrive at a more optimistic, yet at the same time a more informed and rational, answer to the question, What survives?

PART ONE

The Evidence for Survival

Most people assume that belief in an afterlife is strictly a matter of faith. A few may have heard of scientific investigations of reported contacts with deceased persons made through "mediums" at spiritualistic seances; if so, however, they have probably dismissed such reports as instances of fraud or self-delusion. Fewer still are familiar with the great mass of evidence that has been steadily accumulating since the first psychical researchers in England began their investigations into spiritualistic phenomena at the turn of this century.

Colin Wilson, the well-known British writer, is one of the few people who is thoroughly familiar with this evidence. An essay by Wilson begins Part One; in it he describes his own introduction to the facts in the case for survival and how he was gradually converted from skepticism to belief by the sheer weight of the evidence. "A skeptic can usually find some loophole in the most well-authenticated accounts," writes Wilson. "Yet when we read perhaps a hundred accounts, all of which seem to point to the same conclusion, it becomes very hard to feel so certain that they all amount to self-deception or willful mendacity." After presenting some of the most fascinating and compelling cases encountered in his own research for several books, Wilson observes that in his estimation the overall case for survival is so strong that "it would be rather perverse to go on thinking up objections."

In "Survival after Death: Observations from Modern Consciousness Research," Stanislav Grof reports on material he has gathered during more than thirty years of research into nonordinary states of consciousness in government-sponsored LSD research and nondrug

7

experiential psychotherapy. In Grof's view, the data from this and other types of modern consciousness research throws an entirely new light on the issue of the survival of consciousness after death. Among these data are transpersonal experiences, which may involve a sense of reliving dramatic episodes from a previous incarnation; out-of-body experiences, such as the one cited at the beginning of this book in which the participant has the sense of floating above his or her body and watching resuscitation procedures from the ceiling; spiritistic or "astral" phenomena involving encounters and telepathic communication with deceased persons, contacts with discarnate entities in general, and experiences of a realm known in occult literature as the "astral realm"; and apparent memories of past incarnations.

Particularly striking are the reported out-of-body and past-incarnation experiences cited by Grof, which are rich in the kind of detail that makes them extremely difficult to dismiss as instances of fraud. While Grof concedes that such observations cannot be interpreted as unambiguous evidence for the continuity of individual consciousness after death, he concludes that "it is hardly possible for an unbiased and informed scientist to discard this possibility on the basis of metaphysical adherence to a mechanistic worldview."

The philosopher Robert Almeder presents and analyzes further evidence for reincarnation in his essay "On Reincarnation." Focusing on three cases reported by Professor Ian Stevenson in his classic studies of apparent reincarnation memories, Almeder defends the reincarnation hypothesis as the best explanation for Stevenson's data, arguing that alternative explanations proposed by skeptics are more farfetched and implausible than the reincarnation hypothesis. Even those who may be opposed to reincarnation on religious or philosophical grounds will find that the case studies Almeder summarizes make for absorbing reading and raise profound questions.

In "Tests for Communication with the Dead," survival researcher Arthur S. Berger explains the various kinds of "posthumous experiments" that have been carried out over many years by parapsychologists hoping to prove survival after death. Generally these tests involve a researcher's intention to communicate after his or her death, through a medium, secret verifiable facts as a signal that the communicator has survived death. Berger analyzes previous tests that have failed and, based on his own research, describes a new test, currently being carried out, that aims to achieve more satisfactory results.

Probably most of us have heard of the belief that at or near the moment of death one's whole life flashes instantaneously before one's eyes or through one's mind. Is this merely a superstition or an old wives' tale? Or does such a "panoramic life review" really occur and constitute evidence of postmortem survival? According to F. Gordon Greene and Stanley Krippner, there is solid evidence from the emerging field of near-death studies that authenticates the experiential reality of the life review. They also examine several proposed explanations of the life review, including those with both materialistic and "transcendental" implications, and pay particular attention to transcendental models that draw upon the idea of a "fourth dimension" as a theoretical construct.

In "Spontaneous Contact with the Dead: Perspectives from Grief Counseling, Sociology, and Parapsychology," the well-known para-psychological investigator D. Scott Rogo concludes Part One by giving us a more detailed look at some of the "overwhelming evidence" for survival referred to by Colin Wilson in the opening essay. After describing some of the most convincing cases uncovered by the early British investigators of the Society for Psychical Research, Rogo goes on to cite and summarize a large body of data from contemporary research on spontaneous contact with the dead, including reported cases of bereavement visions (apparent contact with a deceased spouse by a grieving partner), sociological surveys of who is most likely to have such visions, and recent surveys on postmortem contacts in everyday life.

"None of the specific cases summarized or cited in this essay, by itself, proves that life extends beyond physical death," writes Rogo. Yet "it is difficult not to be moved and impressed by the stories told by the recently bereaved, to see the utter conviction in their eyes when they repeat their experiences." He concludes that he personally sees "little reason for postulating hypothetical psychological or possibly neurological mechanisms to explain such phenomena." The final judgment about the likelihood of survival based on such evidence, of course, must be left up to the reader.

COLIN WILSON

Glimpses of a Wider Reality

Colin Wilson, author of the best-seller The Outsider, *has written several novels and plays and many books on philosophy, the occult, parapsychology, and crime, including* Afterlife, Beyond the Occult, The Quest for Wilhelm Reich, *and* A Criminal History of Mankind.

The simplest way of explaining my attitude to the question of life after death is to begin with a certain amount of autobiography.

When I was about ten years old, a Sunday newspaper began a series that purported to be the after-death experiences of an airman who had died in the Battle of Britain. I can no longer remember the precise details, but I *can* recall his description of a marvelous land of soft green grass and perpetually flowering trees. I was particularly impressed by his account of going for a swim and feeling that the water was a kind of warm cotton wool in which he floated like a cloud. At that age, I assumed that everything that appeared in print must be literally true and excitedly told all my school friends about these astonishing revelations of what happened on the other side of death. Discovering a section devoted to psychical research in our local library, I soon became an ardent admirer of Harry Price and books like *The Most Haunted House in England* and *Search for Truth*. My maternal grandmother was a Spiritualist, but after one attendance at a Sunday-evening service, I decided that Spiritualism was just as boring as the Church of England and firmly declined to repeat the experience. But I remained totally convinced, in theory, of the reality of life after death.

Then my mother presented me with a chemistry set for my birthday, and an uncle gave me a volume called *The Marvels and Mys-*

teries of Science. From that moment I became a devotee of the religion of Science. By the time I was twelve, I had read Sir James Jean's *Mysterious Universe* and Eddington's *Nature of the Physical World* and had embarked on Einstein's little popular book about relativity. My interest in "the supernatural" fled like a ghost at cockcrow, and the whole question of survival after death became a boring irrelevance. This was not because I had become an out-and-out materialist—I remember becoming infuriated with a fellow student who insisted that free will is an illusion—but it certainly seemed to me that "spiritualism" was simply another name for self-delusion. We have only to observe what happens when we fall asleep to realize that consciousness can be switched off as easily as an electric light. What happens to a light when you turn it off? It simply ceases to exist. Similarly, when I fall asleep, everything that I know as "I" ceases to exist. I might be anybody or nobody. Even my dreams have no real sense of identity: The "I" who observes their scrambled meanings has no more continuity than a breath of air.

At some time in my mid-teens, my faith in science also began to disintegrate as it became increasingly obvious that every attempt to create an indestructible foundation had been a failure. Newton thought that he had discovered the laws of the universe; then Einstein demonstrated that nothing can exceed the velocity of light and that space and time must therefore be relative. Russell and Whitehead thought they had placed scientific logic on an immovable foundation until Godel came along and showed that no logical system can be complete in itself. Quantum theory even argued that a cat could be both dead and alive at the same time. I entered a period of gloomy nihilism in which, like Faust, I felt that the only thing we can know for certain is that we can know nothing. Now my grandmother's faith in Spiritualism seemed only another illustration of the infinite gullibility of human beings.

The nihilism eventually passed, but the skepticism remained. And it had not diminished noticeably when, in the late 1960s, an American publisher asked me if I would like to write a book on "the occult." I accepted for the same reason that I had decided to write an encyclopedia of murder ten years earlier—because I find the oddities of human nature endlessly fascinating. But I had little doubt that, on close examination, most cases of the paranormal would turn out to be either wishful thinking or downright skulduggery. Shortly after I had signed the contract, however, my wife read aloud to me a passage from *Great Morning,* the autobiography of Sir

Osbert Sitwell. He described how, shortly before World War I, he and a group of brother officers had been to see a celebrated London palmist. In several cases, the palmist had looked bewildered and exclaimed: "I don't understand it. It's the same thing again. After two or three months, the line of life stops short, and I can read nothing." Then came the outbreak of war, and the same officers were killed in battle.

I found this story convincing because Sitwell was obviously not a believer in "the occult." (In fact, his father had been instrumental in exposing a famous "medium" in the 1890s.) Again and again I came upon similar cases described by people who had no reason to tell lies. This is why, as I continued to write *The Occult,* I became increasingly convinced of the reality of "second sight," telepathy, precognition of the future, and other matters that had so far struck me as highly dubious. Yet I continued to have my reservations about survival after death. I leaned over backward to present the evidence in an unbiased manner, and in some of the cases I mentioned (such as the death of the son of Bishop James Pike), the evidence seemed very powerful indeed. Yet the very fact that I had found so much evidence for "unknown powers" of the human mind made me aware that the evidence for apparitions could, in fact, be evidence for a kind of self-hypnosis.

In a sequel to *The Occult,* called *Mysteries,* I described the interesting theory propounded by the late T. C. Lethbridge: that so-called apparitions might actually be a kind of "tape recording" of powerful emotions, somehow absorbed by the places in which tragic events have occurred. Lethbridge offers an interesting illustration. He and his wife had gone to a beach in Devon to collect seaweed for the garden. At a certain place where a stream ran down the cliff and onto the beach, both experienced independently a curious feeling of gloom. His wife then went to the top of the cliff to make a sketch and had an odd feeling that someone was urging her to jump. Lethbridge later discovered that a man had, in fact, committed suicide by jumping from this spot. He concluded that the man's depression had somehow "imprinted" itself on the scenery—he suggested that the recording medium might be the electrical field of water— and that he and his wife had simply "tuned in" to the emotion as a radio set might accidentally pick up a foreign station.

I became increasingly inclined to accept this theory when I began to gather information for a book on the subject of psychometry, the curious power possessed by certain individuals to "intuit" the history of an object by holding it in the hands. In the 1840s, an American doctor named Joseph R. Buchanan was intrigued when a bishop told him that he could detect brass in the dark because it produced a peculiar brassy taste in his mouth when he touched it with his fingers. Buchanan began to experiment with his students and discovered that many of them possessed the ability to detect unknown substances even when the substances were wrapped in thick brown paper. His colleague William Denton, a professor of geology, discovered that some of his students could touch geological specimens—again wrapped in thick paper—and describe where they came from. Dinosaur fossils even produced vivid mental impressions of dinosaurs, and a piece of mosaic from a Roman villa conjured up a vision of Roman soldiers. Obviously, a person who unwittingly possessed a high degree of this peculiar power might easily believe that he had seen a ghost when he had only "picked up" some powerful impression from a bygone age.

Yet anyone who takes an intelligent interest in the paranormal continues to stumble upon cases that contradict his most carefully constructed theories. This is what happened to me when I was asked to write a book on the subject of the poltergeist. I had never entertained the slightest doubt about the reality of poltergeists—"banging ghosts"—because the evidence for their existence is exceptionally strong; there are literally hundreds of recorded examples dating back as far as the eighth century. Poltergeists cause objects to fly around the room and specialize in rapping noises and other irritating disturbances. At the beginning of the twentieth century, however, investigators observed how often such cases are associated with the presence of a disturbed adolescent, particularly someone who is passing through the difficult sexual adjustments of puberty. This led one researcher, Nandor Fodor, to suggest that poltergeist effects may be some kind of "unconscious psychokinesis"—in other words, some peculiar form of "mind over matter." By the second part of the twentieth century, most respectable investigators of the paranormal had accepted the unconscious-psychokinesis hypothesis, including myself.

Yet as soon as I began a systematic study of the poltergeist in order to write a book on the subject, I realized that I was taking too much for granted. To begin with, there were a number of cases in which poltergeist phenomena had continued when the same house was occupied by different tenants—even, occasionally, when the house was empty. My wife and I went to look into such a case in

Yorkshire—a case that involved apparitions of a "black monk"—and I had to reluctantly concede that it seemed unlikely that the "ghost" was simply a manifestation of the unconscious minds of the teenage son and daughter. To begin with, the entity manifested itself on two separate occasions, with a two-year interval between them, when first the son and then the daughter reached puberty. And when the daughter described to me how it had thrown her repeatedly out of bed and dragged her upstairs by her hair, I suddenly knew with intuitive certainty that this was not her unconscious mind playing tricks. This creature was an independent entity that was somehow "tied" to the house (which was on the site of a medieval gallows), but that could manifest itself only when it could draw upon the sexual energy of an adolescent on the verge of puberty.

In fact, this alternative to the unconscious-psychokinesis hypothesis was suggested to me by my friend Guy Lyon Playfair, who had investigated poltergeists as a member of the Brazilian Society for Psychical Research. Guy had become convinced that poltergeists are spirits and, what is more, that they can be controlled by witch doctors, or *umbanda* magicians. At first this notion struck me as preposterous. But the more I studied individual cases, the more I recognized that Guy's hypothesis seemed to make sense. Poltergeists behave like mischievous spirits, and the unconscious-psychokinesis hypothesis has to be stretched a long way to fit all the facts. These facts are set out at length in my book *Poltergeist*, and they finally left me convinced, rather to my dismay, that most poltergeists are "spirits."

Even so, the notion that "spirits" exist does not necessarily entail a belief that human beings survive death. A "spirit" might simply be some disembodied form of energy at present unknown to science. It might even be some peculiar combination of physical—or psychic—energy with human thought. The existence of "spirits" is no more evidence of human survival than is the existence of duck-billed platypuses. Besides, I continued to feel that no amount of mere physical evidence could outweigh the logical or philosophical problem of survival. This was expressed with great clarity and force by Bertrand Russell in an article entitled "Do We Survive Death?" Russell argued that a "person" is simply a series of mental occurrences and habits, and that if we believe in life after death, we must believe that the memories and habits that constitute the personality must continue to exist. He states flatly: "It is not rational arguments, but emotions, that cause belief in a future life." And it is true that we are all aware that our personalities change over the years according to what happens to us. I am surely not now the same person that I was at the age of seven and that I shall be if I survive to the age of ninety. Nevertheless, I cannot help feeling that the being who now looks out of my eyes is, in some basic sense, the same individual who opened his eyes on the world fifty-odd years ago, whether or not his "personality" has changed. (After all, he had no personality at all when he was born.) Yet in spite of all this, the fact remains that this person I call "me" seems to vanish into nothingness when I fall into a deep sleep or when I am injected with a dose of anesthetic in the hospital. Thus, it seems logical to assume that when I die, I simply "vanish" permanently—disappear into the same void from which I emerged when I was born.

In 1984, I was commissioned by a British publisher to write a book called *Afterlife*. Once again I settled down to studying the evidence for life after death, this time in more detail than ever before. Like so many writers, I have discovered that writing a book is the best—certainly the most thorough—way to investigate a subject. What happens, of course, is that you are simply forced to immerse yourself in a subject until you have become an expert on it. In doing so, you read all—or as many as possible—of the books on that subject and quickly come to recognize how well the writers have done their homework and how far they have borrowed from one another. I started off with the advantage of just having read and reported on an erudite and far-ranging typescript entitled *Survival: Body, Mind and Death in the Light of Psychic Experience* by a brilliant young researcher named David Lorimer. He not only offers a history of the belief in life after death—primitive man, ancient Egypt, Greece, and Rome—but also studies the views of the philosophers and such modern authorities on the mind-body relation as Sir Karl Popper and Sir John Eccles. In addition to this, he cites dozens of cases of apparitions, out-of-body experiences, and so-called near-death experiences. Lorimer's quotations led me to other books and particularly to the recent literature on the near-death experience. It may be objected that this is not the right way to research a book— merely reading what other people have said. Yet it certainly has one great advantage: You become conversant with so many cases that you begin to see the similarities between them and to become aware of the sheer consistency of the descriptions. I had had the same experience when researching *The Occult*, and again when writing *Poltergeist* and *The Psychic Detective* (a book on psychometry). But then, there is no real conflict between the *logical* possibility of psychometry or poltergeist activity and the physical evidence. But, in considering the possibility of life after death, it is hard to get away from that basic fact that I cannot take "myself" with me into sleep or into unconsciousness. So why should I be able to take it into death?

I must admit I can still see no answer to that objection. On the other hand, the sheer volume of physical evidence for survival after death is so immense that to ignore it is like standing at the foot of Mount Everest and insisting that you cannot see a mountain. This evidence is of many different types—accounts of near-death experiences, out-of-body experiences, and so on—but the most impressive is certainly the evidence of those who believe they have received incontrovertible proof that they have been in contact with a dead friend or relative. This is the type of evidence that we are tempted to dismiss as wishful thinking when we hear about it at second hand. A skeptic can usually find some loophole in the most well-authenticated accounts. Yet when we read perhaps a hundred accounts, all of which seem to point to the same conclusion, it becomes very hard to feel so certain that they all amount to self-deception or willful mendacity.

Obviously, the best way to convince the reader would be to cite a dozen or so cases. This is plainly impractical in an article of this length. But I can at least offer one or two typical samples.

It is not generally realized that although Sir Arthur Conan Doyle, the creator of Sherlock Holmes, was a convinced Spiritualist in later life, he remained a skeptic until he was in his mid-fifties. The event that finally convinced him took place during World War I. He and his wife were looking after a sick girl named Lily Loder-Symonds, who amused herself by practicing automatic writing. The Doyles were convinced that this was simply a manifestation of her unconscious mind. They began to take it more seriously when Lily produced a message that said: "It's terrible. And will have a great influence on the war." That day, a German submarine sank the passenger liner *Lusitania*, an event that led to America's entry into the war.

Soon after this, as Doyle was sitting by Lily's bedside watching her hand scrawl across a sheet of paper, he was fascinated to recognize the writing of his brother-in-law, Malcolm Leckie, who had been killed at Mons. Doyle began to ask questions, and "Leckie" replied. And when Doyle asked a question about a private conversation that had taken place between himself and Leckie, and about which he had told no one else, "Leckie" replied with such accuracy that it was no longer possible for Doyle to doubt that Leckie was, in some sense, still "alive." From then on, he was a believer in life after death.

The standard objection to such a case is that the medium—in this case Miss Loder-Symonds—might have read his mind. (In *The Occult* I cited the experience of a friend of mine, Louis Singer, who was totally convinced that he had influenced the mind of a medium at a seance through telepathy.) But it is difficult to see how that objection applies to the Nils Jacobsen case, cited by Stan Gooch in his book *The Paranormal.* In 1928, Jacobsen's uncle was slammed against a wall by a truck and died three days later without regaining consciousness. Six years later, at a séance, the medium told Jacobsen's father that his dead brother was present. The brother then described the accident and added that he had not died from an injury to the skull—as the family had assumed—but that "it came from the bones." Nils Jacobsen thereupon consulted the hospital and unearthed the records. The postmortem report showed that his uncle had died not from a skull fracture, but from a brain embolism caused by a blood clot from the bone—lower-bone thrombosis. If we can accept Jacobsen's evidence, it is very difficult to see how this story could be explained in terms of telepathy. Gooch, admittedly, points out that the surgeon who performed the postmortem must have known the truth and that it is conceivable that the medium might somehow have picked up this information from his mind; but such a possibility seems more farfetched than the alternative assumption that Jacobsen's uncle somehow survived his own death.

But the case that is usually regarded as the most convincing proof so far of life after death is the one known as the Cross Correspondences. The "spirit" concerned was apparently that of the famous psychical researcher F. W. H. Myers, one of the founders of the Society for Psychical Research and the author of a classic work called *Human Personality and Its Survival of Bodily Death.* Before his death in 1901, Myers had remarked that perhaps the ultimately convincing way to demonstrate life after death would be for the "spirit" to give separate bits of the same message to a number of different mediums, like pieces of a jigsaw puzzle that would make sense only when they were fitted together. Not long after Myers's death, a number of mediums—including the American Leonore Piper; Margaret Verrall, the wife of an Oxford don; and Alice Fleming,

Rudyard Kipling's sister—began receiving bits of the "jigsaw puzzle" from a "communicator" who claimed to be Myers. (Later, two other deceased founding members of the Society for Psychical Research joined in.) The messages are extremely complex and involve classical allusions in several languages, so few skeptics have ever had the patience to study them. But, as in the case of Jacobsen's uncle, it can be explained away only in terms of some absurdly complicated hypothesis about telepathy between mediums in different parts of the world.

Now these, and many similar cases, failed to answer that basic objection about how an individual consciousness could somehow survive the death of the body. Yet by the time I had studied dozens of them and incorporated many in my book *Afterlife,* I had ceased to feel that this was some kind of ultimate objection. Anyone who approaches a question scientifically recognizes that one of the basic problems is that of verification, and that, in the logical sense, it is virtually impossible to be one hundred percent certain about anything. But in such matters we apply common sense. No one has ever seen an electron, but the evidence of their existence is so powerful that no one in his right mind can doubt it. And when I had finished writing *Afterlife,* I felt much the same about human survival of death.

To be honest, I feel that, where I am concerned, the problem has no great relevance. The possibility that I might not survive my own death does not bother me; after all, I accept "annihilation" every night when I close my eyes. I have never had an out-of-body experience or (I am pleased to say) a near-death experience. (That these experiences can be deeply convincing is demonstrated by the recent announcement of Professor A. J. Ayer, a well-known champion of materialistic philosophy, that such an experience has shaken his own skepticism about life after death.) So, as far as I am concerned, the question of belief in life after death is purely a matter of the scientific evidence. I have found, to my surprise, that this evidence is remarkably strong—so strong that I feel it would be rather perverse to go on thinking up objections. I am surprised, and I suppose rather pleased, to find that it seems highly likely that when this body of mine finally breaks down irretrievably, the rest of me will continue to exist—the "essential me" who is now looking out through my eyes. Of course, I could be wrong about this; it may be that all this powerful evidence is some kind of unconscious creation of the human mind— what Jung, referring to flying saucers, called a "projection" (meaning a kind of hallucination). If so, that would not bother me particularly. But of one thing I am fairly certain: All the abundant evidence for survival after death is not some kind of fraud or trickery, the result of some conspiracy to help people overcome their fear of death and their grief at the loss of those they love. It is as strong as—probably stronger than—the evidence for black holes.

Let me conclude with some kind of attempt to express the personal philosophy that has gradually emerged over twenty years of studying the paranormal. I should state, to begin with, that my interest in the paranormal has been a kind of by-product of my interest in a more general problem, that of expanded states of awareness. My first book, *The Outsider*, was a study of men who felt themselves alienated from everyday life because they had experienced brief flashes of some wider and deeper kind of awareness. These "glimpses" made them feel that they were trapped in what Heidegger calls "the triviality of everydayness," and in the nineteenth century, the result was a dissatisfaction that often led to suicide or early death from tuberculosis. What impressed me was the sheer consistency of accounts of states of expanded consciousness, as experienced by poets and mystics. And one of the basic themes to emerge from these accounts was what might be called the idea of "oneness," or "connectedness"—the feeling that it is the laziness and inefficiency of human consciousness that makes us see things as "separate." Who among us has not had some experience in which, in the course of an excited discussion about ideas, we have suddenly seen all kinds of implications that we were unaware of a split second earlier. The same kind of thing often happens when we are setting out on holiday or on a journey: that odd feeling that a veil has been drawn back and we can now see that the world is an infinitely more exciting and complex place than we had realized.

In a recent book called *Beyond the Occult*, I have suggested that we might describe ordinary human consciousness in terms of seven levels, beginning with dream consciousness and ending with what I have christened "Faculty X," that curious ability we possess, in certain moments, to conjure up the total reality of some other time and place. One of the best examples can be found in Proust's novel *Swann's Way*, in which Marcel tastes a cake dipped in herb tea and finds himself almost literally transported back to his childhood. Beyond these seven levels lies so-called "mystical consciousness," of which dozens of descriptions will be found—for example, in

R. M. Bucke's famous treatise *Cosmic Consciousness*. When P. D. Ouspensky described such a state in an essay called "Experimental Mysticism" (in *A New Model of the Universe*), he explained that it was virtually impossible to say anything about the experience, because in order to say anything one would have to say *everything*, for everything is seen to be connected together; nothing is "detachable." Looking at an ashtray in this state, he saw so many "implications" that he made the comment: "One could go mad from one ashtray."

Another comment made again and again by mystics is that in these states they are suddenly able to grasp the meaning of the famous alchemical formula "As above, so below." This seems to be a recognition that there is no real difference between our physical world and the realm of the mystics; the only trouble is that we cannot *see* this latter world. Our gaze is limited, like the gaze of blinkered horses.

Yet it should be possible, in theory, to somehow carry this expanded awareness, or at least its essence, back into everyday consciousness. This is in fact what poets and mystics are attempting to do. The message that seems to emerge from these states of expanded insight is that "all is well," that the chief problem of human beings lies in the negativity of their own minds. We are always "shrinking," running away from problems that could easily be solved with a little effort and optimism.

Then, in the mid-1960s, a medical student named Raymond Moody began talking to patients who had apparently died and then returned to life. He was amazed to discover the basic similarity of their experiences. There was often a feeling of traveling down a tunnel, then of emerging into some tremendous light. There was a sense of revelation—the "Of course!" feeling—followed by an experience of tremendous joy. And when they woke up in the hospital, such people usually continued to experience the sense of marvelous insight, the feeling that life *is* meaningful, and that the fight to evolve to higher levels of awareness is the most basic aim of human existence. Again and again, such patients declared that they now had "the courage to live."

I was struck by the similarity of these near-death experiences to the experiences of the mystics, and it seemed logical to conclude that the two are basically identical; both are glimpses, so to speak, of the "eighth level of consciousness."

It also struck me clearly that my job as a writer is fundamentally the same as that of every other human being: to try to bring this insight "down to earth" and convey it to others. Most of our troubles are due to negativity and "discouragement," the feeling that no effort is really worthwhile. In fact, this is surely the commonest of all human experiences: facing the prospect of some task with a sinking heart and a sense of futility. Yet whenever we give way to this desire to run away, we realize it is stupid. A problem we flee from today has to be faced tomorrow, and as often as not, we have to pay "interest" on the energy we failed to use the day before.

Now, it seems to me that whether we survive the death of the body or not, the insight of these experiences is self-evidently valid. In other words, I have no doubt whatever that the glimpses of a "wider reality" as experienced by the mystics are objectively true. Moreover, we can confirm them by ordinary logic and ordinary psychology. (For example, Abraham Maslow concluded that peak experiences—those sudden experiences of tremendous happiness and courage—are a normal potentiality of all human beings.) And if I can accept the genuineness of these glimpses of a wider reality, and if I concede that Moody's findings are consistent with these insights, it seems to me that I have come very close to accepting the logical reality of life after death. And that is why, in spite of my acceptance of the fact that these findings cannot be regarded as scientifically proven, I now feel perfectly comfortable about acknowledging that I have come to accept the notion of life after death as a virtual certainty.

S T A N I S L A V   G R O F

Survival after Death: Observations from Modern Consciousness Research

Stanislav Grof, M.D., is a world-renowned psychiatrist who special-
izes in altered states of consciousness and spiritual emergency. He is
the author of Realms of the Human Unconscious: Observations
from LSD Research, Beyond the Brain: Birth, Death, and Transcendence in Psychotherapy, *and* The Adventure of Self-
Discovery.

This essay is based on observations from over three decades
of systematic exploration of the heuristic and therapeutic potential of nonordinary states of consciousness induced by psychedelic substances and various nonpharmacological techniques.[1] The
first twenty years involved clinical work with psychedelics in
government-sponsored research. The last fourteen years involved
experimentation with various powerful nondrug alternatives to
psychedelics, especially a psychotherapeutic technique developed
by my wife, Christina, and me that we call *holotropic therapy.*

Holotropic therapy combines controlled breathing, evocative music and other forms of sound technology, focused body work, and
mandala drawing. By using this nondrug approach, we have been
able to induce the entire spectrum of experiences characteristic of
psychedelic sessions and classical shamanic journeys.[2]

The experiences thus induced cannot be accounted for in the
traditional model of the psyche used in psychoanalysis; hence, it
has been necessary to create a new, more extensive and encompassing model of the regions of human consciousness. Besides the traditional biographical-recollective level and the Freudian individual

unconscious, the cartography of the new model includes what I have called the *perinatal* and the *transpersonal* regions of the psyche. The experiences characteristic of the perinatal and transpersonal realms are of special interest to the question of whether consciousness survives after death, because these experiences include the visionary phenomena important in eschatological mythologies, ancient "books of the dead," and other contexts in which the experience of death (and rebirth) plays a significant role.

The belief that consciousness or existence in some form continues beyond biological death is found in all the ancient and non-Western cultures, in their religious and philosophical systems, cosmologies, ritual practices, and various elements of social organization. All these cultures, although differing in their specific concepts of an afterlife, are united in a belief that death is merely a transition or transfiguration, not a final annihilation of the individual. Some spiritual traditions teach that individual consciousness undergoes a complex journey after death, through specific stages, ordeals, and abodes; others teach that following the death of one body, consciousness is reincarnated on earth in a new body. In some traditions, death is regarded as an opportunity for final liberation and merging with the Absolute.

In contrast, Western cultures have a radically different view of death and dying. To one degree or another, most educated Westerners are under the influence of mechanistic science and its assumption that consciousness is a product of the physiological functioning of the brain. The logical implication of this assumption is, of course, that consciousness must cease to exist when the brain dies. According to the mechanistic worldview, belief in any form of afterlife and the concept of "posthumous soul journeys" are expressions of primitive fears, magical thinking, and superstition. Thus, modern society isolates aging, sick, and dying individuals in nursing homes and hospitals, treating the dying in isolation from meaningful human support and merely prolonging life through technological expertise. Similarly, modern psychology and psychiatry until recently exhibited the massive denial of death characteristic of Western civilization in general, showing little interest in the death experience and offering no psychological support for the dying.

Modern consciousness research throws an entirely new light on the issue of the survival of consciousness after death. If we wish to increase our understanding of the universe and of human nature, it is necessary for us to take the data provided by this new research seriously and to review the present attitude of most scientists, who either are unfamiliar with this evidence or choose to ignore it. Psychedelic sessions, experiential psychotherapy, various forms of meditation, and spontaneous nonordinary states of consciousness provide a direct experience of many of the phenomena described in mystico-religious worldviews (perennial philosophy) and in eschatological mythologies—phenomena that support a worldview recognizing the reality of the postmortem survival of consciousness.

In this chapter I will focus on observations from my own research, especially the transpersonal experiences that appear during the course of holotropic therapy. After that discussion I will examine those types that are directly related to the question of whether consciousness survives after death, especially the experiences of ostensible communication with discarnate entities, out-of-body experiences, visions of astral realms, and memories of past incarnations.

The Transpersonal Realm

In one sense, consciousness is characterized by its limits: In our normal waking state, we experience ourselves as existing within certain physical borders circumscribed by our body image; our perception of the external environment is restricted by the range of our sensory organs; and our actions are subject to the usual spatial and temporal boundaries. Ordinarily, we can experience events only in the present moment and in our immediate environment. We can recall the past, and we can anticipate or fantasize about future events; but the past and future are not available for our direct experience.

By contrast, in transpersonal experiences, whether they occur in psychedelic sessions, in holotropic therapy, or spontaneously, one or more of the usual limitations of consciousness appear to be transcended. Such experiences fall into three general categories. The first category involves experiences in which linear time appears to be transcended—experiences interpreted by those who have them as historical regression and exploration of their biological, cultural, and spiritual past, or as historical progression into the future. The second category involves experiences characterized mainly by an apparent transcendence of ordinary spatial boundaries. The third category is characterized by experiential exploration of domains that in Western culture are not considered to be part of objective reality.

For many people, nonordinary states of consciousness are characterized by very concrete and realistic episodes that they identify as fetal and embryonal memories. Under these circumstances, it is not unusual to experience, on the level of cellular consciousness, full identification with the sperm and ovum at the time of one's conception. Historical regression may sometimes go even farther, the person having a feeling of reliving memories from the lives of his or her ancestors, or even of drawing on the memory banks of the racial or collective unconscious. Individuals occasionally even report identifying with various animal ancestors in the evolutionary pedigree, or having a distinct sense of reliving dramatic episodes from a previous incarnation.

Transpersonal experiences involving transcendence of spatial barriers suggest that the boundaries between the individual and the rest of the universe are not fixed and absolute. Under special circumstances, a person may identify experientially with anything in the universe, including the entire cosmos itself. In this group belong experiences of merging with another person into a state of dual unity, of assuming another person's identity, of tuning in to the consciousness of a specific group of people, or of one's consciousness expanding to such an extent that it seems to encompass all of humanity. Similarly, individuals may sometimes report transcending the limits of our specifically human experience, identifying instead with the consciousness of animals, plants, or inorganic objects and processes. It is even possible to experience consciousness of the entire biosphere, of the planet as a whole, or of the entire material universe.

Many transpersonal experiences involve an apparent extension of consciousness beyond the phenomenal world and the time-space continuum as we ordinarily perceive it. In this category we find numerous visions of archetypal personages and themes, of deities and demons of various cultures, of complex mythological sequences, and of the spirits of deceased people, suprahuman entities, and inhabitants of other universes.

Additional examples of this category of phenomena include visions of abstract archetypal patterns, intuitive understanding of universal symbols (cross, ankh, yin-yang, swastika, pentacle, six-pointed star), experiences of the meridians and of the flow of *ch'i* energy as described in Chinese philosophy and medicine, and the arousal of the "serpent power" (*kundalini*) and the activation of various centers of psychic energy, or chakras, as described in Tantric yoga. In some cases, individual consciousness can identify with cosmic consciousness or the Universal Mind, or—at its furthest reaches—with the Supracosmic and Metacosmic Void, the mysterious primordial emptiness and nothingness that is conscious of itself and contains all existence in a germinal and potential form.

Because transpersonal experiences can convey instant intuitive information about any aspect of the universe in the present, past, and future, they appear to violate some of the most basic assumptions of mechanistic science, implying that, in a yet unexplained way, each human being contains information about the entire universe, has potential experiential access to all its parts, and in a sense *is* the whole cosmic network.

Out-of-Body Experiences

According to the Western mechanistic worldview, because consciousness is a product of the body (i.e., the brain), it is absurd to think that consciousness could detach from and exist independently of the body. Yet this is precisely what seems to occur in many well-documented cases of so-called out-of-body experiences (OBEs). Such experiences can take various forms and degrees: OBEs can be isolated episodes, or they may occur repeatedly as part of a psychic opening or other type of transpersonal crisis.

Circumstances particularly conducive to OBEs are vital emergencies, near-death situations, experiences of clinical death, sessions of deep experiential psychotherapy, and ingestion of psychedelic substances, especially the dissociative anesthetic ketamine hydrochloride (Ketalar). Classical descriptions of OBEs can be found in spiritual literature and philosophical texts of all ages, particularly in the Tibetan Book of the Dead and other similar literature.

Research by Raymond Moody,[3] Kenneth Ring,[4] Michael Sabom,[5] and Elisabeth Kübler-Ross,[6] my own study,[7] and the work of many others have repeatedly confirmed that people considered clinically dead can have OBEs during which they accurately witness the resuscitation procedures from a position near the ceiling, or perceive events in remote locations. Modern thanatological research thus confirms the descriptions in the Tibetan Book of the Dead, according to which an individual after death assumes a "bardo body" that transcends the limitations of time and space and can freely travel around the earth.

Psychedelic research, holotropic therapy, and other types of experiential psychotherapy similarly provide observations that confirm the possibility of genuine OBEs during the types of visionary states reported in various mystical sources and anthropological literature. The authenticity of OBEs has been demonstrated in controlled clinical experiments by the well-known psychologist and parapsychologist Charles Tart at the University of California at Davis.[8]

A remarkable illustrative example of an out-of-body experience including accurate perception of a remote location is reported by Kimberly Clark, a social worker in Seattle who found the circumstances of this case so extraordinary and convincing that she developed a lasting interest in OBEs:

"My first encounter with a near-death experiencer involved a patient named Maria, a migrant worker who was visiting friends in Seattle and had a severe heart attack. She was brought into the hospital by the rescue squad one night and admitted to the coronary-care unit. I got involved in her case as a result of her social and financial problems. A few days after her admission, she had a cardiac arrest. Because she was so closely monitored and was otherwise in good health, she was brought back quickly, intubated for a couple of hours to make sure that her oxygenation was adequate, and then extubated.

"Later in the day I went to see her, thinking that she might have some anxiety about the fact that her heart had stopped. In fact, she was anxious, but not for that reason. She was in a state of relative agitation, in contrast to her usual calmness. She wanted to talk to me about something. She said: 'The strangest thing happened when the doctors and nurses were working on me: I found myself looking down from the ceiling at them working on my body.'

"I was not impressed at first. I thought that she might know what had been going on in the room, what people were wearing, and who would be there, since she had seen them all prior to her cardiac arrest. Certainly she was familiar with the equipment by that time. Since hearing is the last sense to go, I reasoned that she could hear everything that was going on, and while I did not think she was consciously making this up, I thought it might have been a confabulation.

"She then told me that she had been distracted by something over the emergency-room driveway and found herself outside, as if she had 'thought herself' over the emergency-room driveway and, in just that instant, she was out there. At this point, I was a little more impressed, since she had arrived at night inside an ambulance and would not have known what the emergency-room area looked like. However, I reasoned that perhaps at some point in time her bed had been by the window, she had looked outside, and this had been incorporated into the confabulation.

"But then Maria proceeded to describe being further distracted by an object on the third-floor ledge on the north end of the building. She 'thought her way' up there and found herself 'eyeball to shoelace' with a tennis shoe, which she asked me to try to find for her. She needed someone else to know that the tennis shoe was really there to validate her out-of-body experience.

"With mixed emotions, I went outside and looked up at the ledges but could not see much at all. I went up to the third floor and began going in and out of patients' rooms and looking out their windows, which were so narrow that I had to press my face to the screen just to see the ledge at all. Finally, I found a room where I pressed my face to the glass and looked down and saw the tennis shoe!

"My vantage point was very different from what Maria's had to have been for her to notice that the little toe had worn a place in the shoe and that the lace was stuck under the heel and other details about the side of the shoe not visible to me. The only way she would have had such a perspective was if she had been floating right outside and at very close range to the tennis shoe. I retrieved the shoe and brought it back to Maria. It was very concrete evidence for me."

Spiritistic or "Astral" Phenomena

In this category of experiences we find phenomena that have been the main focus of interest to participants in spiritistic séances, to parapsychologists researching possible cases of survival after death, and to writers of occult literature. These experiences involve encounters and telepathic communication with deceased persons, usually relatives and friends, contacts with discarnate entities in general, and experiences of a domain referred to in occult literature as the astral realm.

Experiences of this kind sometimes have certain extraordinary aspects that are not easy to explain, as the following two examples indicate. The first occurred during the psychedelic treatment of a young depressed homosexual patient whom I shall call Richard.[9]

In one of his LSD sessions, Richard had a very unusual experience involving a strange and uncanny astral realm. It had an eerie luminescence and was filled with discarnate beings that were trying to communicate with him in a very urgent and demanding manner. He could not see or hear them; however, he sensed their almost tangible presence and was receiving telepathic messages from them. I wrote down one of these messages that was very specific and could be subjected to subsequent verification.

It was a request for Richard to contact a couple in the Moravian city of Kromeriz in Czechoslovakia and let them know that their son Ladislav was doing all right and was well taken care of. The message included the couple's name, street address, and telephone number. All of these data were unknown to me and the patient. This experience was extremely puzzling; it seemed to be an alien enclave in Richard's experience, totally unrelated to his problems and the rest of his treatment.

After some hesitation and with mixed feelings, I finally decided to do what certainly would have made me the target of my colleagues' jokes had they found out. I went to the telephone, dialed the number in Kromeriz, and asked if I could speak with Ladislav. To my astonishment, the woman on the other line started to cry. When she calmed down, she told me with a broken voice: "Our son is not with us anymore; he passed away, we lost him three weeks ago."

A second example involves my close friend and former colleague Walter N. Pahnke, who was a member of our psychedelic research team at the Maryland Psychiatric Research Center in Baltimore. His deep interest in parapsychology, especially in the question of life after death, led him to work with many famous mediums and psychics, including his friend Eileen Garrett, president of the American Parapsychological Association. He was also the initiator of an LSD program for patients dying of cancer.

In the summer of 1971, Walter went with his wife, Eva, and his children for a vacation in a cabin in Maine, situated right on the ocean. One day he went scuba diving by himself and did not return from the ocean. An extensive and well-organized search failed to find his body or any part of his diving gear. Under these circumstances, Eva found it very difficult to accept and integrate his death. Her last memory of Walter when he was leaving the cabin involved seeing him full of energy and in perfect health. It was hard for her to believe that he was not part of her life anymore and to start a new chapter of her existence without a sense of closure of the preceding one.

Being a psychologist herself, she qualified for an LSD training session for mental-health professionals offered through a special program in our institute. She decided to have a psychedelic experience with the hope of getting some more insights and asked me to be her sitter. In the second half of the session, she had a very powerful vision of Walter and carried on a long and meaningful dialogue with him. He gave her specific instructions concerning each of their three children and released her to start a new life of her own, unencumbered and unrestricted by a sense of commitment to his memory. It was a very profound and liberating experience.

Just as Eva was questioning whether the entire episode was merely a wishful fabrication of her own mind, Walter appeared briefly once more, with the following request: "By the way, I forgot one thing. Would you please do me a favor and return a book that I borrowed from a friend of mine? It's in my study in the attic." He then proceeded to give her the name of the friend, the name of the book, the shelf, and the sequential order of the book on this shelf. Following the instructions, Eva was actually able to find and return the book, about which she had had no previous knowledge.

Earlier during his life, Walter had made an agreement with Eileen Garrett that after her death she would try to give him an unquestionable proof of the existence of the beyond. Thus, it would certainly have been completely consistent with Walter's lifelong search for a scientific proof of paranormal phenomena to add a concrete and testable piece of information to his postmortem interaction with Eva to dispel her doubts.

Memories of Past Incarnations

This category of transpersonal experiences is probably the most fascinating and controversial of all. Ostensible memories of past incarnations in many ways resemble ancestral, racial, and collective experiences. They are, however, usually very dramatic and associated with an intense emotional charge. Their essential experiential characteristic is a convinced sense of remembering something that happened once before. The subjects undergoing these dramatic experiences maintain a sense of individuality and personal identity, but experience themselves in another form, at another place and time, and in another context.

There are two distinct categories of ostensible past-life experiences, each characterized by the quality of the emotions involved. The first category reflects highly positive connections with other persons—deep friendship, passionate love, spiritual partnership, teacher-disciple relationship, blood bonds, life-and-death commitment, extraordinary mutual understanding, or nourishing and supportive exchange. The second category, which is more frequent, involves dramatic negative emotions. The experiences belonging to this category cast subjects into various internecine past-life situations characterized by agonizing physical pain, murderous aggression, inhuman terror, prolonged anguish, bitterness and hatred, insane jealousy, insatiable vengefulness, uncontrollable lust, or morbid greed.

Certain specific aspects of past-life experiences are extremely interesting and deserve the serious attention of researchers of consciousness and of the human psyche. The persons who experience karmic phenomena often gain amazing insights into the time and culture involved, and occasionally even acquire knowledge of specific historical events. In some instances, it is absolutely clear that they could not possibly have acquired this information in the conventional way, through the ordinary sensory channels. In this sense, past-life memories are transpersonal experiences that share with other transpersonal phenomena the capacity to provide instant and direct extrasensory access to information about the world.

In rare instances, transpersonal experiences that seem to support the reality of reincarnation can be very specific. A small fraction of transpersonal past-life memories involve very unambiguous information about the personality and life of the individual to whom the subject feels karmically connected. This information may consist of names of persons and places, dates, descriptions of objects of unusual shapes, and many other facts. Occasionally, the nature of this material allows for independent testing. In these cases, historical research often brings extraordinary surprises in terms of verifying these experiences down to minuscule details.

In the following, I will illustrate some important aspects of past-life experiences by an interesting case history. The person who is the protagonist in this story, Karl, started his self-exploration in a primal-therapy group. Later, he participated in one of our monthlong seminars at the Esalen Institute in Big Sur, California, where we used the technique of holotropic breathing.

During the time in primal therapy when Karl was reliving various aspects of his birth trauma, he started experiencing fragments of dramatic scenes that seemed to be happening in another century and in a foreign country. They involved powerful emotions and physical feelings and seemed to have some deep and intimate connection to his life; yet none of them made any sense in terms of his present biography.

He had visions of tunnels, underground storage spaces, military barracks, thick walls, and ramparts that all seemed to be parts of a fortress situated on a rock overlooking an ocean shore. These images were interspersed with images of soldiers in a variety of situations. He felt puzzled, since the soldiers seemed to be Spanish, but the scenery resembled Scotland or Ireland.

As the visionary process continued, the scenes became more dramatic and involved, many of them representing fierce combats and bloody slaughter. Although surrounded by soldiers, Karl experienced himself as a priest and at one point had a very moving vision that involved a Bible and a cross. At this point, he saw a seal ring on his hand and could clearly recognize the initials that it bore. As he was recovering bits and pieces of this story, Karl was finding more and more meaningful connections with his present life. He was discovering that many emotional and psychosomatic feelings, as well as problems he was experiencing in interpersonal relationships at that time in his everyday life, were clearly related to his inner process, involving the mysterious event in the past.

A turning point came when Karl suddenly decided on an impulse to spend his holiday in Ireland. After his return, he was showing for the first time the slides that he had shot on the western coast of Ireland. He realized that the place that attracted his attention was the ruin of an old fortress called Dunanoir, or Forte de Oro (Golden Fortress).

Suspecting a connection with his experiences from primal therapy, Karl decided to study the history of Dunanoir. He discovered, to his enormous surprise, that at the time of Walter Raleigh, the fortress was taken by the Spaniards and then besieged by the British. Raleigh negotiated with the Spaniards and promised them free escape from the fortress if they opened the gate and surrendered to the British. The Spaniards agreed on these conditions, but the British did not keep their promise. Once inside the fortress, they mercilessly slaughtered all the Spaniards and threw them over the ramparts to die on the beach.

In spite of this absolutely astonishing confirmation of the story that he laboriously reconstructed in his inner exploration, Karl was not satisfied. He continued his library research until he discovered a special document about the battle of Dunanoir. There he found that a priest accompanied the Spanish soldiers and was killed with them. The initials of the name of the priest were identical with those that Karl had seen in his vision of the seal ring and had depicted in one of his drawings.

The observations from holotropic therapy that I have discussed here deserve systematic and careful research as evidence related to the question of the postmortem survival of consciousness. While such observations cannot be interpreted as unambiguous evidence for the continuity of individual consciousness after death, it is hardly possible for an unbiased and informed scientist to discard this possibility on the basis of metaphysical adherence to a mechanistic worldview. Although the assumption of postmortem survival is not the only imaginable interpretation of the data in question, a serious reexamination of this data is certainly important in the interest of scientific objectivity, honesty, and progress. Moreover, such an endeavor could have important social and political implications. The status of consciousness in the scientific worldview and the question of its survival after physical death are among the most critical matters influencing the human hierarchy of values, ethical standards, moral codes, and behavior. In view of the current global crisis and impending danger of collective suicide, this is a factor that should not be underestimated.

ROBERT ALMEDER

On Reincarnation

Robert Almeder, Ph.D., is associate professor of philosophy at Georgia State University. He is currently writing a book, Death and Personal Survival: The Evidence for Life after Death.

The academic world was shocked and highly skeptical when Professor Ian Stevenson of the University of Virginia published his now-classic book *Twenty Cases Suggestive of Reincarnation.*[1] Stevenson argued that the hypothesis of reincarnation offers the best available explanation of a large body of data that, until recently, has been generally ignored, overlooked, or rejected for various unacceptable reasons. This data consists of a number of case studies (described in great detail in *Twenty Cases* and elsewhere), all of which typically share the following core features:

1. A young person, usually between the ages of four and nine, claims to remember living an earlier life as a different person. This person then provides a detailed description of his alleged earlier life, a description including (but not restricted to) where and when he lived, his name, the names and characteristics of his relatives, highly selective historical events that could be known only by the person he claims to have been in that earlier life, the way he lived, and the specific details of the way in which he died.

2. These memory claims are of two types: (a) those that can be verified in terms of available information; and (b) those that can be verified, but not in terms of available information. For example, if a young person from Evanston, Illinois, claims to remember having lived an earlier life as Lazarus Smart, born approximately in 1630 in Boston, Massachusetts, to Mary and Abraham Smart, who lived on Boylston Street during the Boat

Fire of 1642, the fact that Lazarus Smart did exist under this description could be verified easily in terms of available birth records, historical documents, and other information publicly accessible. But if the same person claims to recall having secretly buried a silver spoon with the initials L.S. in the concrete pier under the northwest corner of the Boylston Street Church when it was rebuilt in 1642, that sort of claim would be verifiable, but not in terms of known or existing information.

3. The person claiming to remember living a past life is interviewed (and taped) at great length, asked to provide information one would expect him to know if indeed he did actually live that earlier life, and he indeed provides such information.

4. Investigators independently confirm both sorts of memory claims, and, in some cases, family members are interviewed and confront the person, who reminds them of various details of the life they allegedly spent together.

5. The person claiming to remember living a past life also manifests certain skills possessed by the person in the alleged earlier life such as speaking fluently a foreign language or dialect, of playing an instrument—which the person claiming to have lived the earlier life could not have acquired in this life. For example, if a person claims to remember having lived in medieval Sweden, and if that person in a hypnotic trance begins to speak and describe his earlier life in a difficult but clear dialect of medieval Swedish, that person (assuming we can document that he has not learned or been exposed to medieval Swedish) manifests skills not acquired in this life.

6. The real possibility of deception by way of fraud or hoax on the part of the person claiming to have lived a past life cannot be substantiated.

According to Stevenson, in cases having all these characteristics, the only available explanation that plausibly fits the data is reincarnation.

Not surprisingly, philosophers and scientists of a materialistic bent have been quick to attack Stevenson's hypothesis with a barrage of objections and alternative explanations. We will examine some of these objections and alternative explanations later. Before we do so, however, let's take a quick look at three of the most striking cases reported by Stevenson.

The Case of Bishen Chand

Bishen Chand was born in 1921 to the family of Gulham in the city of Bareilly, India. At the age of about one and a half, Bishen began asking questions about the town of Pilibhit, some fifty miles from Bareilly. Nobody in the Gulham family knew anybody in Pilibhit. Bishen asked to be taken there, and it became obvious that he believed he had lived there during an earlier life.[2]

As time passed, Bishen talked incessantly of his earlier life in Pilibhit, and his family grew increasingly distressed with his behavior. By the summer of 1926 (when he was five and a half years old), Bishen claimed to remember his previous life quite clearly. He remembered that his name had been Laxmi Narain, son of a wealthy landowner. He claimed to remember an uncle, Har Narain (who turned out on later investigation to be Laxmi Narain's father). He also described the house in which he lived, saying it had a shrine room and separate quarters for women. Frequently, he had enjoyed the singing and dancing of Nautch girls, professional dancers who often functioned as prostitutes. He remembers enjoying parties of this sort at the home of a neighbor, Sander Lal, who had lived in a "house with a green gate." Indeed, little Bishen one day recommended to his father that he (the father) take on a mistress in addition to his wife.

Because Bishen Chand's family was poor (Bishen's father was a government clerk), Bishen's memories of an earlier and wealthier life only made him resentful of his present living conditions with the Gulham family. He sometimes refused to eat the food, claiming that even his servants—in his former life—would not eat such food. He demanded meat and fish, and when his family would not provide it, he sought it out at the house of neighbors. He threw aside the cotton clothes given to him by his family, demanding to be dressed in silk and saying that cotton clothes were not fit for his servants. He also demanded money from his father, and cried when his father would not give it to him.

One day Bishen's father mentioned that he was thinking of buying a watch, and little Bishen Chand said: "Papa, don't buy. When I go to Pilibhit, I'll get you three watches from a Muslim watch dealer whom I established there." He then provided the name of the dealer.

His sister, Kamla, three years older than he, caught Bishen drinking brandy one day (thus explaining the dwindling supply of alcohol kept in the house for medicinal purposes only). In his typically superior way, the child told her that he was quite accustomed to drinking brandy, because he had drunk a good deal of alcohol in his earlier life. Later, he claimed to have had a mistress in his former life (he knew the difference between a wife and a mistress), saying that her name was Padma. And, although this woman was a prostitute, Bishen seemed to have considered her his exclusive property, because he proudly claimed to have killed a man he once saw coming from her apartment.

Bishen Chand's memory claims came to the attention of K. K. N. Sahay, an attorney in Bareilly. Sahay went to Bishen Chand's home and recorded the surprising things the young boy was saying. Thereafter, he arranged to take Bishen Chand, along with his father and older brother, to Pilibhit. Not quite eight years had elapsed since the death of Laxmi Narain, whom this little boy was claiming to have been in his earlier life. Crowds gathered when they arrived at Pilibhit. Nearly everyone in Pilibhit had heard of the wealthy Narain family and the profligate son, Laxmi, who had been involved with the prostitute Padma (who still lived there), and how in a jealous rage Narain had shot and killed a rival lover of Padma's. Although Narain's family had been influential enough to get the charges dropped, Narain died a few months afterward of natural causes at age thirty-two.

When taken to the old government school in Pilibhit, Bishen Chand ran to where "his" former classroom had been. Somebody produced an old picture in which Bishen recognized one of Laxmi Narain's classmates who happened to be in the crowd; and when the classmate asked him about the teacher, he correctly described him as a fat, bearded man.

In that part of town where Laxmi Narain had lived, Bishen Chand recognized the house of Sander Lal, the house he had described before being brought to Pilibhit as having a green gate. The lawyer, Sahay, when writing a report later for the national newspaper *The Leader* in August 1926, claimed that he had seen the gate himself and verified that its color was green. The boy also pointed to the courtyard where he said the Nautch girls used to entertain with singing and dancing. Merchants in the area verified the boy's claims. In the accounts published by *The Leader*, Sahay wrote that the name of the prostitute with whom the boy associated in his previous life was repeatedly sought by people in the crowd follow-ing the boy. When he mentioned the name "Padma," the people certified that the name was correct. During that remarkable day, the boy was presented with a set of tablas, or drums. The father said that he (Bishen Chand) had never seen tablas before; but to the surprise of his family and all assembled, Bishen played them skill-fully, as had Laxmi Narain much earlier.

When the mother of Laxmi Narain met Bishen Chand, a strong attachment was immediately apparent between them. Bishen Chand correctly answered the questions she asked (such as the time in his previous life when he had thrown out her pickles), and he successfully named and described Laxmi Narain's personal servant. He also gave the caste to which the servant had belonged. He later claimed that he preferred Laxmi Narain's mother to his own.

Laxmi Narain's father was thought to have hidden some treasure before his death, but nobody knew where. When Bishen Chand was asked about the treasure, he led the way to a room of the family's former home. A treasure of gold coins was later found in this room, giving credence to the boy's claim of having lived a former life in the house.

In examining this case, Ian Stevenson urges that it is especially significant because an early record was kept by a reliable attorney at a time when most of the principals were still alive and capable of verifying Bishen's memory claims. Many of the people who knew Laxmi Narain were still alive and well when Bishen was making his memory claims. They verified nearly all the statements Bishen made before he went to Pilibhit. Moreover, according to Stevenson, the possibility of fraud is remote because Bishen Chand's family had little to gain from association with the Narains. It was well known that the Narains had become destitute after Laxmi Narain had died. As with most cases similar to this, the events could not be explained in terms of anticipated financial gain for the family.

The Case of Swarnlata

In 1951, an Indian man named Mishra took his young daughter, Swarnlata, and others on a 170-mile trip south from the city of Panna, in the district of Madhya Pradesh, to the city of Jabalpur, also in the same district. On the return journey, as they passed through the city of Katni, fifty-seven miles north of Jabalpur,

Swarnlata unexpectedly asked the driver to turn down a certain road to "her house." The driver quite understandably ignored her request. Later, when the same group was taking tea in Katni, Swarnlata told them that they would get better tea at "her" house nearby. These statements puzzled Mishra because he knew that neither he nor any member of his family had ever lived near Katni. His puzzlement deepened when he learned that Swarnlata had told other children in the family further details of what she claimed was a previous life in Katni as a member of a family named Pathak. In the next two years, Swarnlata frequently performed for her mother—and later in front of others—unusual dances and songs that, as far as her parents knew, Swarnlata had not had any opportunity to learn. In 1958, Swarnlata met a woman from the area of Katni whom she claimed to have known in her earlier life. At this time, Mishra first confirmed numerous statements his daughter had made about her "previous life."[3]

In March 1959, a parapsychologist named Banerjee from the University of Rajasthab in Rajasthan began to investigate the case. From the Mishra home in Chhatarpur, Banerjee traveled to Katni, where he became acquainted with the Pathak family of which Swarnlata claimed to have been a member. He had noted, before journeying to Katni, some nine detailed statements Swarnlata had made about the Pathak residence. These statements he confirmed upon his arrival.

Banerjee also found that the statements made by Swarnlata corresponded closely to circumstances in the life of Biya, a daughter of the Pathak family and the deceased wife of a man named Pandley, who lived in Maihar. Biya had died in 1939—eight years before the birth of Swarnlata.

In the summer of 1959, members of the Pathak family and of Biya's marital family traveled to Chhatarpur, where the Mishra family lived. Swarnlata, without being introduced to these people, and under conditions controlled by parapsychology investigators, recognized them all, calling them by name and relating personal incidents and events in which both they and Biya had taken part—events that, according to these relatives, only Biya could have known. For example, Swarnlata claimed that, as Biya, she had had gold fillings in her front teeth. Biya's sister-in-law confirmed as much. The Pathaks eventually accepted Swarnlata as Biya reincarnated, even though they had never previously believed in the possibility of reincarnation.

After these visits, in the same summer of 1959, Swarnlata and members of her family went first to Katni and then to Maihar, where Biya had spent much of her married life and where she died. In Maihar, Swarnlata recognized additional people and places and commented on various changes that had occurred since the death of Biya. Her statements were independently verified. Later, Swarnlata continued to visit Biya's brother and children, for whom she showed the warmest affection.

The songs and dances that Swarnlata had performed presented some problem, however. Biya spoke Hindi and did not know how to speak Bengali, whereas the songs Swarnlata had sung (and danced to) were in Bengali.

After a careful examination of this case, Ian Stevenson concludes that it is very difficult to explain the facts involved in it without admitting that Swarnlata had paranormal knowledge. After all, how otherwise could she have known the details of the family and the house? These details—including the fact that Biya had gold fillings in her teeth, which even her brother had forgotten—were by no means in the public domain. Moreover, how otherwise could we explain her recognition of members of the Pathak and Pandley families? How can her knowledge of the former (as opposed to the present) appearances of places and people be explained? Her witnessed recognitions of people amount to twenty. As Stevenson notes, most of these recognitions occurred in such a way that Swarnlata was obliged to give a name or state a relationship between Biya and the person in question. On several occasions serious attempts were made to mislead her or to deny that she gave the correct answers, but such attempts failed.

Could there have been a conspiracy among all the witnesses in the various families (the Mishras, the Pathaks, and the Pandleys)? Might not all of them have conspired to bring off a big hoax? Not likely in this case, says Stevenson, who notes that a family of prominence such as the Pathaks, with far-reaching business interests, would be unlikely to participate in a hoax involving so many people, any one of whom might later defect. If a hoax occurred, it is more likely that it came from the Chhatarpur side. But even here, Mishra had nothing to gain from such a hoax. He even doubted for a long time the authenticity and accuracy of his daughter's statements, and he made no move to verify them for six years. Most agree that Mishra had nothing to gain but public ridicule.

But even if we suppose that there was some attempt at fraud, who would have tutored Swarnlata for success in such recognitions? Who would have taken the time to do it? Apart from Swarnlata, Mishra was the only member of the family who received any public attention from Swarnlata's case, and he was none too happy about that attention. Also, how could Mishra have gotten some of the highly personal information possessed by Swarnlata about the private affairs of the Pathaks—for example, about Biya's husband taking her twelve hundred rupees?

Might Swarnlata have been tutored by some stranger who knew Katni and the Pathaks? If so, how could he have gotten access to Swarnlata? As Stevenson notes, Swarnlata, like all children in India, especially girls, had her movements very carefully controlled by her family. She never saw strangers in the house alone, and she was never out on the street unaccompanied.[4]

Apart from the legal documentation and methods used in Stevenson's examination of this case, its most interesting feature is the fact that it is only one of very many similar cases. Is there any alternative explanation that can more plausibly account for the facts in such cases than the hypothesis of reincarnation? As we shall see later, there does not seem to be.

Responsive Xenoglossy: The Lydia Johnson Case

Xenoglossy refers to an ability to understand a foreign language not learned by the speaker in a normal way. This phenomenon has occurred in cases similar to the Swarnlata case and constitutes a special kind of evidence in favor of reincarnation—evidence beyond the sort offered in the Swarnlata case. In a book titled *Xenoglossy*, Ian Stevenson presents the case of Lydia Johnson.[5] This case is referred to as an instance of *responsive* xenoglossy, which occurs when the person can respond in a language not previously taught to him, thereby showing an ability to understand the language spoken. It is thus distinguished from *recitative* xenoglossy, which occurs when a person can merely speak, or "recite," a language not previously taught to him but does not know what the words mean or how to respond in the language.

In 1973, Lydia Johnson (not her real name) agreed to help her husband with his experiments in hypnotism. As it turned out, she was an excellent subject because she could easily slip into a deep trance. Dr. Harold Johnson (also a pseudonym) was a distinguished and quite respected Philadelphia physician. He had taken up hypnotism in 1971 to help treat some of his patients. As his experiments with his wife were working so well, he decided to try a hypnotic regression, taking her back in time. In the middle of the regression, however, she suddenly flinched as if struck, screaming and clutching at her head. He ended the session immediately, but his wife had a headache that would not go away. Twice Johnson repeated the session, each time with the same result: On both occasions, Lydia awoke from the trance saying that she had visualized a scene in which old people seemed to be forced into a body of water to drown. She had felt herself being pulled down, then felt a blow to her head, screamed, and awoke from the trance with a headache.

As a result of all this, Dr. Johnson called in another hypnotist, Dr. John Brown (also a pseudonym). Dr. Brown repeated the regression, but before the pain could strike again he told Lydia, "You are ten years younger than that." Suddenly Lydia began to talk—not in sentences, but in words and occasional phrases. Some of it was in broken English, but much of it was in a language that nobody present could understand. Her voice, moreover, was deep and masculine. Then, from the mouth of this thirty-seven-year-old housewife came the words "I am a man." When asked her name, she said "Jensen Jacoby." In this trance she began, in hesitating English punctuated with foreign words, to describe a past life. In this session, and in others that followed, speaking in a low masculine voice, she told of living in a small village in Sweden some three centuries ago. The sessions were tape-recorded, and careful notes were kept. Swedish linguists were called in to translate "Jensen's" statements. In the later sessions, "he" spoke almost exclusively in medieval Swedish, a language totally foreign to Lydia. When asked, "What do you do for a living?" he answered, in sixteenth-century Swedish, "A farmer." To the question, "Where do you live?" he answered: "In the house." And when asked, "Where is the house?" he answered, again in Swedish, "In Hansen." These last questions were also asked in Swedish.

According to all reports, Jensen showed a simple personality quite consistent with the peasant life he described. He showed little knowledge of anything beyond his own village and a trading center he visited. He raised cows, horses, goats, and chickens. He ate goat's cheese, bread, milk, salmon, and poppy-seed cakes made by his wife, Latvia. He had built his own stone house, and he and Latvia had no children. He was one of three sons, his mother had been Norwegian, and he had run away from home.

Certain objects were brought in while Lydia was entranced. She was asked to open her eyes and identify the objects. As Jensen, she correctly identified, in Swedish, a model of a seventeenth-century Swedish ship, a wooden container used then for measuring grain, a bow and arrow, and poppy seeds. She did not, however, know how to use modern tools—for example, pliers.

Why Reincarnation? Proposed Alternative Explanations

At this point, Stevenson's argument for reincarnation is very simple: What would be a better or more plausible explanation for these cases than to assume that the human personality, whatever it is, is reincarnated? Those who are skeptical of reincarnation must provide an equally plausible or better explanation for the data if they are to effectively undermine Stevenson's claim that the best available explanation for these cases is reincarnation. Let's take a brief look at some proposed alternative explanations.

Assume for the moment that cases such as that of Swarnlata and Bishen Chand do exist, and that deception, fraud, or hoax are not plausible explanations for the facts such cases involve. Then there are only three reasonable alternative explanations:

1. Clairvoyance plus subconscious impersonation. According to this explanation, a skeptic may claim that the subjects in each of the above cases are unknowingly clairvoyant—that is, although they do not know it, they have paranormal knowledge (ESP) of certain past events and persons, even though the subjects were not alive at the time of those past events or persons, and even though nobody has told them what happened. According to this view, the subjects, for some reason or other, subconsciously identify with a particular person who lived in the past—a person whose life and beliefs the subject clairvoyantly understands. The subject subconsciously impersonates or dramatizes that person, because the subject sincerely believes that he is in fact that person.

Is this a reasonable alternative to the reincarnation explanation? Not really. In such cases as we have described, children with memories of an alleged earlier life do not, as a rule, show *any* signs of being gifted with clairvoyance. Furthermore, if their memories are

instances of clairvoyance, what would account for its being exhibited in such a specialized, narrow way? As far as we know,
clairvoyance is a general ability, and people who are clairvoyant are
not generally clairvoyant with respect to *one* past event or series of
past events in *one* person's family.

But even if we could explain the "memories" in such cases as
some highly specialized form of disguised clairvoyance, children
such as Swarnlata and Bishen Chand would need to be credited
with *super*-clairvoyance in order to acquire such a large number of
correct details about the life, relatives, and circumstances of a dead
person. Clairvoyance of this special kind does not occur without a
great deal of practice. In other words, this alternative explanation is
problematic because it requires a highly restricted form of clairvoyance not generally encountered.

Besides, even if narrowly restricted forms of clairvoyance did exist, the best clairvoyants make a predictable number of mistakes—
whereas Swarnlata and Bishen Chand made virtually no mistakes in
their memory claims. The frequency of error associated with the
memories of Swarnlata and Bishen Chand is just too low to fit our
general understanding of clairvoyance. Thus the evidence strongly
suggests that clairvoyance is out of the question as a way of explaining how Swarnlata and Bishen Chand acquired knowledge of the
past events they so accurately described. But neither could they
have gotten the information from some third party through natural
means.

This proposed alternative explanation also involves some highly
dubious claims about unconscious impersonation. After all, can
anybody honestly believe that Swarnlata was so good at impersonat-
ing Biya that nobody in Biya's family—neither her brothers, sisters,
father, mother, nor husband—could detect it as a clever bit of subconscious impersonation? It seems very unlikely that she could
have duped the whole family. Of course, some will suggest that
they were all duped because they all believed in reincarnation. But
in this case, as in most other similar cases, the family members did
not believe in reincarnation.

We should also remember that some parts of a person's character
defy successful impersonation over a long period of time. For example, a look, a way of walking, a peculiar sense of humor, or the way
one laughs are all sufficiently personal to require only the most
competent of impersonators to imitate or dramatize. In other words,

the skeptic's proposed explanation requires the existence of a very specialized ability—the ability to impersonate flawlessly the most personal traits of only one person. Can we plausibly attribute such an ability to Swarnlata in view of the fact that she never showed a general ability to successfully imitate anybody else? Surely, if the "clairvoyance/unconscious impersonation" explanation were credible, we would expect to find in subjects like Swarnlata and Bishen Chand a general ability to successfully imitate the difficult traits of other personalities as well. But that is not what we find. Thus, even if we accept the general phenomenon of clairvoyance and "multiple personality," the skeptic's first alternative explanation is unconvincing. And the case for reincarnation is even stronger when we consider cases involving xenoglossy.

2. *Clairvoyant xenoglossy and clairvoyant skills.*   What is important about the Lydia Johnson case, and other similar cases, is that the skeptic cannot begin to explain such an ability by appealing to ESP or clairvoyance. Knowing *how* to do something—like knowing how to speak a foreign language—is quite different from knowing that something or other is so. And knowing how to speak a foreign language (or a different dialect), unlike knowing that something or other happened in the past, defies explanation in terms of ESP or clairvoyance. In order to explain the acquisition of such skills by appeal to clairvoyance, we would have to redefine the nature of clairvoyance as it is now known. Outside of cases such as those we have been examining, clairvoyance has no history of ever being associated with acquired skills, like speaking a language or playing an instrument.

3. *Genetic memory.*   A skeptic might still suggest, however, that we need only suppose that everybody is born with a certain kind of "genetic memory"; that just as one genetically inherits the physical traits of one's ancestors, so the *memories* of our ancestors are also coded in our genes. If so, this explanation goes, under certain circumstances the inhibitors of these traits may be relaxed, allowing the memories of our ancestors to emerge—memories experienced by the subject as though they were the subject's own memories. This explanation asks us to believe that Swarnlata, for example, had inherited Biya's memory and mistakenly identified the memories of Biya as her own. Similarly, Lydia Johnson had inherited the mem-

ory of Jensen, and this extended to her remembering how to speak Jensen's language. In each case, both subjects obviously mistakenly believed that what they were remembering were events in their own respective past lives. In fact, however, they were merely remembering events in the lives of others who passed those memories on to their ancestors in and through the gene pool. Of course, this same explanation is also used to account for the fact, in the Bishen Chand case, that Bishen had an unlearned facility to play the drums.

This third alternative explanation, however, is no more forceful than the earlier ones. If appeal to the phenomenon of genetic memory were the proper explanation of Swarnlata's knowledge of Biya's life, we would expect Swarnlata to be in Biya's genetic line, though clearly she was not. This point was emphasized by Stevenson,[6] and this seems to be an important consideration in cases in which no genetic connection is discernible between a subject and the alleged ancestor whose language the subject can speak. In the case of Lydia Johnson and "Jacob Jensen," tracing the genetic line is pretty much out of the question. But in some of the strongest other cases, it is possible to determine that no genetic line connects the person to the alleged ancestor. In the Bishen Chand case, for example, there was no genetic link between Bishen Chand and Laxmi Narain. This is a decisive reason for setting aside the "genetic" explanation.

Materialist Objections

In a recent extended essay on reincarnation, Paul Edwards, a well-known philosopher of materialism, offers a number of objections to Stevenson's claim that reincarnation offers the best explanation of the data in question. Edwards begins by presenting a general argument to the effect that if Stevenson's case studies are evidence for reincarnation, they must also be evidence for certain other assumptions that are just too incredible for a rational person to take seriously. He says, "What these objections enable us to see is that somebody who opts for reincarnation is committed to a host of collateral assumptions, the most important of which I will now enumerate.

"When a human being dies, he continues to exist not on earth but in a region we know-not-where as a pure disembodied mind or else as an astral or some other kind of 'nonphysical' body; although deprived of his brain, he retains memories of life on earth as well as some of his characteristic skills and traits; after a period varying from a few months to hundreds of years, this pure mind, or 'non-physical' body, which lacks not only a brain but also any physical sense organs, picks out a suitable woman on earth as its mother in the next incarnation, invades this woman's womb at the moment of conception of a new embryo, and unites with it to form a full-fledged human being; although the person who died may have been an adult and indeed quite old, when he is reborn he begins a new life with the intellectual and emotional attitudes of a baby; finally, many of the people born in this way did not previously live on earth, but (depending on which version of reincarnation one subscribes to) in other planes or on other planets from which they emigrate (invisibly of course), most of them preferring to enter the womb of a mother in a poor and overpopulated country where their life is likely to be wretched. The collateral assumptions listed so far are implied by *practically all forms* of reincarnationism, but in Stevenson's case there is the additional implication that the memories and skills that the entity took over from the person who died and that are transmitted to the new regular body appear there for a relatively short time during childhood to disappear forever after.

"If Stevenson's reports are evidence for reincarnation they must also be evidence for the collateral assumptions just mentioned. These assumptions are surely fantastic if not indeed pure nonsense; and, even in the absence of a demonstration of specific flaws, a rational person will conclude either that Stevenson's reports are seriously defective or that his alleged facts can be explained without bringing in reincarnation. An acceptance of the collateral assumptions would amount, to borrow a phrase from Kierkegaard, to the 'crucifixion' of our understanding."[7]

Prior to examining Stevenson's argument, Edwards had argued that we have no known evidence of consciousness existing independently of the brain, and that the very idea of its existing between reincarnated lives in an "astral" body—that is, a "nonphysical" body that sees without eyes, hears without ears, and thinks without a brain—is absolutely incredible.

Edwards's argument has the disturbing ring of a dogmatic materialism committed to showing that, owing to the incredible nature of the reincarnationist thesis, the cases offered by Stevenson *must* be instances of fraud, hoax, or delusional imagining on the part of Stevenson.

But we do *not* know that consciousness cannot exist without a brain. And, unless we simply beg the question, we *do* have evidence that consciousness can exist independently of a brain. Indeed, since no one has shown that Stevenson's cases are instances of fraud, hoax, or delusion, these cases themselves must be considered some of the strongest evidence we have that human personality does in fact survive death and that, by implication, human consciousness *can* exist independently of the brain, flourish for a period without a body as we know it, and be reincarnated. Thus, Edwards's charge that all this is just too incredible for any rational person to believe is simply a blatant bit of question-begging. Moreover, Stevenson's claim that reincarnation is the best explanation of the data implies nothing specific about the nature of an "astral body," where it goes during the period between incarnations, how it is reincarnated, why it is reincarnated, how frequently it is reincarnated, whether every-body is reincarnated, or what the point of it all is. Stevenson's cases imply only that core elements of human personality survive death and are reincarnated.

The Vindication of Stevenson's Reincarnation Hypothesis

In a last-ditch effort, other skeptics of a materialistic persuasion have objected that Stevenson does not take seriously the possibility of fraud on the part of the various parties involved in these cases. Anybody who reads *Twenty Cases* and later works, however, cannot help but be impressed with the seriousness of Stevenson's effort to detect fraud in each of the major cases.[8] For example, in two of the cases cited at the outset of this essay, the case of Swarnlata and the case of Bishen Chand, Stevenson raises straightforwardly the question of fraud. In the Bishen Chand case, it is of course possible that the two families conspired and tutored little Bishen. But for Steven-son, a fraud of that sort would need to involve a number of people in both families as well as strangers (Laxmi Narain's classmates)—and the likelihood of such a fraud being subsequently detected is pretty high. More important, neither family had anything to gain financially from a fraud (just as Bishen had nothing to gain), be-cause both families were poor. Indeed, both families were embar-rassed by the notoriety, wished it hadn't occurred, and, in the case of Bishen's family, did everything possible to keep the case from becoming public. Furthermore, neither family believed in reincarna-tion as a matter of religious or philosophical commitment before the children started telling their stories. And, although Bishen's accomplished drum playing could have been taught to him secretly by his father, that is precisely the sort of thing that is very difficult to do without somebody knowing about it.

Certainly there is some possibility of fraud in every case. The question ought to be, however, whether there is in each case a *reasonable likelihood* of fraud or hoax. Short of subjecting everybody to polygraph examinations (which a good skeptic would not take seriously anyway), what else could Stevenson have done to detect a possible fraud or hoax? For those who think that fraud must be involved in each of these cases, let them establish it in at least a sufficient number of cases to warrant the inference that it is likely in the remaining cases also. Until then, we have only the *suspicion* of fraud, and no reasonable skeptic will be able to detect actual fraud in any of the richer cases. After actually examining the cases, the unbiased reader may well come to view the charge of fraud as a peculiar throwback to the dogmatic attitude behind the refusal of the Roman cardinals to look through Galileo's telescope. If the opponents of reincarnation keep insisting that they will accept *no* evidence for the thesis because it is just too incredible to believe, we must conclude that their opposition is purely dogmatic, perhaps motivated by various kinds of intellectual or emotional investment in materialism.

Finally, still other critics have objected that Stevenson's cases must be "culturally fabricated" because they occur only where people already believe in reincarnation.[9] There are, however, several replies to this objection. First, although the earlier cases Stevenson investigated occurred in cultures where a large number of people believe in reincarnation, many of the richer cases involved families and children who did not believe in reincarnation. Second, even if these cases always involved people who had an antecedent belief in reincarnation, one simply cannot *fabricate* the data that confirms the hypothesis originally accepted for religious reasons. (After all, how does one fabricate, for example, Swarnlata's ability to recognize, without prompting, randomly selected members of Biya's family when the investigators were trying to deceive her? Or, how does one fabricate a subject's ability to speak in an unlearned foreign language or play an instrument unlearned?)

As of 1990, there are literally hundreds of cases, varying in their degree of richness, currently under investigation and documented in Great Britain and North America. Naturally, if one never found any reincarnation cases except in cultures where belief in reincarnation was strong, one might have *some* reason for being suspicious. But, as the body of data comprising cases similar to those we have seen above grows, the grounds for such suspicion dissolve. Hence we must conclude that as things currently stand, for all the reasons we have examined above, there is good reason to suppose that the hypothesis of reincarnation is the best explanation of the cases documented by Ian Stevenson.

ARTHUR S. BERGER

Tests for Communication with the Dead

Arthur S. Berger, Ph.D., is the director of the International Institute for the Study of Death and president of the Survival Research Foundation. Among his many publications are Aristocracy of the Dead: New Findings in Postmortem Survival *and* Lives and Letters in American Parapsychology: A Biographical History, 1850–1987.

Tests for survival after death and communication with the dead are not new. Almost everyone knows of the test involving the great showman and magician Erich Weiss, who achieved fame under the name of Harry Houdini. In an attempt to prove that he still lived after his death, Houdini is supposed to have told his wife, Beatrice, while on his deathbed, that he would send her the message "Rosabelle, believe" in a code they had used in Houdini's mind-reading performances. Three years after Houdini's death from peritonitis, the public was electrified when the medium Arthur Ford claimed to have received this message. The case made sensational headlines but, in reality, provides a sad example of a test that failed. Its value was destroyed by four factors: reports of collusion between Ford and Mrs. Houdini, who supposedly planned to use the famous séance to promote a proposed circuit of lecture halls and theaters; the strong possibility that Ford had used trickery, since evidence of fraud in other séances was uncovered by his biographers after his death;[1] Beatrice Houdini's later repudiation of the message and denial that Houdini had ever communicated with her through a medium; and the fact that she knew what the message was supposed to be, thus allowing the possibility that Ford might have obtained it from her through telepathy.

Long before Houdini, and since the early days of psychical research (parapsychology), people before death have arranged certain "posthumous experiments" with the intention of communicating after death, through a medium, secret verifiable facts as a signal that the communicator, as an identifiable personality, has survived death. What follows is a description of these experiments or tests of survival, old and modern, along with a few suggestions, based on my own research, about how to improve the quality of such tests.

The investigation of the survival question involves tentative acceptance of the possibility of survival and communication after death. These are merely working hypotheses. Words like *medium* and *communicator* are therefore used in this chapter only for the purpose of clarity, not necessarily to imply any belief that survival and communication have already been proven. Indeed, the whole object of the posthumous experiments is to see whether they can be.

First Tests

In 1934 a book was published with the peculiar title *Extra-Sensory Perception*. By "extra-sensory perception," the author, Joseph B. Rhine, meant perception without the use of the senses. The book gave a full account of card-guessing experiments that he and his colleagues had carried out at Duke University to investigate telepathy. In the next five years, the book produced what Rhine called a "hullabaloo," becoming a Book of the Month Club selection and a best-seller.[2]

Rhine's apparent demonstration of telepathy among the living tempts many people to suppose that telepathy was "discovered" in the 1930s, when the public and scientific sectors in twentieth-century America became aware of it. But, in fact, nineteenth-century researchers were already familiar with telepathy and were ready to accept it as a counterhypothesis to mediumistic communications from the dead. If facts known to a deceased person were known to someone alive—no matter how far away from a medium—it was assumed possible that the medium had used telepathy to pick up the facts from that person's mind. This recognition of what has since been called "super-ESP," or "extended telepathy," led people of that era to start their search for empirical evidence of survival using tests involving the communication of facts that were not known to any living person but that could be verified.

One of the first experimental attempts to obtain such survival evidence was made in 1866 in Rockland, Massachusetts, by a brother and sister named Benja and Julia. In this case, the two had talked about life after death and spirit communication. Benja devised an experiment in which an ink mark was made on a brick that was then broken in two, one piece being given to Julia, the other kept by Benja. He hid his piece in a place known only to himself. His plan was to come back as a spirit after he died and tell Julia where his piece of brick was hidden. If he could communicate to her the location of his piece, and if the two pieces matched, they thought it would be proof that Benja had indeed returned in spirit form and communicated with Julia.

After Benja died, Julia and her mother tried for months to communicate with Benja by table-tipping, a spiritualistic procedure in which participants at a séance lightly rest their hands on top of a small table, which then begins to move or "tip" (forward or backward) allegedly by spirits who use the motions to spell out a message. Finally, the table rapped out a message: "You will find the piece of brick in the cabinet under the tomahawk. Benja." Julia went to the cabinet, unlocked it, and found a piece of brick under the tomahawk. It corresponded exactly with the piece of brick she had retained. Benja had returned.

In 1891, twenty-five years after the event and after her mother's death, Julia wrote to Richard Hodgson, secretary of the American Society for Psychical Research, to describe what had happened. Frederick W. H. Myers, one of the leading lights of the English Society for Psychical Research, was so impressed by the story that he described it as one that "narrates the success of a direct experiment."[3] This description, however, is somewhat overly enthusiastic—since we cannot be sure that the facts actually occurred as they were reported. The case depends entirely on Julia's unconfirmed report of an event that had taken place many years before. Her reliability as a witness and the accuracy of her memory and testimony are open to question. In addition, we cannot rule out the possibility of fraud or normal explanation. Benja could have disclosed the location of the brick to Julia, or she could simply have found it while cleaning or looking in the cabinet.

A less suspect and also very early experimental test to obtain survival evidence was initiated by Myers himself. He devised an experiment in which the facts contained in a message were not to be revealed to any living person but were to be communicated by him after death through a medium. He sent a sealed envelope containing his message to his close friend Sir Oliver Lodge with the intention of posthumously communicating its contents. Myers died in 1901, and in 1904, a script obtained by "automatic writing" through Mrs. A. W. Verrall seemed to contain allusions to the envelope left by Myers. The envelope was subsequently opened in the presence of the members of the council of the Society for Psychical Research in London and the communication compared to it. Was it right or wrong? According to the SPR, there was no resemblance between the contents of the envelope and what the Verrall script said it contained. Their conclusion was therefore that "this one experiment has completely failed."[4] It has since been argued, however, that if the meaning of the Verrall script is stretched and interpreted, then, although it may not have a *literal* relation to the contents of the envelope, it will be seen to have a clear *connection* to it.[5]

It is exactly this kind of argument, however, that makes the test faulty. Myers wanted a result that would be clearly and unambiguously right or wrong. Instead, the result was anything but clear and unambiguous, producing doubt and debate over whether the message that the medium received was the one that Myers had placed in his envelope.

From the view of an experimentalist like myself, there were other problems with the sealed-envelope test as well. In the first place, Myers gave himself only one chance to communicate the contents of the envelope. Once the envelope was opened, its value as a test ceased permanently. This is because any later message received, even if correct, could be explained away on the normal grounds that the contents of the envelope were already known.

But there is still another disadvantage of using tests like those of Benja, Julia, and Myers. Although they may have all been familiar with telepathy, none of these early experimenters recognized or took precautions against the possibility of clairvoyance—extrasensory perception of some event or object. Thus, both experiments were laid open to the counterexplanation that a psychic person—as Julia might have been, and as Mrs. Verrall certainly was—had used clairvoyant powers to detect the brick or obtain information from inside the envelope.

Cipher and Lock Tests

Clearly, an ideal test would involve a simple scheme that would allow the posthumous communication of verifiable data to be tested any number of times; it would involve data that were known to no one on earth, that were not left in writing, and whose meaning was not open to doubt or interpretation.

The first attempt to develop such a test was made by the British psychologist and parapsychologist Robert H. Thouless.[6] Elsewhere I have described him as the "father" of other tests, because he inspired them with his own.[7] Thouless's test consists of a message in cipher prepared by the use of a standard method of coding—in this case, a method known as the Vigenere letter square. The encipherment is done with a key passage that, in turn, is reduced to a random sequence of letters that is, in turn, the basis for an enciphered message left with survival researchers. The key passage is not left with anyone, or even left in written form. It is this key passage that the communicator must remember through life and communicate after death.

Thouless's test overcame many of the problems of the sealed-envelope test. For example, whereas that test lost its value once the envelope was opened and its contents were revealed, the theory behind the Thouless test is that the message left behind can be examined any number of times and tested without being compromised.

But the test has disadvantages. It is far from simple in its preparation, and it presents researchers with enormous difficulties: Not only must they determine whether a received passage breaks a test message and is right or wrong, they must also overcome the real problem of knowing exactly what passage Thouless intended to communicate, because he planned not to give the passage itself, but merely to indicate it by a literary title or include it in such a title. Thouless died in 1984. These reasons (and one more to be mentioned) may explain why his test has not succeeded.

Because of the demands and complexities presented by Thouless's scheme, Professor Ian Stevenson, a leading investigator of survival and reincarnation evidence, developed a combination-lock test to make less work for possible subjects of the experiment and for researchers.[8] In Stevenson's test, a subject selects a verbal key consisting of a six-word phrase or six-letter word. A formula is provided by which the letters of the key are translated into numbers and the lock is set to this combination of numbers. The key is not disclosed or left in writing by the lock setter. If communicated after death through a medium, the key word or phrase can be converted back into numbers that will open the lock. The advantage of

Stevenson's scheme is that it completely circumvents the two faults of the sealed-envelope test: A lock can be subjected to a large number of trials by the wrong combination of numbers without spoiling the test; and a combination is either right or wrong—there is no ambiguity.

The disadvantage with the lock test arises from the fact that the lock used involves a delicate mechanism whose design requires absolute precision to set, and this may be too trying, particularly for the fingers of the elderly. Even when he was not elderly, the late J. G. Pratt, a noted parapsychologist and colleague of Stevenson's, used the lock test and had difficulties with the lock because he had forgotten an intricate alignment.[9]

Recent experiments with the Thouless and Stevenson tests suggest that both may suffer from an additional disadvantage: They may be exposed to false or fraudulent keys—that is, keys other than the subjects' that would seem to be correct because they could make test messages readable or unlock the lock.[10]

The By-the-Numbers Test

In order to circumvent the disadvantages of the Thouless and Stevenson tests, I have developed another "cipher" test that I think presents fewer obstacles for subjects and researchers. One advantage of this new test is that only one word—not a key passage—needs to be remembered. A second advantage is that the test requires only a simple counting procedure instead of tedious and complicated encipherment procedures or intricate lock mechanisms. A third advantage is that it needs no expensive and sophisticated lock, but merely an ordinary dictionary available without charge in libraries, offices, and homes. A final advantage is that it does not seem to be subject to decipherment by a false key.[11]

In this test, a dictionary is opened at random and one word chosen as the key. Each letter in the word and in the definition that follows it is numbered consecutively. Then a test message is enciphered using the single key word and its definition. *Enciphered* here means that numbers are substituted for the real letters of a message, so that the message cannot be read by anyone who doesn't have the key to decipher it. The individual who enciphers the message must keep the verbal key to himself or herself and not reveal it to anyone. He or she will not even write down the key. All the individual needs to do is remember it, because it is essential to deciphering the message. The message itself, however, need not be remembered. Such an individual intends, after death, to recall and reveal through a medium the key word used so that the message he or she has left can be deciphered. The basic premise of the test is that, without a verbal key known to an individual alone, a test message enciphered by that person with that key cannot be deciphered. It is the furnishing of a key that no one else could have known that will stand as prima facie evidence both of the survival of the individual and of his or her identity as the same person who coded and deposited a message, because that person was the only one who knew the deciphering key. Even Anthony Flew, the British philosopher and redoubtable skeptic who denies the logical possibility of survival, recognizes that such a by-the-numbers experiment makes it possible to show that a postmortem person is identical with a premortem one.[12]

After converting their messages into ciphers with the verbal key, people, before they die, will deposit the messages with researchers, together with the name and edition of the dictionary they used in the test. An example of a message that might be deposited is 98 6 18 106 29 12 32 26 21 39 53. This jumble of numbers, of course, is meaningless, and the message behind the numbers cannot be read by anyone without the correct key. The numbers were meant to be meaningless. This secret writing—the kind used by spies and diplomats—now, for the first time, can be used to test whether the person who enciphered the message has survived death. The message cannot be deciphered without the one correct key word selected out of a dictionary containing hundreds of thousands of other words. But should the person who enciphers the test message reveal the key after death, researchers would be able to determine easily if it is the right key and verify the test. This checking can be done at once. If the verbal key makes sense out of the coded numbers, it is the right key. There can be no doubt about it.

As did the Thouless and Stevenson tests, this test avoids the difficulties of a sealed envelope, because the enciphered test message can be tried with one incorrect word after another and the test will not be invalidated. There can never be any doubt or room for interpretation. A word will either break or not break the test message. In the example given, only the key world *builder* in the dictionary the subject used—no other—will permit researchers to set up a sequence of numbers that will decipher 98 6 18 106 29 12 32 26 21 39 53 into the subject's message, "We have souls." *Builder* is, therefore, unquestionably the right key.

An unabridged dictionary, say, the second edition of *Webster's New International Dictionary*, will contain about 600,000 words. The chance of finding the key word by a random guess would therefore be 1 in 600,000—odds great enough to suggest that any posthumous success with this test could not reasonably be attributed to chance. Even abridged dictionaries can be used, however, since most of them contain about 150,000 words, and the odds thus remain high enough to make a chance explanation improbable.

If, after the death of a subject, there is a purported message from him or her, it may be a problem to decide if a word in the message relates to that person's by-the-numbers test. So it is hoped that subjects using the test will introduce their keys with a signal that will tell others that the keys are related to their tests, such as the word *test*, or the word *message* and the subject's name or the name of the researcher with whom a test message has been left. In addition to the key word, therefore, the signal should be remembered.

The test also calls for conducting premortem experiments with psychics who try over and over again to learn the keys of living subjects. Since it would seem easier to obtain the key by telepathy while the subject is alive rather than after the subject's death, failures of premortem trials followed by a postmortem success will make less likely the counterexplanation that a key had been obtained telepathically from a subject while alive. Such failures will also suggest that what brought about the postmortem success was new elements that entered the picture—the death of the subject and a willingness now to supply the secret key word.

The test also creates multiple-blind conditions, in which information and responsibility are split among the different groups making up the project—that is, the subjects, mediums, and experimenters—in order to render the possibility of fraud highly unlikely.

Communicators

Gardner Murphy, an eminent psychologist and a leader of parapsychology in America, was once asked what the next step in survival research should be.[13] He wrote that "the discovery of powerful mediums is our most immediate task."[14] But Murphy described only half of the next step in survival research. After all, it always takes two to tango. Even if mediums with paranormal powers of high quality are brought out of hiding, they cannot produce evidence of high quality without the active cooperation of communicators powerful enough to use these mediums and then to supply evidential material. It has seemed to me, therefore, that the second step in survival research—or, in any case, a parallel and simultaneous step—lies in discovering powerful communicators.

That we have not yet understood the necessity of discovering powerful communicators is illustrated by the research efforts to obtain the key of Thouless and Pratt. After Thouless's death, the English Society for Psychical Research undertook fourteen sittings with eight presumably powerful mediums in order to make contact with him. But none produced Thouless's key. The Survival Research Foundation has been engaged in intensive research efforts to obtain Thouless's key as well. We have used mediums and have offered throughout the world a two-thousand-dollar reward to charity for receipt of the correct key. But, in spite of enormous expenditure of energy and resources, the Thouless key has not been received.

Pratt, who died in 1979, has also failed to communicate his key to open a lock. Although Stevenson has made many attempts to reach him through good mediums, and although other researchers and I have conducted an experiment intended to reach him, these efforts have all been unsuccessful.[15]

One valid interpretation of the failures of these experiments is that Thouless and Pratt were weak communicators or noncommunicators who should never have been subjects participating in the tests. Both cases bring to mind Richard Hodgson's observation in his lengthy study of the medium Leonora Piper that, even through such a powerful medium, some classes of people will always fail to communicate, whereas others will succeed.[16] This important observation has never been pursued, but it suggests to me that communicators are as different as the fat, pompous Oliver Hardy was from the skinny, bumbling Stan Laurel. Hodgson's work suggests these questions: If people do survive death, who will be the Oliver Hardys—strong communicators with whom mediums may succeed and who may produce evidential material—and who will be the Stan Laurels—weak communicators or noncommunicators with whom mediums will fail as they have failed in the cases of Thouless and Pratt? And how can we tell the difference between the two classes?

I took the next research step in order to attempt to determine what distinguishes strong from weak communicators. I wanted to know what, if any, correspondences may exist between peoples' personal characteristics and life histories, on the one hand, and their being good communicators after death, on the other. What, for example, are the roles of religion, sex, and personal aptitudes? I have elsewhere reported at length on how I made an in-depth examination of the biographies of twelve apparent mediumistic communicators and reanalyzed a mass of key cases in the literature of parapsychology in order to answer these questions.[17] From extensive comparisons and statistical analyses of qualities, characteristics, and circumstances relating to communicators, I was able to combine the data into the first composite profile of the "ideal" communicator: He will be a male who persists in his interests and endeavors; he will be an artist or man with an aptitude for poetry or music; he will have a strongly pessimistic or doubtful attitude toward the possibility of human survival after death; when he dies, his death will be painful or unpleasant; and he will die leaving work unfinished.[18]

Although one of the twelve biographies I studied was of an excellent female communicator, and although many good female communicators were found in my mass survey of reports in the literature, there was a great predominance of males (78 percent). Thus, for the best communicators and more promising results, researchers should focus mainly on males who match this profile.

Neither Thouless nor Pratt seems to have approximated this composite. So, if we select deceased people who do fit this profile as targets for survival experiments, and if we choose living people of this type as participants in the "by the numbers" test, we can perhaps prevent the types of foredoomed tests represented by Thouless and Pratt, save much time and expense, and produce high-quality survival evidence. I have tested the hypothesis that the selection of favored or gifted communicators (i.e., those who match my ideal profile) as research subjects would produce a greater chance of success. The experiment I conducted, which I have described elsewhere, was aimed deliberately at a deceased person who met my model of the powerful communicator: The result was the receipt of evidence that was very suggestive and of high quality.[19]

F. GORDON GREENE
STANLEY KRIPPNER

Panoramic Vision: Hallucination or Bridge into the Beyond?

F. Gordon Greene is a scholar of theoretical parapsychology and consciousness research. He is currently writing a book linking the imagery structures of otherworld passage as found in myths, fairy tales,
and fantasies to the phenomenological structures of otherworld passage as found in out-of-body experiences and near-death experiences.
Stanley Krippner, Ph.D., is professor of psychology and director of
the Center for Consciousness Studies at Saybrook Institute, San Francisco. His works include Human Possibilities, Healing States (as
editor), The Realms of Healing, and Dreamtime & Dreamwork
(in press).

Among the myths, legends, and superstitions whose origins will
probably remain obscure is the belief that at or near the moment of
death one's whole life flashes instantaneously before one's eyes or
through one's mind. Until approximately fifteen years ago, many
people would probably have questioned the reality of this fleeting
vision, regarding belief in it as a common superstition or old wives'
tale. Recently, however, newly gathered evidence from the emerging
field of near-death studies has authenticated the experiential reality
of the life review, also called *panoramic memory recall*.

As a consequence of the new scholarly interest in near-death
experiences (NDEs) that has developed over the last two decades,
reseachers have dusted off the history books and have begun to
look for NDE cases in bygone eras. They have discovered that a
number of people in various historical periods have reported experi-

encing NDEs very similar to those documented in contemporary times. The phenomenon of panoramic memory recall, like other prominent characteristics of contemporary NDEs, has also been discovered in the accounts of earlier historical periods. It is now clear that numerous people in both historical and contemporary times who have come close to but eluded physical death have reported experiencing this fleeting yet personally astonishing flashback.[1]

While the vast majority of people reporting life reviews believed that they were on the verge of death at the time of the vision, there is also a reported tendency for the life review to occur among epileptics during the preseizure aura signaling the onset of epilepsy.[2] Panoramic memory recall has also reportedly taken place among people who have ingested powerful psychedelic substances.[3] And at least one person reports that he has witnessed a panoramic vision of his life while dreaming.[4]

Among literary classics there is perhaps no better portrayal of the life review than in Charles Dickens's *A Christmas Carol*. In this story, Mr. Scrooge not only travels into his past but also experiences a "flash forward" in which he sees his own gravestone in a "possible future," a future that inspires him to transform his life in order to avoid the dismal fate he sees awaiting him. Fiction aside, in a small number of actual cases, a flash-forward component does form a part of the panoramic vision. In contemporary literature, Kurt Vonnegut's satirical best-seller *Slaughterhouse Five* is based on elements of the panoramic vision. The central character of the story, Billy Pilgrim, becomes "unstuck in time" and ranges, in no particular order, through the course of his life. Interestingly, Billy Pilgrim's episodes of time travel share some fascinating parallels with one person's actual panoramic vision.[5]

Characteristics of the Life Panorama

Raymond Moody aptly summarizes the characteristics of the life review as follows:

> This review can only be described in terms of memory, since that is the closest familiar phenomenon to it, but it has characteristics which set it off from any normal type of remembering. First of all, it is extraordinarily rapid. The memories, when they are described in temporal terms, are said to follow one another swiftly in chronological order. Others recall no awareness of temporal order at all. The remembrance

was instantaneous; everything appeared at once, and they could take it all in with one mental glance. However it is expressed, all seem in agreement that the experience is over in an instant of earthly time.[6]

Moody goes on to report that despite its rapidity, the life review is almost always described as a display of visual imagery that is incredibly vivid and real. He mentions that in some cases the images are reported to be in vibrant color, three-dimensional, and even containing movement.

Examining the life review in more detail, we may add that some people report that this vision is supervised by a higher spiritual presence, whereas others mention no such presence. The review is sometimes reported to begin in early childhood and then to trace forward to the moment of the near-death crisis. With others, the review begins at the moment of the near-death crisis and traces backward into early childhood. The review sometimes encompasses an entire life, while at other times only the major portions or highlights of a life are observed. Sometimes visual images of the past become superimposed over the scene of the present life crisis, creating a visual montage. In other cases, one perceives only the most memorable of life events at first, and then, as the vision develops, more and more events come into view until the entire life is simultaneously encompassed.

Associated with this last pattern of development is a tendency for the vision to be described as flashing by rapidly at first, after which it takes place in an aura of timelessness as one's whole life springs into simultaneous view. The review may occur after the person's consciousness appears to have separated from his or her physical body. In other cases, the review occurs after the person appears to have passed down a long dark tunnel and has begun to emerge out the other side. At yet other times, no out-of-body experience (OBE), tunnel passage, or any other common experiential component of the NDE is reported in conjunction with the review. Occasionally, people report a sense of plural consciousness as they appear to be present in each scene of their life while simultaneously observing these events as if from a third-person perspective.

People report that mental activity during this panoramic vision vastly accelerates: Thoughts are processed at a rate that is so indescribably swift as to be inconceivable to people who have not directly experienced this state of consciousness. In contrast to this mental acceleration, and in some sense apparently correlated with it, people report impressions of outer or environmental time slowing down: In these cases time seems to be drawing out or expanding while the life events under scrutiny appear to be happening in continually slower motion. As the vision develops, the person's ability to see and comprehend things greatly expands. As a consequence of this expansive understanding, people believe that they are able to take in and intellectually digest, all at once, the whole of their lives emerging into panoramic view.

Yet another striking feature of the life review is the assessment that people often make of their life behavior while witnessing the vision. Often they believe that they are in some sense judging themselves, scrutinizing how well they have lived and how much they have learned while living. Others report a sense of being judged or held accountable for their lives, at least sometimes by an apparent higher spiritual presence. While most NDEers are awestruck during the act of perceiving the life review and remember the vision in a positive or even ecstatic light, at least one came to believe that she was damned after witnessing the vision.

Undoubtedly, one of the most curious effects of the life review, reported in a small number of cases, is the person's sensation of perceiving not only a flashback but also a flash-forward encompassing possible future events that may or may not subsequently occur as envisioned. Some claim, for instance, that they have subsequently lived through flash-forwards contained in the vision, even though at the time of the vision they could not make sense of these seeming future events. They might, for instance, believe that they have accurately perceived a future mate, the children they are to have together, and the home in which they are destined to live, even though they have yet to meet this mate.[7] This last finding would seem to challenge the conceptual viability of looking upon the life panorama purely as a form of memory, although the vision undoubtedly must be assumed to be intimately related to memory. As a result of this flash-forward component, the term *life overview* may be descriptively more appropriate than the terms *life review* and *panoramic memory*. (Henceforth we will refer to the vision as the *life panorama* and continue using the term *panoramic vision*.)

The state of consciousness in which the life panorama takes place also has a tendency to grow at its terminal end—that is, in its farthest point of development away from ordinary waking consciousness—into a classic mystical experience. Visions of all-encompassing knowledge, feelings of having utterly transcended space and time, and the sense of having communed with (or even having become engulfed within) divine intelligence are reported.[8] Some NDEers, we should note, pass directly into this transcendent condition without experiencing either an overview of their life or an OBE.

An occasional outgrowth of personal flash-forwards is visions of a prophetic order possessing potentially immense planetary significance. Those NDEers who have witnessed prophetic visions sensed that they have perceived one or more of the following possible futures: nuclear disasters, polar shifts, increased incidents of earthquakes coupled with heightened volcanic activity, worldwide famines, or other scenarios of planetary death and destruction. Some have envisioned a new, more spiritually evolved planetary culture emerging out of this period of tumultuous upheaval.[9]

Frequency and Likelihood of the Life Panorama

Although the life panorama is commonly experienced during NDEs, it is, like all other facets of the NDE, not a universal feature. For example, of the forty-eight NDEers whose cases are analyzed in Michael Sabom's *Recollections of Death,* only two reported experiencing life panoramas.[10] Most studies, however, have reported a higher frequency of panoramic visions among participating NDEers. The best indication as to the frequency of panoramic visions during NDEs comes from the largest and presumably most representative NDE survey yet compiled. In their 1982 book, *Adventures in Immortality,* George W. Gallup and William Proctor report the findings of their nationwide survey of NDEs. An estimated 8 million Americans have, according to these researchers, undergone NDEs. Of these people, an estimated 2.5 million have experienced "the impression of reviewing or reexamining [their] past life in a brief, highly compressed period of time."[11] Thus, while the life panorama is not universally experienced during NDEs, it appears to be a surprisingly common occurrence, especially in view of the fact that such experiences were relegated to the dark corners of superstition less than a generation ago.

Based on a number of studies of the NDE, including those reviewed above, it appears that between 20 and 30 percent of the NDEer population experiences panoramic vision. The reason for this particular figure is unknown, although the fact that only a minority of NDEers experience this vision is in keeping with the experiential pattern of the NDE as a whole. Aside from common mood elevations associated with NDEs, all other facets or phases of this state of consciousness almost never appear together in a single case. Of the five or six most noted experiential facets of the NDE— the sensations of the OBE, the tunnel experience, the meeting with spirits, the life panorama, and the voyage into heaven—usually only two or three, in any particular combination and in varying developmental orders, are present in any actual case. This patchwork mixture of experiential components and juxtaposing of developmental sequences in NDEs constitutes one of the greatest mysteries surrounding these states of consciousness. To account for this experiential pattern for the NDE, we offer the following explanation.

The quality of consciousness possessed by a person during this apparently transcendent and otherworldly voyage may not share enough experiential ground with our ordinary state of consciousness to enable memories of this excursion to be thoroughly integrated into our ordinary memories. The radical changes in time sense reportedly experienced during NDEs may be of critical importance in this regard. In ordinary consciousness, our lives are ordered inside more or less fixed temporal parameters. During NDEs and related mystical states of consciousness, however, this fixed order is broken, and each succeeding instant may seem to grow, or even contract, in duration. Indeed, time is sometimes reported to become irrelevant, and people often cannot be sure if everything is happening at once or if, on the contrary, the events they experience have become frozen in eternity. Considering such circumstances, we may begin to appreciate why different people remember different developmental sequences for the NDE and why they are able to "remember" or "forget" different phases of it. The life panorama, accordingly, may be witnessed by a much larger percentage of NDEers than those who are able to bring recollection of it back with them into ordinary consciousness.

Whatever the plausibility of the preceding speculation, a more solid basis for inference does exist concerning the question of who, among the NDE population in general, is most likely to experience a life panorama. Russell Noyes and Roy Kletti report that "women experienced it more frequently than men, as did persons age twenty or less. Those who nearly drowned were more likely to report a revival of memories than were persons who suffered falls."[12] These findings, it should be remembered, point only to tendencies. One of the most famous panoramic visions on record was experienced by the Swiss geologist Albert Heim, over forty at the time, who slipped off an Alpine mountainside and fell approximately sixty feet to a snow-covered ledge below.[13] Other researchers have come to believe that panoramic visions have occurred most frequently during NDEs that began suddenly or unexpectedly—for example, during sudden accidents or while the person was suffering unexpectedly from a condition such as cardiac arrest.

Three Approaches

While the authenticity of the life panorama and the frequency with which it occurs are no longer subject to debate, there is still no consensus among researchers about how best to account for it. One approach to explaining the life panorama utilizes materialistic constructs drawn from biology, neurology, and biochemistry. This approach usually regards the survival of human consciousness beyond the death of the physical body as impossible.

A second approach utilizes psychological constructs drawn from the fields of psychology, psychiatry, and philosophy. Such theories may maintain a positive, negative, or neutral perspective on the question of survival. The choice has to do with the theorists' view of the human mind—that is, whether he or she believes that the mind may be looked upon as an entity distinct from the physical body and brain. Granting the separateness of mind from matter, the question then becomes whether human consciousness, as a mental entity, may exist separately from matter in a "mind-dependent world."

A third approach involves theories that unquestionably do support a survivalistic interpretation of the NDE and life panorama. This third class, which includes but is not limited to psychological theories of mind-dependent worlds, may be termed "transpersonal" or "transcendental." It presumes the existence of other worlds or dimensions outside the material universe into which it is possible for human consciousness to pass temporarily during NDEs, OBEs, and other mystical states of consciousness, or permanently upon the demise of the physical body.

When the materialistic approach is directed specifically to attempts at understanding the life panorama, investigators often call attention to the research of S. K. Wilson, who reported that panoramic visions sometimes occur among people undergoing epileptic seizures.[14] This finding has been construed by some NDE researchers as suggesting that temporal-lobe excitation may induce the vision.

Vivid memory recall has also been elicited by Wilder Penfield in patients undergoing electrode probes to the cerebral cortex during open brain surgery.[15] Penfield's research has also frequently been cited by those seeking a neurological basis for the life panorama.

Most recently, the neuropsychiatrist Vernon Neppe and the neuropsychologist Michael Persinger have investigated the possible relationship between epilepsy, NDEs, OBEs, other unusual states of consciousness, and purported anomalous activities (that is, telepathic, clairvoyant, or precognitive impressions). Persinger, for example, is quoted as saying that in epilepsy "an electrical discharge takes place at a particular focal point [in the temporal lobes]. Because temporal-lobe neurons are so sensitive, that single lightning stroke soon spreads into an energetic storm."[16] This storm, interestingly, may spread to the hippocampus, deeply buried in the temporal lobes and known as the "gateway to the memory." The inference here seems to be that stimulation to the hippocampus via epileptic seizure somehow retrieves and lucidly replays before the conscious mind a vast array of past experiences at such a phenomenal rate as to seem instantaneous.

What may be the most significant discovery spawned by this new research is the identification of "temporal-lobe sensitives." In this view, promoted in particular by Persinger, all human brains may be said to lie along a continuum of temporal-lobe sensitivity. Clinical epileptics occupy one extreme along this continuum. Numerous other temporal-lobe sensitives may undergo neurophysiological excitations similar to epileptic seizures, but not powerful enough to gain medical attention or to require medical treatment.

The notion of temporal-lobe sensitivity may turn out to be one of the most fruitful ideas ever proposed to explain why different people are "experientially launched" from such diverse embarkment points as dreaming, fantasizing, mortally dangerous circumstances, psychedelic-drug intoxication, and even ordinary waking consciousness into states of consciousness possessing profoundly similar phenomenological correlates. Perhaps in each of these different mind/body conditions, temporal-lobe sensitivity is a critical common denominator. Although this has not yet been demonstrated, the possible relationship between temporal-lobe sensitivity and anomalous experiences may be one of the most exciting areas for parapsychological investigation in the 1990s.

In a neurophysiological analysis of the NDE, Daniel Carr examines the possible role of the underlying limbic-lobe region of the brain in the generation of complex NDE-related visions.[17] Carr traces the possible routes and modes of modulation that various peptide neurotransmitters undergo in their movement through the limbic lobes during moments of extreme duress or potentially mortal danger. The resulting limbic-lobe hyperactivity may be elaborated in the cerebral cortex to produce the complex visions associated with NDEs and related states of consciousness. Many of the neurotransmitters he discusses are known to have a profound influence upon mood and memory. His approach may enable researchers to better understand the remarkable elevations in temperament and increased capacities for memory retrieval associated with NDEs.

In psychological theorizing directed to the life panorama, several variants on psychoanalytic thought have been employed. Johann Christop Hampe, for example, draws upon Freud's theory of a "censor" lodged in the human unconscious. Hampe proposes that this censor is an aspect of the unconscious that suppresses "our judgments about our wrong actions."[18] The censor ceases operation during the flooding forth of countless past memories that create the panoramic vision. These approaches draw upon different aspects of psychoanalytic theory.

Noyes and Kletti draw upon another of Freud's constructs—his assertion that it is impossible for human beings to conceive of their own deaths.[19] In Freud's view, whenever we try to imagine our personal death, we do so from the vantage point of a surviving spectator. Freud believed that everyone is unconsciously convinced of his or her own immortality. Noyes and Kletti adapt this idea as an explanation for the life panorama, arguing that people who believe they are confronted with their own imminent demise psychologically withdraw, or dissociate, from the scene of the impending disaster by engaging in a hallucinatory escape into the past. In this way such people attempt to place themselves in the safety and comfort of the life they once knew so as to avoid what appears to be the ghastly fate rapidly overtaking the physical body. The report of one subject, studied by Noyes and Kletti, seems to support this view. Commenting on the time she fell from a horse, this subject stated,

"To ease the horrible, gruesome thoughts [that death was nearly upon her] an involuntary situation of my mind took over. It was much more pleasant to see wonderful past times flash through."[20]

The documented existence of negative panoramic visions would, however, seem to take away with the second hand what this Freudian speculation has given us with the first.[21] When the life panorama offers an even more unsettling presentation for consciousness than the experience of one's own death, why would one be motivated to "escape" from the first unenviable circumstance into a second, even more unpleasant circumstance? We might also point out that Noyes and Kletti attempt to buttress their thesis on the basis of one person's statement, while entirely ignoring the beliefs of the vast majority of NDEers on the meaning and significance of the NDE. Most NDEers believe that their experiences offered them an actual glimpse into a life beyond material existence.

Finally, we shall examine a few variants on the transpersonal or transcendental theory. Each of these approaches supports the belief that NDEers and other "ecstatic voyagers" have actually gained a glimpse into an afterlife realm that transcends the material universe. This general approach has been developed along a number of different lines. Inspired by conceptions of the afterlife derived from "channeled sources," some writers interested in the question of human survival of bodily death have proposed the following possibility. Upon the death of the physical body, human consciousness "merges" with the unconscious mind—or, rather, incorporates the unconscious mind into an expanded mental framework. In the words of one purported communicator from beyond:

> On our own sphere . . . I seem to have but one memory. I have the ordinary memory of physical things that I had on earth, and this is merged into the subliminal memory which operates consciously here. When one passes over, one's subliminal memory operates consciously . . .
>
> [Here] we do not recall memory, because it is present. All is upon the one page. Past is present in that sense with us. It is impossible to forget anything; not that we are always looking at the past, but it is there for us to read in our memory. It is there without any striving for it.[22]

In other words, freed in death from the constraints of space and time, the human psyche is able to embrace all of the forgotten experiences of the past and link them together with the conscious mind, creating an expanded or superconscious state of awareness.

When we shift our attention from psychological constructs to questions regarding the type of "environment" capable of housing such a superconscious state of being, we come to the second variant on this theoretical approach. Stanislav Grof and Joan Halifax briefly touch upon this second variant in suggesting that panoramic vision may possess "holographic" properties in instances where the vision displays "different periods of life . . . simultaneously as part of a single continuum."[23] Kenneth Ring elaborates upon this suggestion in formulating his "holographic/four-dimensional" theory of human consciousness. In Ring's view, during NDEs and related states of consciousness, human consciousness ascends into a fourth dimension that is organized, in some sense, upon holographic principles. Ring looks upon the panoramic vision as a "holographic phenomenon par excellence" because during it "everything is happening all at once, synchronously."[24]

We will conclude this section by examining one additional transcendental explanation for panoramic vision, which also draws upon the fourth dimension as a theoretical construct. To begin to appreciate this approach, imagine a one-dimensional being confined to a line world. This being may move in either of the two available directions in which his or her line extends. If this line is vertical, these directions would be up and down; if horizontal, they would be back and forth. Our line-lander knows of no other possible directions for spatial movement.

Now let us suppose that unknown to this one-dimensional being, the whole line-world is moving at right angles to itself across a two-dimensional plane—like an uncooked spaghetti noodle rolling uniformly across a flat tabletop. Sections of the plane that have already intersected with our line-lander's world will be referred to by him or her as "time past"; sections currently intersecting with it are "time present"; and sections that have yet to intersect with it will be "time future." Now let us imagine that the consciousness of this linear being somehow expands to occupy a position above the plane. What this line-lander had perceived of his or her life *successively* while embedded in the line world would now be seen simultaneously from the vantage point of this more spacious, dimensionally superior position.

If our own world of three dimensions traces through a higher four-dimensional space in a manner analogous to the image pictured above, then each instant in our earthly lives may be regarded as a three-dimensional cross-section of this higher dimension. Our past and future, then, are literally laid out behind and in front of us within this fourth dimension. As our attention expands out of that part of us embedded in three-dimensional space—prompted, let us suppose, by some life-threatening circumstance—we experience what is commonly called "out-of-body travel," which could be conceived as the first step into higher space. During this extradimensional extension, our sense of a "present moment" undergoes expansion, also moving out from three-dimensional space into four-dimensional space, until it overlaps with the time span of our entire life spread out in time. Thus we are afforded, in one simultaneous vista, a miraculous glimpse that encompasses the whole of our physical lives. Time has, in a sense, "spatialized" into a fourth dimension. Upon returning to the physical body following the cessation of this threat to our life, our consciousness and our sense of a "present moment" collapse back down into the fixed parameters of space and time perceived from within the material universe.

A detailed analysis of how the various specific features of the life panorama, reported by individuals, correlate with this higher-space theory lies beyond the scope of the present essay. We will offer at least some indication, however, of how the two fit together in the following brief discussion.

The vast acceleration in mental processes, the tracing backward from the precipitating life crisis toward childhood, coupled with the impression that the future and past have come into view, offer to our mind's eye an image of human consciousness surging out beyond the confines of brain-filtered awareness and dilating into the past and future.[25] The sense of perceiving one's life in part and fleetingly, after which the vision becomes timeless and all-encompassing, also suggests a rapid swelling of human awareness from a location that is inside time to a timeless position, wherein life- and time-bound states of being are observed as if from eternity. The sense of time becoming "drawn out" or "expansive" to the point where time stands still also suggests an expansion of the present moment. This expansion begins within our time-bound region of the cosmos and culminates in the emergence of human consciousness into a four-dimensional "spatialized time" region of the cosmos. In a reverse manner of sorts, the sensation of the life panorama beginning in early childhood and tracing forward to the life crisis may be construed as an instance where people are withdrawing or contracting back down into the physical universe. In this view such people have already experienced, though perhaps they do not remember it, the expansive phase of this extradimensional excursion.

Human Eschatology: Judgment and Transcendence

Two additional facets of the life panorama warrant attention when pondered within the context of survival theory. These are the sense that people are engaged in a judgment of their lives and the sense that they possess an expansive understanding during the vision. The judgment theme, correlated with the life panorama, forms an essential part in the eschatological teachings of many religions. As far back as the ancient Egyptian religious text *The Instruction of King Meri-ka-re* (circa 2500 B.C.), the judgment theme has been linked with the whole of the human life perceived in a greatly compressed period of time. In the relevant passage from this text, a council of deities judges the life of newly deceased people, deities who regard a human life as if it had transpired in but an hour.[26]

In the Tibetan Book of the Dead, the Lord of Death is said to observe the life of newly deceased people as reflected in the "mirror of karma." The life behavior recorded therein determines the afterlife destiny of the soul. Souls of the deceased will then pass into any one of a number of different spiritual worlds, heaven worlds or hell worlds, depending upon the life conduct recorded in the karmic mirror. After periods of residence in these spiritual worlds, these souls are destined to return once again, on the wheel of karma, into physically embodied existence. Only those people who have attained enlightenment—that is, who have come to a personal realization of the indescribable condition of nirvana—are able to extricate themselves from the wheel of karma. In Buddhism, paradoxically, attainment of nirvana involves the realization that there is, in an ultimate appreciation of reality, no "self" or "soul" to be absolved from karmic debt.

In *The City of God*, the early church father Saint Augustine offers a Christian perspective on the themes of judgment and panoramic vision, drawing upon the concept of the life panorama to interpret the "Book of Life" in Revelations 13:8. He believes that the biblical mention of this book refers to a certain divine power present in the human soul that becomes activated during judgment. The light of

God's presence, says Augustine, infuses souls of the deceased with a higher spiritual illumination that enables them to observe the whole life with a marvelous rapidity. The knowledge absorbed from this vision then either excuses or accuses that soul's conscience. Eternal salvation or eternal damnation follows the acquisition of this knowledge from the "Book of Life."

The thought that each of us, as spiritual beings destined to transcend the death of our physical bodies, might actually be faced with a judgment of our life is an undeniably unsettling prospect. In fact, few thoughts could be more unsettling to all but the most saintly of human beings. If we are to examine the life panorama and related eschatological beliefs in light of survival theory, however, we cannot help but attend to this issue: If we do find ourselves in such a judgment, will it be we ourselves, some higher spiritual aspect of ourselves, some other higher spiritual being (or council of beings), or a supreme being that conducts the judgment? What of the consequences of this judgment? Do we face a continuing circuit on some sort of karmic wheel, or do we find ourselves lodged eternally in heaven or hell? And what of free will? Is our whole life laid out in front of us inside a higher four-dimensional space, as some flash-forward cases would seem to suggest? Or, as other cases may seem to suggest, are there a number of possible futures situated in higher dimensions of space, some of which are to be actualized within our own three-dimensional space while others are not, depending upon the life choices we make?

Those of us who are uncertain as to our spiritual status may perhaps be consoled in the knowledge that mystical experiences seem, as a matter of course, to follow panoramic visions. It could be argued that such patterns would not be expected if the cosmos were so structured as to allow only a predestined few to attain heavenly salvation or the transcendence of material existence.

In the mystical-experience/higher-space perspective, the panoramic vision may be regarded as a condition of consciousness, or as a level of being, positioned at a critical juncture between time and eternity. Upon our physical demise, having ascended out of the material universe into this intermediate cosmic region, we might then be in a position to transcendentally encompass the lower life we have just lived. Having examined and profited from our experiences of this life below, and having incorporated these insights into our higher spiritual essence, we might then wish to direct our gaze upward from time-bound states of being onto the transcendental reality unfolding before us.

Perhaps only when we have ascended into this higher world will we be able to fully comprehend the meaning of our lives, the meaning of our relationship to the wider cosmos, to time and eternity, to God and immortality, and to other unfathomable mysteries. Perhaps it is true that "now we see through a glass darkly; but then face to face: Now I know in part; but then I shall know even as I am known."[27]

D. SCOTT ROGO

Spontaneous Contact with the Dead: Perspectives from Grief Counseling, Sociology, and Parapsychology

D. Scott Rogo is a well-known researcher, educator, and writer in the field of parapsychology. Among his twenty-nine books on parapsychology are The Welcoming Silence, The Infinite Boundary, *and* Life after Death.

Consider the following three cases of reported spontaneous contact with the dead or dying:

The year was 1970, and it was a sad time for Romer Troxell, who was driving from his home in Pennsylvania to Portage, Indiana. The sojourn was a heartbreaking ordeal, since he was making the drive to identify his son's body, which had been found by a deserted road. But from the moment he entered the city he could sense his son's presence, which seemed to "speak" inside his mind. The voice proceeded to give him directions where to find his (son's) stolen car. By following these instructions, Mr. Troxell drove to nearby Gary, Indiana, and began searching for the vehicle. The guidance from his son directed him through many streets until the car was spotted. Mr. Troxell executed a quick U-turn and began to follow his son's likely murderer. With the help of a relative (who was making the drive with him), they pressured the car to stop. Mr. Troxell engaged the

This work is dedicated to the memory of Kenneth Honeychurch, with whom I often discussed these reports. News of his untimely death in Orinda, California, at the age of thirty reached me within an hour of my completing this essay, so it is befitting that it should be used to acknowledge the contributions he made to the lives of his many friends.

driver in some innocuous conversation while the relative phoned the police. The driver was duly arrested and later convicted of the murder.

Romer Troxell later told reporters, "Charlie left me after we caught the killer. Charlie's in peace now. The police were onto the killer, though. I came to realize what they uncovered in their investigation. But when I heard my son guiding me, I acted. Maybe the Lord wanted it that way."[1]

The redistribution of the small estate left upon the death of Mr. James L. Chaffin is probably the most unique in contemporary legal history. The events leading to the distribution began in 1921, when the elder Chaffin died in North Carolina. His formal will (written in 1905) lopsidedly bequeathed his property solely to his third son, Marshall, which left his other sons and wife virtually disinherited. Why he showed such favoritism has never been made public, but in 1925 the spirit, soul, or whatever of Mr. Chaffin became restless. One day late at night, his son James P. Chaffin received a visitation from the deceased man. The younger Chaffin would later explain that he couldn't determine whether he was waking or dreaming when the apparition materialized. The visitations continued and the phantom finally spoke to him. Pointing to the overcoat he wore, the phantom said, "You will find my will in my overcoat pocket."

The message so impressed James P. Chaffin that he searched for the overcoat, which was in the possession of yet another brother. They found the inside lining sewn, and, ripping it open, they discovered a handwritten note that said: "Read the 27th chapter of Genesis in my Daddy's old Bible." The chase continued!

The Bible was still in the possession of their mother, who had stored it with other memorabilia in her attic. In the presence of two witnesses, Chaffin opened the Bible, which broke into three pieces. Hidden within the pages of the Book of Genesis was a handwritten will that Chaffin Sr. had written in 1919. This revised document distributed the estate equally and provided for his wife. Since the handwriting was clearly Chaffin's, it was not contested when filed with the court, and the property was redistributed.[2]

Few people will ever experience the utter shock and bewilderment felt by Mr. and Mrs. Grant Oyler, a Mormon couple living in Carmel, California, when they learned that their little son Ben had AIDS. Because he was born with hemophilia, his parents often gave him injections of a clotting factor to control his bleeding. These injections—derived from blood pooled from hundreds of donors—were given before such blood could be checked for contamination. Ben eventually suffered the consequences as his parents stood by hopelessly, supported only by their strong religious convictions.

After a series of hospitalizations and other medical interventions, Ben died on July 4, 1986. During these last terrible days, the boy's brother Aber (short for Abraham) was staying with his grandparents. Sometime near two o'clock in the morning, the little boy came into his grandparents' room to say, "There's a little ghost flying around my room." The elderly couple explained that his experience was merely a dream and escorted him back to his room. The child responded firmly, "It was Ben. He came in here and told me he won't have to hurt anymore 'cause he's got only one more day here."

Ben Oyler died three hours later.[3]

These three distinctly different cases represent a small fragment of the literature on spontaneous contact with the dead or dying. Relatively little of this literature is known to the general public, because much of it dates from an early period (1880–1930) and remains buried in the obscure annals of psychical research (or parapsychology; see below). Despite this situation, this huge body of literature is vastly important to the study of immortality and should be examined by anyone who is seriously interested in the case for life after death.

People who report these contacts rarely seem confused by their experiences. Indeed, such episodes bring with them an utter conviction that life extends beyond the grave. I would like to briefly review here the kinds of spontaneous cases that point to survival of bodily death and to examine several surveys on the subject.

Historical Research on Spontaneous Contact with the Dead

Humanity, both in modern Western society and in technologically unsophisticated cultures, has been perennially fascinated with the idea of the "return" of the dead and our prospects for spiritual immortality. Cases of the dearly departed appearing to their friends and relatives—perhaps to say good-bye or to right some wrong they suffered—crop up repeatedly in the folklore and popular history of different cultures. The critical study of such experiences dates only from the late 1800s, however, when several intellectuals and scholars in Great Britain began investigating reports of people who could "communicate" in trance with the dead, as well as reports of telepathy, haunted houses, and other psychic phenomena. These phenomena were popularly espoused and promoted by Spiritualism, a controversial religious movement that migrated to Great Britain from the United States in the 1850s and whose ideas seemed opposed to Victorian materialism. Yet few scientists had made a collective effort to study these incredible stories in order to ferret out the truth from the nonsense. So in 1882 a group of intellectuals—Professor Henry Sidgwick of Cambridge, F. W. H. Myers, Edmund Gurney, and others—organized the Society for Psychical Research. (This organization is still in existence and regularly publishes in the field of *parapsychology*—a term that replaced the older term *psychical research* in the 1930s.)

It wouldn't be possible within the scope of this essay to summarize much of the society's early work, which by the turn of the century consisted of fifteen lengthy volumes of research. Several committees were set up within the SPR to investigate and evaluate different forms of psychic phenomena, and one of these committees began collecting cases of spontaneous psychic phenomena reported by the general public. The collection and investigation of these cases eventually resulted in the publication in 1886 of the two-volume *Phantasms of the Living*, written by Edmund Gurney with the help of Frank Podmore and F. W. H. Myers.[4] Several of the cases contained in the book directly suggested the possibility of personal immortality. The SPR investigators discovered that many people experienced "crisis" apparitions similar to the Aber Oyler case summarized earlier: Either shortly before or subsequent to a person's death, his/her visible form was seen by a friend or relative living in a distant city or country. In some of these instances, the witness did not know that the deceased person was sick; at other times, the phantom was seen by two people simultaneously.

The following report is typical of several published in *Phantasms of the Living*. The reporter was a servant to a family living in London:

> I sat one evening reading, when on looking up from my book, I distinctly saw a school friend of mine, to whom I was very much attached, standing near the door. I was about to exclaim at the strangeness of her visit when, to my horror, there were no signs of anyone in the room but

my mother. I related what I had seen to her, knowing she could not have seen, as she was sitting with her back toward the door, nor did she hear anything unusual, and was greatly amused at my scare, suggesting I had read too much or been dreaming.

A day or so after this strange event, I had news to say my friend was no more. The strange part was that I did not even know she was ill, much less in danger, so I could not have felt anxious at the time on her account, but may have been thinking of her; that I cannot testify. Her illness was short, and death very unexpected. Her mother told me she spoke of me not long before she died. . . . She died the same evening and about the same time that I saw her vision, which was the end of October 1874.

The servant's mother certified to the SPR that she was told the story before they learned of the friend's death.

Despite the simple nature of these cases, the effort to determine their meaning was fraught with difficulties. Did they or didn't they indicate that some element of consciousness survives death? The SPR researchers were soon hopelessly divided on the matter. F. W. H. Myers felt that these apparitions probably represented the dying person's consciousness, released by death or oncoming death, manifesting itself spatially in the distant location. Especially convincing to him were collective cases in which two or more people saw the figures.

But other SPR luminaries came to different conclusions. Edmund Gurney in particular felt that such cases could be explained by telepathy. It seemed likely to him that the witnesses received subconscious telepathic messages from the dying patients, which they projected outward in the form of realistic hallucinations. Collective cases could possibly evolve from some sort of psychic contagion between the witnesses.

In light of such possibilities, Myers began turning his interest to postmortem cases in which the apparition appeared days, weeks, or even months after the person's death. Especially provocative to him were cases in which the figure communicated important information to the friend or relative. The SPR scholar published a selection of such cases in 1892, which included the following report:

Elizabeth Conley, the subject of so much comment in the various papers, was born in Chickasaw Township, Chickasaw County, Iowa, in March 1863. Her mother died the same year. Is of Irish parentage; brought up, and is, a Roman Catholic; has been keeping house for her father for ten years.

On the 1st day of Feburary, 1891, her father went to Dubuque, Iowa, for medical treatment and died on the 3rd of the same month very suddenly. His son was notified by telegraph the same day, and he and I started the next morning after the remains, which we found in the charge of Coroner Hoffmann.

He had 9 dollars 75 cents, which he had taken from his pocketbook. I think it was about two days after our return she had the dream, or vision. She claimed her father had appeared to her, and told her there was a sum of money in an inside pocket of his undershirt. Her brother started for Dubuque a few days afterward, and found the clothes as we had left them, and in the pocket referred to found 30 dollars in currency. These are the facts of the matter as near as I can give them.[5]

Included in the evaluation of the case were statements from the local pastor, who personally spoke with the witness, and certifications from her brother. Letters testifying to the good faith of the people involved in the incident were also published.

Of course, criticisms of the SPR's early work were published in the popular press. As a result, their chief investigators replicated their study of spontaneous cases and published a second report with even better-documented cases in 1894.[6]

Contemporary Research on Spontaneous Contact with the Dead

The reports presented so far in this chapter exemplify the way cases concerning contact with the dead were collected and studied in the nineteenth and early twentieth centuries: Reports were examined case by case, and evaluating the specific evidence of each story was the researcher's primary concern.

While these investigations represent a considerable body of fascinating material, more far-reaching issues that emerged from their study had to be bypassed. For example, is purported contact with the dead a rare phenomenon? What sort of people report such experiences? Does the cultural background of the witness influence the experience?

These issues could be neither explored nor resolved until the rise of sociology and the employment of proper demographic research. While the purely parapsychological study of cases of contact with the dead continued (and continues to this day), the exploration of such experiences as a cultural phenomenon gradually rose within the social sciences.

Bereavement Hallucinations

This psychosocial phenomenon first came into prominence when psychologists specializing in bereavement counseling noticed that widows and widowers often mentioned such experiences.[7] These episodes consisted of everything from visual materialization of the departed person to the simple sense that the deceased was present, though not sensorily detectable. To the best of my knowledge, the first consideration of this phenomenon—pointing out its frequency—appeared in P. Morris's book *Widows and Their Families*, published in 1958.[8] A year later, a team of Japanese researchers decided to see if experiences of contact with the dead were common in their own country, a possibility they believed to be likely because Japanese cultural beliefs—which involve respect for the continued existence of departed relatives—could feasibly encourage such experiences. In order to implement their study, they sampled fifty-four widows living in Tokyo, but could interview only twenty of them. Ninety percent reported some sort of contact with their deceased spouses. Most notable was the fact that none of the widows found the experiences frightening or psychologically threatening—perhaps, the researchers speculated, because Japanese religious beliefs provide a socially sanctioned framework for such experiences.[9]

The Japanese researchers were incorrect, however, in their belief that these experiences were especially common in their country. Subsequent research has shown that these experiences may be a normal part of the grieving process, whether they represent psychological or genuinely paranormal episodes. This finding was the result of a project undertaken by Dr. W. Dewi Rees, a Welsh psychiatrist who conducted a detailed study of bereavement contacts that was published in 1971.[10]

Dr. Rees was then a physician practicing in Wales, and he extended the scope of the Japanese study by interviewing 293 widows *and* widowers in a selected region in Wales. His goal was to interview every bereaved spouse in the district in order to gain exact baseline statistics on experiences of contact with the dead. He came close, successfully talking with 94.2 percent of them. Nearly half of these people reported such experiences. It was particularly interesting that men reported these contacts no less frequently than women. Nor did Dr. Rees find that these experiences necessarily occurred during the most critical phases of grieving—i.e., during the first six months of the bereavement process.[11] Such contacts were slightly more common during the first decade after the loss, but reports by people whose spouses had been dead twenty years or longer were common in the study.

Dr. Rees also discovered that visual manifestations of the dead occurred more commonly during the first decade of bereavement, but this finding was just barely statistically significant. Other findings of the study:

1. Young people reported postmortem contacts slightly less frequently than people bereaved in middle age. But this, too, was a borderline finding.
2. Childless couples experienced postmortem contacts slightly less frequently than widows/widowers with children.
3. Probably the strongest finding in the entire study was that the likelihood of experiencing a bereavement hallucination was directly correlated with the length of the marriage.

When Dr. Rees reported these fascinating findings in the *British Medical Journal* in 1971, he posited that there was nothing pathological in these experiences:

> It seems reasonable to conclude from the study in mid-Wales that hallucinations are normal experiences after widowhood, providing helpful psychological phenomena to those experiencing them. Evidence supporting this statement is as follows: Hallucinations are common experiences after widowhood; they occur irrespective of sex, race, creed, or domicile; they do not affect overt behavior; they tend to disappear with time; there is no evidence of associated illness or abnormality to suggest they are abnormal features; they are more common in people whose marriages were happy and who became parents; and people are able to integrate the experience and keep it secret.[12] Evidence supporting the claim that these experiences are helpful is twofold: Most people feel they are helped; and among the people least likely to be hallucinated are those widowed below the age of forty, yet it is known from the evidence that people in this younger age group are particularly likely to die soon after widowhood.

It may seem from this remark that the psychiatrist considers these experiences purely psychological in nature. Dr. Rees does hold open the possibility, however, that some of these experiences represent genuine contacts with the departed.

A confirmation of the pioneering Welsh study was briefly reported in 1974 by Richard A. Kalish of the Graduate Theological

Union, in Berkeley, California, and David K. Reynolds from the University of Southern California, in Los Angeles. They were primarily interested in studying whether a series of psychological factors—such as belief in immortality and so forth—changed during widowhood. Their survey was extensive because it consisted of a cross-ethnic examination of these factors, in which representative people (in both the bereaved and control groups) from the white, black, Japanese, and Latino communities in Los Angeles were interviewed.[13] While the study was not designed specifically to replicate the Rees study, the following item was included on their survey form: "Have you ever experienced or felt the presence of anyone after he had died?"

Nearly 60 percent of the widows reported such experiences, and 24 percent claimed multiple contacts. While not specifically stated by the researchers, these contacts were presumably with the respondents' deceased spouses. This finding contrasted with the data contributed by the control subjects, of whom less than a third reported contacts with the dead. This finding could suggest that such experiences are linked specifically to the bereavement process, but such an interpretation does not necessarily preclude the possibility that some of these experiences represent genuine paranormal incidents. A person who has recently died, if survival really takes place, might have an especially ardent desire to reestablish contact with his or her spouse.

It is unfortunate that relatively few formal studies of bereavement hallucinations have been conducted by psychologists or related counselors. This is surprising because the existence of such postmortem contacts is mentioned in most books on grief and bereavement. In this respect, it is interesting that clinicians specializing in grief counseling sometimes offer conflicting interpretations of the phenomenon. Some of them offer purely psychological explanations, suggesting that the experience is based on the desire to be reunited with the departed.[14] Other experts who work directly with the bereaved have, however, come to the conclusion that some of these encounters could be ontologically real.[15] Still other psychologists seem completely confused over the reports they have heard. My favorite discussion reflecting this consternation can be found in a recent book on coping with grief. The author—a California counselor specializing in grief therapy—offers a standard psychodynamic explanatory model for bereavement hallucinations. But she then explains that a client (personally known to her) once saw her deceased husband's form in a doorway wearing his favorite robe. Her mother-in-law was sitting in the room, but the primary witness did not report the sighting to the elderly woman. She later learned, however, that her mother-in-law had seen the figure wearing the same bathrobe. The counselor wisely concludes from such cases that "the explanations of *why* these experiences occur are less important than the fact that they are very real to the people who experience them."[16]

Whatever the nature of the experience, bereavement counselors maintain that such encounters do not represent pathological reactions to grief and can be helpful to the bereaved person.

Surveys of the General Public

The study conducted so thoroughly by Kalish and Reynolds improved on the earlier Welsh and Japanese studies in one respect: they tried to determine whether contact with the dead was specifically linked to bereavement. Their results indicate that while related to bereavement, contact with the dead is commonly reported by the public in general.

Probably the most comprehensive study on postmortem contacts also comes to us from Kalish and Reynolds. Their research on psychological changes caused by widowhood was merely a small part of a lengthy research project exploring psychocultural influences on death and dying, which resulted in the publication of their book *Death and Ethnicity* in 1976.[17] Since they heard so many reports of contacts with the dead during their study, they devoted a great deal of space to this phenomenon in their book and other publications.[18] Pooling the results of the widows and widowers with the other participants in the study, they found that over 50 percent of the women and over 30 percent of the men reported some sort of contact with the dead.

By far the most commonly reported form of contact with the dead mentioned in the Kalish/Reynolds study was especially significant dreams. But some people (like those in the study conducted by Dr. Rees) reported more realistic "visitations" from the departed. They reported visual sightings, sensing the presence of the deceased, or hearing his or her voice. These experiences were extremely private, but in a separate publication Kalish acknowledged that, on rare

occasions, other people present with the witness shared the experience.[19] I find it rather humorous that, having made this concession,
the researcher never considered the possible implications of such
cases.

In the long run, Kalish came to the conclusion that these experiences represent nothing supernatural. He stated in 1979:

> I do not believe that these people have engaged in conversation with the
> dead. . . . However, I do believe that the experiences are both very vivid
> and seem very real, that they are neither dreams nor indication of
> emotional disturbance. Rather, they are signals that the intensity of the
> loss or other experience is extremely great and extremely enduring, and
> that the previously formed associations with the dead person were
> extremely strong. As a result, minimal stimuli in the form of a familiar
> room or chair or even in the form of a memory become sufficient to re-
> create an apparent reality in the form of the person who had died.[20]

It is little wonder, in this respect, that Kalish shied away from discussing those rare reports where other people who were present
shared the experience.

Some further statistics on contact with the dead were collected
during the same period that Kalish and Reynolds were publishing
their results. This project was undertaken by the National Opinion
Research Center in Chicago in 1973.[21] By surveying a sample of
close to fifteen hundred people, researchers found postmortem contacts reported by 25 percent of the general public. The likelihood of
encountering such contacts did not seem related to chronological
age, religious denomination, ethnicity, or education.

It is extremely unfortunate that neither the Kalish/Reynolds team
nor the National Opinion Research Center was particularly interested in the contents of the cases reported to them. Their reports
focused primarily on the statistical findings emerging from their
studies. Because both of these projects were basically sociological
studies, perhaps this oversight can be forgiven. But would an experientially oriented study of the reports themselves support the
Kalish/Reynolds bias that we are dealing with an exclusively psychological phenomenon?

Recent Surveys of Postmortem Contacts in Everyday Life

The oversight that characterizes the Kalish/Reynolds and National
Opinion Research Center surveys was partially corrected in 1980

when Julian Burton decided to study cases of spontaneous contact with the dead within a more phenomenological/humanistic framework. The researcher was working toward his doctorate in psychology and used his survey as the basis for his dissertation.[22] The study grew from a dramatic personal event that Burton experienced shortly after his mother died in 1973 from a massive stroke:

> My wife and I were entertaining relatives. I was in the kitchen cutting a pineapple when I heard what I thought were my wife's footsteps behind me to the right. I turned to ask the whereabouts of a bowl but realized that she had crossed to the left outside my field of vision. I turned in that direction to repeat my question and saw my mother standing there. She was fully visible, looking years younger than at the time of the death. She was wearing a diaphanous pale-blue gown trimmed in marabou which I had never seen before. . . .
>
> The figure gradually dissolved, but the real denouement came the following day. The next morning I called my sister Jean and told her what had happened. She was upset and began to sob, asking why our mother had not come to *her*. I felt bad about this and asked her if she believed what I had told her, whereupon she said she *knew* it was true. Why was she so certain? She replied that she and Mother had gone shopping together two weeks before the stroke and Mother had tried on the pale-blue gown I had described. Although Mother looked attractive in the dress and wanted it very much, she had balked at paying two hundred dollars for such a garment.

Even though he was forty-two years old when this incident took place, Burton decided to finish his education and doctorate, focusing on people claiming similar experiences. He initiated his research by preparing a survey form that asked people whether they had experienced contacts with the dead. Specific items on the form requested information on the respondent's relationship to the departed, the frequency of the experiences, and so forth. Because opportunities for distributing the survey were limited, Burton first handed it out to small psychic-study classes in the Los Angeles area. He changed his strategy, however, when he saw the extraordinarily high percentage of confirmations he was receiving. Suspecting that his informants were biased by their interest in psychic matters, the researcher sent out the forms to the psychology departments of three Los Angeles colleges. Fifty percent of the students *still* reported postmortem contacts. Burton collected data from fifteen hundred respondents by the time he finished his project.

The results of Burton's research confirmed several of the findings described in the preceding section. The elderly are especially prone to such contacts, but they certainly have no franchise on the experience. Most of the respondents reported either dream contacts or the subjective feeling that the departed ones were present, but other more vivid stories of disembodied voices, waking visions, and full-blown sightings of the deceased were also described. These experiences were extremely meaningful for the witnesses, because 60 percent of the respondents changed their feelings about death on the basis of them.

What especially impressed Burton were the cases themselves, because some were similar to his own. For example, the following report involved his own housekeeper:

> While cleaning my bedroom one day, Lita heard a "wolf whistle." Thinking a workman outside the window was looking in (although I live on the third floor), she continued her work. The whistle sounded again. When she looked up she heard a woman's voice call her twice by name. She looked through the other rooms and found no one. Despite a cold chill and goose bumps, she thought no more of it until she arrived home to find a letter from El Salvador with the news of the death of her best friend. Her friend's mother wrote that Lita's gift of a pair of new shoes arrived three hours before the death. This news triggered Lita's memory; the wolf whistle had been a girlhood signal between her friend and her.

Another case was contributed by a young college student and concerned the death of his great-aunt. The fact that they obviously didn't share the type of relationship that ordinarily gives rise to strong emotional bonds makes the episode even more provocative:

> I heard of her death as soon as I got home from school. I had to hurry off, however, to go to my catechism class. I went up to my room to get my book, and as I was reaching for it, I stopped and slowly turned around. Sitting on my other bed was a slightly transparent woman with her hands folded in her lap. She just sat there smiling at me. I had not seen her since I was six months old, but somehow I knew it was my great-aunt who had just died. We had corresponded for years through letters, and I still correspond with her sister, with whom she lived. I realized what was happening, but I wasn't frightened because I was almost overwhelmed with this intense feeling of love. There was nothing threatening or disturbing about the experience at all. I stood very still and purposefully started memorizing details of what she looked like, what dress she was wearing, and so on. When she was gone, I went downstairs and told my mother and sister what had happened. If I was ever afraid of death, I'm not anymore. I strongly believe

in some sort of life after death. I'm not sure that if another family member had had an experience, they would have said so.

Burton came to feel that the results of his research bear significantly on the practice of psychotherapy and bereavement counseling. It is his opinion that such experiences are rarely reported by the grieving, a conclusion certainly consistent with the findings of Dr. Rees in Wales. This problem has been exacerbated, claims the psychologist, by certain counselors who try to "explain away" such incidents and refuse to validate their experiential reality.

Because Burton's research was never published except for a short piece in a popular magazine, it is a sad fact that few grief counselors will ever learn about it.[23] But there is a sidelight to his work that simultaneously confirms the earlier research of Reynolds, Kalish, Rees, and others. Based on a sample population of 1,473 people taken in 1984, the National Opinion Research Council conducted a second study of experiences of contact with the dead by the general public. The results of this poll showed that 67 percent of people with deceased spouses report such contacts, while a total of 42 percent of the general public makes similar claims.[24] Certainly an unexplained phenomenon that is reported by nearly half of the American public deserves the recognition and respect of conventional psychology.

What Survives?

None of the specific cases summarized or cited in this essay, by itself, proves that life extends beyond physical death. Each suffers from certain evidential weaknesses or can be explained by theories other than psychic survival. Many people who report such contacts could be experiencing brief and nonpathological hallucinations or illusions, especially if they experienced their encounters while grieving. But this isn't to say that *some* bereavement "hallucinations" and *some* contacts with the dead couldn't be paranormal— that is, real extrasensory contacts of some unknown nature. But even if we consider a few of the cases reported in this chapter to be genuinely paranormal, such a consideration still only *suggests* that postmortem communication took place. The reason is as follows:

Scientists and psychologists who study psychic phenomena have learned that extrasensory perception is a common human capability. Some parapsychologists even believe that every case pointing to survival can be explained on this basis. Let's take a look at the three cases that opened this chapter and interpret them from this perspective:

1. Perhaps the voice that Romer Troxell heard in his mind was his own subconscious, which psychically "knew" the location of his son's stolen car.
2. Perhaps the disappointed and disinherited James P. Chaffin clairvoyantly learned of his father's second will and the message in his overcoat. This information emerged in the form of realistic dreams of his father's return from death.
3. Perhaps little Aber Oyler received a telepathic signal from his brother, which he "translated" into a "ghost" in his room— i.e., something similar to an eidetic projection produced by the boy's subconscious upon receiving the message.

This is not to say that such explanations are correct, only that they remain logical possibilities that cannot be dismissed.

If the cases and data surveyed in this chapter do point to survival, they still reveal relatively little concerning *what* survives. Is it the soul? Cases such as the discovery of the Chaffin will and the restless phantom described by Myers show that, possibly, some earthly memory survives death relatively intact. Whether this survival is permanent or temporary cannot be determined, even though the case of the Chaffin will suggests that personal survival could last for years.

It is my personal conviction that some reports of contact with the dead *do* represent genuine contacts with our deceased friends and relatives. I further believe that while bereavement hallucinations probably represent psychological effects, some such reports could be real communications from the beyond. It is difficult not to be moved and impressed by the stories told by the recently bereaved, to see the utter conviction in their eyes when they repeat their experiences—much the way my own late grandfather took me aside during a family get-together: With utter simplicity he told me that, a few weeks previously, he had seen my deceased grandmother standing in the kitchen smiling at him. The event took place several months after his grief over her death had lifted. I see little reason for postulating hypothetical, psychological, or possibly neurological mechanisms to explain such phenomena.

But these are personal ruminations that will not impress the skeptic, nor has that been my goal in this chapter. What I have tried to show is that a belief in spiritual immortality can be based on more than religious faith. Searching for evidence of psychic survival can and should be a scientific endeavor. The research presented here represents the results of this search and the provocative information it has gathered. The specific interpretation of this information is for the readers to determine.

PART TWO

The Challenge of Materialism

D avid Lorimer begins this section by tracing the age-old opposition between the materialists and the survivalists in the West, examining attitudes toward death from the time of the Homeric Greeks and the Old Testament Hebrews through the rise of modern scientific materialism and the theories of Darwin, Marx, and Freud. In contrast to the well-known view of these latter thinkers that consciousness is merely a "by-product" of the activity of the brain, Lorimer draws our attention to the lesser-known opposing view propounded by F. C. S. Schiller, William James, and Henri Bergson: that consciousness is not actually *produced* by the brain, but is rather *transmitted through* the brain and is therefore not necessarily destroyed when the brain dies. "The transmissive theory fits facts rejected as supernatural by materialism," Lorimer points out; hence, it is able to attain an explanation that is, in Schiller's words, "ultimately tenable instead of one which is ultimately absurd."

Recent research devoted to the near-death experience gives us a glimpse into the death process and throws considerable light on the possible validity of the transmissive theory of consciousness, Lorimer maintains. Citing a typical near-death case in which a person, while lying apparently unconscious on a bed, is actually in a state of extremely heightened and expanded awareness that transcends normal space-time boundaries, Lorimer points out that the accuracy of information received while in such a state can be explained only by the transmissive theory, and that the burden of proof is on the materialist to provide an alternative explanation.

Rupert Sheldrake is a well-known biologist who subscribes to a variation of the transmissive theory of consciousness. In his piece

Sheldrake critically examines the materialistic assumption that memories are localized and somehow "stored" inside the brain, and concludes that all such theories are either unproven or incoherent. He then describes a new model of memory based on his own theory of "morphogenetic fields"—that is, fields associated with living things that help mold developing cells, tissues, and organisms and that connect similar things, through "morphic resonance," across space and time. According to Sheldrake's theory, memory can be explained as an organism's "tuning in" to its own past states through morphic resonance with its own morphogenetic fields.

Sheldrake uses the analogy of a transistor radio to explain the difference between the "localized memory trace" theory and his own version of the transmissive theory: Damage to the radio may lead to distortion or loss of the music it transmits, but this does not mean the music is actually produced or stored within the set. It means only that the radio has lost its ability to accurately transmit sounds. Similarly, damage to the brain may lead to distortion or loss of memory, but this does not prove that the lost memories were stored inside the brain. Sheldrake posits that "the damage might simply prevent the brain from tuning in to its own past states."

Sheldrake's model does not automatically lead to the conclusion that survival after death occurs, because it could be interpreted within a materialistic framework in which the conscious self is regarded as identical with the functioning of its brain. Nevertheless, if Sheldrake's theory is interpreted within a framework in which the conscious self is not regarded as identical with the functioning of its brain, but rather *interacts* with the brain through resonance with its morphogenetic fields, "then it is possible that the conscious self could continue to be associated with these fields even after the death of the brain, and retain the ability to tune in to its own past states." Sheldrake's conclusion is, therefore, that "a field theory of the mind could be developed that is compatible both with a new scientific understanding of memory and with the possibility of a conscious survival of bodily death."

Clearly there are profound philosophical differences separating those who deny and those who assert the possibility of survival after death. But is there any way in which these opposing viewpoints might be reconciled? In "Beyond Dualism and Materialism," the philosopher Mark B. Woodhouse examines this question and attempts to develop a new way of thinking about the survival issue that transcends the traditional opposition between materialists and survivalists. Calling his model "energy monism" and basing it on the concept of "energy consciousness" rather than on the concept of "mind" (as in classical dualism and idealism) or "matter" (as in classical materialism), Woodhouse argues that energy monism provides a better explanation of near-death and out-of-body experiences, extrasensory perception, apparitions of the dead, and so forth than either materialism or dualism.

Woodhouse also asserts that "at certain phases in the evolution of species, there is a convergence of cycles that makes for large-scale shifts in perspective over comparatively short periods of time." Maintaining that we are now in such a convergence of cycles—a period of great transformation of consciousness—he predicts that the idea of survival of physical death is going to become "progressively less problematic in contexts where previously it has been." Additionally, he believes, growing numbers of persons will begin choosing to intentionally "leave their bodies." Parapsychological research, including reincarnation investigations, will enjoy increased support. Past-life emotional-release work will gradually be incorporated into mainstream psychotherapy. And the care of terminally ill patients will reflect a clear awareness of the dynamics of the impending transition. "The actual dynamics of survival will remain open to debate well into the future," Woodhouse asserts, "but the question of *whether* we survive the death of our bodies will be taken by a majority to have been settled."

Woodhouse's predictions are of course based on the assumption that present research interests and trends will continue well into the future. Meanwhile, the debate between the survivalists and materialists can hardly be considered settled and continues in full force. In the final chapter of this section, the well-known consciousness researcher and psychologist Charles T. Tart presents a powerful challenge to the materialist side of the debate in a trenchant critique of the materialistic worldview, which he bases on the data of parapsychological research.

Tart observes that the reality of "psi phenomena"—telepathy, clairvoyance, precognition, and psychokinesis—has been firmly established by parapsychological experiments. This is important to the question of survival after death because such phenomena are manifestations of *mind* that have resisted all attempts to reduce them to known physical forces. Thus they are potent counterexamples to the materialistic thesis that the mind is identical with the brain. "These psi phenomena do not 'prove' postmortem survival,"

Tart grants, "but they do at least refute the claim of materialistic science that the survival of consciousness after death is impossible in principle."

Tart then considers potential scenarios of what our state of consciousness might be like if we do survive death. First he notes that "ordinary consciousness," our usual sense of "I," is quite changeable and composed of many different "I"'s, or subselves, that do not long "survive" the small changes of ordinary life—for example, intense emotions, fatigue, alcohol intoxication, and so forth. He argues that ordinary consciousness is not likely to survive the vastly greater change of death. Thus, if we do "wake up" after death, we should not be too surprised if we find ourselves in an altered state of consciousness, perhaps analogous to the dream state or to some of the altered states of consciousness known to shamans, yogis, and other mystics.

All in all, the evidence and arguments marshaled by the authors in this section should lay to rest the hard-core materialist dogma that the survival of human consciousness after death is somehow impossible in principle—as if the very idea were an oxymoron. But, of course, the more positive thesis—that survival not only is possible but actually occurs—will be much more difficult to support.

DAVID LORIMER

Science, Death, and Purpose

*David Lorimer is director of the Scientific and Medical Network, an
international group of scientists and doctors who wish to broaden the
framework of science and medicine beyond materialistic reductionism.
He is also chairman of the International Association for Near-Death
Studies (U.K.) and the author of* Survival? Body, Mind and Death
in the Light of Psychic Experience *and* Whole in One *(in press).*

> Death is the hardest thing from the outside and as long as we
> are outside of it. But once inside you taste of such completeness
> and peace and fulfillment that you don't want to return.
>
> C. G. Jung, *Letters,* vol. 1

> Man must at last wake out of his millenary dream and discover
> his total solitude, his fundamental isolation. He must realize
> that, like a gypsy, he lives on the boundary of an alien world; a
> world that is deaf to his music, and as indifferent to his hopes as
> it is to his suffering or his crimes.
>
> Jacques Monod, *Chance and Necessity*

The two statements above were made by two great scientists of our
century. Yet their underlying worldviews were diametrically opposed. Jung was one of the great pioneers of our understanding of
the inner world, which he explored in detail for over sixty years.
The quotation comes from a letter written in 1945, after a heart
attack he experienced the previous year. While he was recovering
he had a series of visions that amounted to an initiation and
changed the way he related to the three-dimensional space-time
world, after which he used the Platonic language of the body as the
"tomb of the soul"—a limitation on the form of consciousness. He
did not at first wish to return to the physical world, but had the

unusual experience of meeting a delegation protesting against his premature departure from the world. If he had in fact died in 1944, then much of his most interesting work during the 1950s on synchronicity, alchemy, good and evil, and so forth would have remained unwritten. The inner world is the dimension of meaning that enables us to find significance in our experience of outer life. Jung could not help finding meaning even in certain kinds of coincidence, as elaborated in his theory of synchronicity—meaningful coincidence.

Monod, a biologist, would have substituted the word *mere* for the word *meaningful* above. He inherited the traditional twentieth-century aversion to purpose, or teleology, shunning the question "Why?" in favor of answers to the question "How?" In observing the purposeful behavior of animals, however, even he was obliged to admit some degree of purpose, yet he coined the world *teleonomy* to distinguish his observation from the idea of there being any intrinsic purpose in life.

Monod's explorations were devoted to the public, objective world of biology: Instead of directing his gaze inward, like Jung, he looked outward through the microscope. His lens was purpose-blind, like Nelson at the Battle of Copenhagen who, putting the telescope to his blind eye, is said to have remarked: "I see no ships." In seeking to achieve a stance of clinical detachment and impartiality, science has cut itself off from the inner dimension of meaning. It is hardly surprising, therefore, that it looks out into a world that seems alien and purposeless, without values: Such is the lens.

Apart from his near-death visions of 1944, Jung had many experiences that led him to believe that a part of the psyche or mind is not confined to space-time, but is capable of overcoming its limitations in demonstrations of telepathy and precognition. He asserted that although valid proof of the continuance of the soul after death could not be marshaled, "there are experiences which make us thoughtful."

One such experience concerned a visitation from a friend whose funeral Jung had attended the previous day. His friend beckoned Jung to accompany him in his imagination to his house. On arrival they went up to the study, where his friend climbed on a stool and showed him the second of five books with red bindings on the second shelf from the top.

Overcome with curiosity, Jung visited his friend's widow the following morning and asked if he could look something up in his friend's library, a room he was not familiar with. There he discovered the stool and spotted the five books with red bindings on the second shelf from the top. They were translations of Zola, and the second volume was entitled *The Legacy of the Dead*. This must surely have been one of the experiences that made Jung "thoughtful," because he had gained information through channels other than the senses—and the title of the book seems peculiarly apposite!

What would Monod have said of this incident? Mere coincidence? A fantasy on Jung's part resulting from chemical imbalance in his brain after attending the funeral? One is reminded of the famous lines by Coleridge:

> What if you slept, and what if in your sleep you dreamed,
> And what if in your dream you went to heaven
> And then plucked a strange and beautiful flower,
> And what if when you awoke
> You had the flower in your hand.
> Ah!
> What then!

How could Jung fail to conclude that a part of his mind was functioning outside the normal confines of space-time? What if death is simply the liberation of the mind from the shackles of the space-time dimension? Viewed from the outside, we cannot tell whether the mind is extinguished at death, or whether it becomes permanently absent from a physical body that it no longer animates or organizes. It is not for nothing that the Latin word for "soul" is *anima*.

Worldviews and the Nature of Explanations

What constitutes a satisfactory explanation? Why are some explanations regarded as "unsatisfactory"? It all depends on the assumptions and categories used. Although dictionary definitions of the word *explanation* are expressed in terms of "making things clear or intelligible," etymologically the word means "to unfold." What is unfolded was already implicit or enfolded. So, to explain something is to unfold or unpack its implications. An explanation has been defined by Basil Willey as a "restatement of something—event, theory, doctrine, etc.—in terms of the current interests and assumptions." Thus, to be satisfied with an explanation means accepting certain terms and categories as ultimate, as incapable of further explanation. Theories based on such presuppositions are regarded as intelligible and "plausible," while theories based on rival assumptions may be derided as unintelligible or "implausible." (In this connection, it is revealing that the word *plausible* is derived from the Latin *plaudere*, meaning "to clap the hands in approval.")

If the plausibility of an explanation depends on our presuppositions, these in turn depend on our training—itself a feature of the prevailing intellectual climate. From time to time, argues Willey, there arises a general demand for a restatement, indicating "a disharmony between traditional explanations and current needs." The seventeenth-century scientific revolution was one such movement, in which naturalistic explanations superseded supernatural and theological ones. Primacy was accorded to matter and materialistic explanations, today referred to as "scientific." As we shall see in more detail below, this meant explaining mind and consciousness as a by-product of matter, thus making the possibility of a life beyond death unintelligible. Put simply, the proposition runs: Consciousness is produced by the physical brain; therefore brain death marks the extinction of consciousness. But before examining the origins of such views in greater detail, we need to go back to the roots of Western thought concerning death and immortality.

Origins of Western Thinking on Death

In the course of his monumental study of the belief in immortality, the early anthropologist Sir J. G. Frazer remarks that

> it is impossible not to be struck by the strength, and perhaps we may say the universality, of the natural belief in immortality among the savage races of mankind. With them a life after death is not a matter of speculation and conjecture, of hope and fear; it is a practical certainty which the individual as little dreams of doubting as he doubts the reality of his own existence. He assumes it without inquiry and acts upon it without hesitation, as if it were one of the best ascertained truths within the limits of human experience.

One should add that such immortality is strongly identified with a sense of continuity with the ancestors of the tribe, and that a distinct sense of individuality has not yet been developed.

There are striking similarities between the beliefs of the Old Testament Hebrews and the ancient Homeric Greeks about a life beyond death. All the Hebrew dead were committed to Sheol, where they persist as *rephaim*, or shades. Sheol is a cheerless place, described by Job as "a land of deep darkness . . . of gathering shadows, of deepening shadow, lit by no ray of light, dark upon dark." The dead continue an atrophied existence, being "weakened editions," so to speak, of their former selves. The Greek Hades is no more attractive, and has been variously depicted as "totally unrelieved gloom" or a "murky underworld" where the condition of the inhabitants is described as one of "grim pathos." On his epic journey to the underworld, Odysseus is able to communicate with the dead only when they have been revitalized through the singularly repulsive ritual of drinking the blood of sacrificial sheep. The implication of these two traditions is that human beings are indissoluble psychophysical organisms and that death, as the shattering of the psychophysical unity, can permit only a feeble persistence, not a desirable form of immortality.

By the time we reach Plato at the turn of the fourth century B.C., we encounter a considerable development of ideas about the soul and immortality. His formulation of the alternatives is succinct: "Death is one of two things. Either it is annihilation, and the dead have no consciousness of anything; or, as we are told, it is really a change: a migration of the soul from this place to another."

Plato inherited the intellectual traditions of Orphism and Pythagoreanism, which may in turn have been influenced by Indian ideas of karma and reincarnation. The Platonic model of the human being differed from that of the early Hebrews and Greeks: The essential person was regarded no longer as psychophysical, but rather as an immortal soul in a mortal body. The soul was the essence, the body a vehicle for the soul in its successive incarnations and return to a pure state of being. Because it was divine in origin and essence, the soul was by definition imperishable, in contrast to the mortal body.

This idea of the immortality of the soul was uneasily absorbed into Christianity, but stripped of its context of reincarnation. The Greek notion also injected dualism of soul and body into Western thought, paralleled by a similar distinction between spirit and flesh that lies at the basis of monastic ascetic practices.

Early Christian faith, especially that of Paul, was underpinned by the resurrection of Jesus from the dead. The exact nature of this resurrection is still the focus of intense theological debate in our time. Was it literally a resurrection of the flesh? If so, will this apply to us in a similar fashion? Or should the resurrection be understood as spiritual regeneration—a new life in Christ? The New Testament texts are hard to unravel and may well have been tampered with in order to favor a literal or spiritual interpretation. On the one hand, we read of Thomas actually being able to touch the body of Jesus, who had just eaten a piece of fish; while on the other, Jesus seems capable of materialization and dematerialization, is not instantly recognized by his friends, and instructs Mary not to touch him in the garden. This is not the place to discuss such issues in detail, but it is worth pointing out the tension between the idea of the resurrection of the flesh—implying that the human being cannot be divided into soul and body—and the immortality of the soul advocated by Plato.

The Greek atomists were the first philosophical school to define the soul in terms of material atoms, specifically those of breath and heat. Epicurus (342–270 B.C.) stresses the complete dependence of soul on body, so that the dissolution of the whole structure marks the dispersion and extinction of the soul. This position is most cogently argued by the Roman poet Lucretius (99–55 B.C.), who maintains that death is the end of life and sensation. The detailed arguments advanced—for instance, in terms of the effects of brain damage and senility—differ little in substance from twentieth-century versions. They lead inexorably to the same conclusion—namely, that death "concerns us not a jot, since the nature of mind is proved to be mortal." The self is simply extinguished.

In summary, then, we can distinguish four variants:

1. Soul and body are inextricably linked, so that death marks the beginning of a diminished existence (Sheol, Hades).
2. Soul and body are inextricably linked and, although parted at death, come together again in the resurrection (early Christianity).
3. The soul is divine and immortal, housed in the perishable vehicle of the physical body (Plato).
4. The soul is entirely dependent on the body and perishes at bodily death (atomists).

The Rise of Materialism and the Denial of a Life beyond Death

Descartes formulated a dualism similar in structure to that of Plato and has been the butt of philosophers ever since, who have vainly been trying to work out the nature of the interaction between the supposedly incompatible substances of incorporeal mind and mechanical body. The strongest trend, however, has involved the systematic attempt to exclude consciousness from the picture by explaining all "mental" processes entirely in terms of material brain processes. Behind this trend lie a number of critical changes in modes of thought, which originated in the seventeenth century.

God and moral order.   The medieval outlook saw God as the Ground of Being and the Supreme Good toward which human beings were moving. He was the Creator and Sustainer of the Universe, who occasionally intervened in human affairs in a providential manner. Galileo made God into the Great Mechanical Inventor who set the universe in motion at the beginning of time. For Newton, God became the Supreme Clockmaker, the designer and regulator of physical laws and processes. God grows increasingly remote in space and time (with the earth viewed as an insignificant speck) until Laplace dispenses with the idea of God completely in his famous riposte to a jibe by Napoleon: "I do not need that hypothesis."

The idea of God as guarantor of a just moral order received a severe blow following the Lisbon earthquake of the mid-eighteenth century, when thousands of innocent people perished: How could a just, omnipotent, and loving God permit or cause such a thing? The debate has continued into our own century with its examples of natural and man-made disasters, which for many people represent a strong argument against the existence of God. Such examples might, however, demand the compensation of a life after death. But they are not usually viewed in this light. The problem of evil is too complex to pursue at length in this context. Modern science substitutes nature, chance, and necessity for God.

From purpose to cause.   Another title for this section might be "From metaphysics to physics," or "From why to how." Galileo was the most influential thinker on the topic, with his mechanical studies of bodies in motion, for which there was no need to postulate a metaphysical explanation. Mechanistic explanations came to be regarded as "scientific" and teleological ones as "unscientific," even in the study of mind and consciousness. Purpose was thus excluded. It is scarcely surprising that human evolution and, therefore, life came to be seen as intrinsically meaningless in an accidental world. As one physicist put it: "The universe is just one of those things that happen from time to time."

Primary and secondary qualities.   This distinction was elaborated by Galileo and has had far-reaching philosophical consequences. Primary qualities are inherent in the object and include shape, position, motion, and number; they are real and objective, constituting the stuff of scientific knowledge; they are quantifiable and therefore measurable. Secondary qualities, such as taste and odor, are "added"; they are subjective and based on opinion rather than knowledge. The result of this distinction is effectively to define consciousness as a secondary quality ultimately dependent on the matter of the primary qualities. Thus, the qualitative is defined in terms of the quantitative, the subjective by the objective, the inner by the outer, consciousness as a product of matter.

At this point it is worth mentioning three key figures whose theories have contributed toward the elaboration of a secular and materialist viewpoint: Darwin, Marx, and Freud. Descartes had already insisted that animals have no souls, but it was left to Darwin to complete the argument by establishing a continuum in the evolution of species, so that there was no obvious break between Homo sapiens and the rest of life, thus making it difficult if not impossible to draw a line showing where souls come into evolution.

Many psychologists, if they did not follow Pavlov and Watson down the road of behaviorism (where psychology is said to have "lost consciousness"!), found a congenial home in Freud's view that religion is an infantile projection of the father image and that the idea of an afterlife is merely wish fulfillment. Such psychologists, however, have not often delved very deeply into the phenomenology of religion, and they neglect the somewhat less-comforting illusion of hell, which is, of course, rather difficult to explain as wish fulfillment. They also ignore the moral demands exerted by a doctrine of personal accountability.

Marxism asserts that consciousness is the product of the brain and that human beings are simply products of society. Following in the footsteps of Feuerbach, Marx regarded religion as a social creation and called for its abolition as the illusory happiness of the people, who could then concentrate on creating the conditions for this-worldly happiness without counting on an afterlife—an impossible illusion from a materialist standpoint.

Modern neuroscience uses materialism as the basis of its increasingly sophisticated research program, assuming all along that no form of consciousness can exist apart from brain processes. As outlined above, such a view entails the proposition that consciousness is a by-product of the brain that cannot survive the brain's dissolution at bodily death. There is, however, a rival philosophical view that dates back to the last decade of the nineteenth century and the work of F. C. S. Schiller, William James, and Henri Bergson. According to this view, consciousness is not actually *produced* by the brain (the "productive theory"), but is rather *transmitted through* the brain, which normally permits only certain types of consciousness to filter through. The corollary of this transmissive theory is that consciousness might be changed or expanded at death, and that bypassing the normal filter might permit various forms of ESP. The transmissive theory, therefore, provides a framework for understanding anomalies of human consciousness that remain inexplicable in terms of conventional materialistic thought.

Schiller's book *Riddles of the Sphinx* appeared anonymously in 1891. The author signed himself a "troglodyte" (cave dweller), explaining that he would risk "the barren honors of a useless martyrdom" were he to reveal his name. He likens himself to the man returning to Plato's cave after glimpsing the truth and vainly attempting to persuade the inmates of the validity of his larger vision. He complains that materialism has inverted the relationship between matter and consciousness, asserting that "matter is not what *produces* consciousness but what limits it and confines its intensity within certain limits: Material organization does not construct consciousness out of arrangements of atoms, but contracts its manifestations within the sphere which it permits."

The transmissive theory, says Schiller, fits facts rejected as supernatural by materialism, and "thereby attains to an explanation which is ultimately tenable instead of one which is ultimately absurd." He goes on to comment on the "spurious self-evidence of death," maintaining that our view is necessarily imperfect.

> For we contemplate it only from the point of view of the survivors, never from that of the dying. We have not the least idea of what death means to those who die. To us, it is a catastrophic change, whereby a complex of phenomenal appearances, which we call the body of the dead, ceases to suggest to us the presence of the ulterior existence which we called spirit. But this does not prove, nor even tend to prove, that the spirit of the dead has ceased to exist. It merely shows that he has ceased to form part of our little world. . . . It is at least as probable

that this . . . is to be ascribed to his having been promoted or removed, as to his having been destroyed.

A good deal of recent research has been devoted to the near-death experience (NDE), which gives us a glimpse into the inside of the death process referred to by Schiller. While NDEs do not constitute proof of survival, the experiencers themselves are generally emphatic that they entered into the first stages of dying and emergence into a non–space-time dimension. An early case of this kind was the personal experience of Lord Geddes; it throws considerable light on the possible validity of the transmissive theory.

Geddes had become so ill in the middle of the night that he was unable even to ring for assistance, his pulse and breathing having become completely irregular. He then realized that his consciousness was separating into two, and that what he called his "A-consciousness," with which he now identified himself, seemed to be altogether outside "his" body, which it could see. "Gradually," Geddes reports, "I realized that I could see, not only my body and the bed in which it was, but everything in the whole house and garden . . . in fact wherever my attention was directed." The explanation of this phenomenon, he thought, was that he was free in a time dimension of space "wherein 'now' was in some way equivalent to 'here' in the ordinary three-dimensional space of everyday life." In this state of consciousness, Geddes was able to see his wife enter the bedroom and the doctor arrive in due course. He "saw" the doctor's thoughts, rather than hearing his voice, and observed the injection that drew him back into his body. Once he was back, "all the clarity of vision of anything and everything disappeared, and I was possessed of a glimmer of consciousness, which was suffused with pain."

While all this was going on, Geddes was apparently unconscious on the bed, yet his senses were extended and sharpened as he seemed to transcend normal space-time awareness. It is also striking that his consciousness was contracted as he reentered his body, causing him to lose his clarity of thought and become aware of pain.

The ESP issue is central to the debate about the nature of the NDE: Can people acquire correct information about events going on while they are unconscious and unable to reconstruct the scene from what they might hear? The evidence suggests that they can and that such an occurrence can be explained only by the transmissive theory. The burden of proof is on the materialist to provide an adequate alternative explanation. In a more general sense, NDE research has certainly aroused a new interest in the question of a possible life after death.

Mysticism, Death, and Purpose

Our discussion so far has concentrated on the relationship between mind, or soul (psyche), and the body, without introducing the spirit, or pneuma. This moves us from a two-dimensional to a three-dimensional scheme, although strict scientific materialism would have to interpret experience of the divine in physical terms as well, thus reducing what are potentially three levels of experience to a single one: The vertical is collapsed into the flatland of the horizontal.

We have already seen how NDEs seem to remove the filter of our ordinary reality, allowing access to an enlarged consciousness. Research also shows how removal of a further filter opens the experiencers to unitive or mystical experiences, which may have a lot to do with the loss of the fear of death. Nona Coxhead, in *The Relevance of Bliss*, cites a woman who describes a spontaneous mystical experience without being near death: "My ego had drowned in boundless being. Irrefutable intimations of immortality came welling up. I felt myself becoming an indestructible part of indestructible eternity. All fear vanished—especially fear of death. I felt death would be the beginning of new, more beautiful life."

Compare the above with Tennyson's impressions, quoted by W. T. Stace in *Mysticism and Philosophy*:

All at once as it were out of the intensity of the consciousness of individuality, individuality itself seemed to dissolve and fade away into boundless being, and this was not a confused state but the clearest, the surest of the sure, utterly beyond words—where death was an almost laughable impossibility—the loss of personality (if so it were) seeming no extinction but the only true life.

The encounter with the light, or the being of light, in reports of NDEs such as those cited in Coxhead's book involves not only a dissolution of normal ego boundaries and an identification with the being of light, but also a sense of feeling flooded with love, joy, warmth, peace, and security. It is as if the person suddenly perceives the universe from the inside through the consciousness of God. The person quoted in *The Relevance of Bliss* continues:

Extraordinary intuitive insights flashed across my mind. I seemed to comprehend the nature of things. I understood that the scheme of the universe is good, it was only man that was out of harmony with it . . . neither time nor space existed on this plane. I saw into the past and observed man's endless struggle toward the light.

Mystics and near-death experiencers agree that the purpose of life, when understood from the inside, is to grow in wisdom and love. Science, focused as it is on the outer and on external observation, can say nothing about the meaning and purpose of life revealed in the inner dimensions. Scientists look through microscopes and telescopes, perceiving at best the apparent self-organizing capacities of matter/energy. The mystical encounter with ultimate reality can be neither weighed nor measured, but is nevertheless a universal and irreducible item of human experience. We must "look within for the living God," whose existence is proved by the existence of love. A materialistic science reflects death and purposelessness; the inner mystical encounter reveals life and purpose.

RUPERT SHELDRAKE

Can Our Memories Survive the Death of Our Brains?

Rupert Sheldrake, Ph.D., a biologist and Fellow of the Royal Society, is creator of the hypothesis of formative causation and morphogenetic fields. His books include A New Science of Life *and* The Presence of the Past.

Most people in the Western world take for granted the assumption that memories are somehow stored inside the brain. The idea that experiences leave traces or imprints or "engrams" in brain tissue has a long ancestry. Aristotle expressed this idea by comparing memories with the impressions left by seals in wax. From time to time the analogies have been updated, the latest in terms of holograms.

Memory and Survival

Clearly, if our memories are stored inside our brains, then our memories must decay with the decay of our brains after death. Therefore, memories cannot survive bodily death. This means that conscious survival of bodily death is impossible in principle, unless we can imagine some kind of conscious survival without memory. I find such a possibility inconceivable: Stripped of all my memories, conscious and unconscious, I would not be me, and I cannot imagine how I would retain any kind of conscious identity.

Theories of survival of bodily death presuppose, at least implicitly, that some sort of memory remains after the decay of the brain. Even theories of reincarnation, although they do not require conscious memories of previous lives to be recalled in subsequent incarnations, still suppose that habits, interests, and dispositions are carried over from one life to another, which means that there must be some transfer of memory.

The conventional theory of memory traces is in fact an *assumption* that follows from the currently orthodox theory of life—the mechanistic theory, according to which all aspects of life and mind are ultimately explicable in terms of the known laws of physics and chemistry. If the mind is nothing but an aspect or an epiphenomenon of physical processes going on in the brain, then memories *must* be located in the nervous tissue. But how well is this assumption supported by scientific evidence?

The Elusiveness of Memory Traces

A vast amount of effort has been expended in an attempt to localize and identify the hypothetical memory traces, and tens of thousands of experimental animals have been expended in this process. Nevertheless, the traces have so far eluded detection.

The classical investigations were made by Karl Lashley, using rats, monkeys, and chimpanzees. For over 30 years he tried to trace conditioned-reflex paths through the brain and to find the locus of specific memory traces, or engrams. To do this, he trained animals in a variety of tasks, ranging from simple conditioned reflexes to the solution of difficult problems. Either before or after the training, he surgically cut nerve tracts within their brains, or portions of their brains were removed, and the effects on initial learning or postoperative retention were measured.

He first became skeptical of the supposed path of conditioned-reflex arcs through the motor cortex when he found that rats trained to respond in particular ways to light showed no reduction in accuracy of performance when almost the entire motor cortex was cut out. Likewise, most of the motor cortex of monkeys was removed after they had been trained to open various latch boxes. Though this operation resulted in a temporary paralysis, after eight to twelve weeks they recovered sufficiently to be able to make the movements required to open the latches; they were then exposed to the puzzle boxes and opened them promptly without random exploratory movements.

Lashley then showed that learned habits were retained if the associative areas of the brain were destroyed. Habits also survived a series of deep incisions into the cerebral cortex which destroyed cross-connections within it. Moreover, if the cerebral cortex was intact, removal of subcortical structures such as the cerebellum did not destroy the memory, either.

With more complex types of learning that involved remembering the way through a maze, rats lost the ability if more than half the cerebral cortex was removed. The amount of loss, measured in terms of the practice required for relearning, was on average proportional to the amount of cortex destroyed. It did not seem to matter which parts of the cortex were destroyed; what mattered was the quantity.

Lashley started out as an enthusiastic supporter of the idea of localized memory traces, but at the end of his career he was forced to abandon this idea:

> It is not possible to demonstrate the isolated localization of a memory trace anywhere within the nervous system. Limited regions may be essential for learning or retention of a particular activity, but within such regions the parts are functionally equivalent.[1]

In reviewing the types of human memory loss that follow brain damage, he came to a similar conclusion:

> I believe that the evidence strongly favors the view that amnesia from brain injury rarely, if ever, is due to the destruction of specific memory traces. Rather, the amnesias represent a lowered level of vigilance, a greater difficulty in activating the organized pattern of traces, or a disturbance of some broader system of organized functions.

Lashley did not consider the possibility that memories might not be stored inside the brain at all. He interpreted the evidence against localized traces in terms of multiple representation of traces throughout an entire functional area. He thought his work indicated that

> the characteristics of the nervous network are such that when it is subject to any pattern of excitation, it may develop a pattern of activity, reduplicated through an entire functional area by spread of excitations, such as the surface of a liquid develops an interference pattern of spreading waves when it is disturbed at several points.

He suggested that recall involved "some sort of resonance among a very large number of neurons." These ideas have been carried further by his former student Karl Pribram in his proposal that

memories are stored in a distributed manner analogous to the interference patterns in a hologram.[2]

Analogous experiments have shown that even in invertebrates
such as the octopus, specific memory traces cannot be localized.
Observations on the survival of learned habits after the destruction
of various parts of the brain have led to the seemingly paradoxical
conclusion that "memory is both everywhere and nowhere in
particular."[3]

Not only have the hypothetical memory traces proved to be spatially elusive, but their physical nature has also remained obscure.
The idea of specific RNA "memory molecules" was fashionable in
the 1960s, but has now been more or less abandoned. The theory of
reverberating circuits of electrical activity, giving a kind of echo,
may help to account for short-term memory over periods of seconds
or minutes, but cannot plausibly explain long-term memory. The
most popular hypothesis remains the old favorite that memory depends on modifications of the synaptic connections between nerve
cells in a manner still unknown.

If memories are somehow stored in synapses, then the synapses
themselves must remain stable over long periods of time. Indeed,
the nervous system as a whole must be stable if it is to act as a
memory store. Until recently this was generally assumed to be the
case, even though it has long been known that there is a continuous
process of cell death within the brain. But recent evidence suggests
that the nervous system may be more dynamic than previously
supposed.

Studies of the brains of canaries, and in particular those parts
involved in the learning of song, have shown that not only do many
new connections between nerve cells continue to develop, but many
new nerve cells appear. In males, the number of neurons increases
as the birds mature in the spring, but then decreases by about 40
percent by the autumn. As the new mating season approaches, the
number of nerve cells increases again, and so on. Such changes
have also been found in other parts of the brains of canaries, and
there is now evidence that in adults of other species there is a
turnover of neurons in the forebrain, the "seat" of complex behavior
and learning, with new cells being formed while others die.[4]

Brains also appear to be more functionally dynamic than previously thought. Recent studies of monkeys have shown that sensory areas of the brain that "map" different parts of the body are
not "hard wired" or anatomically frozen, but are unexpectedly

fluid. In one series of experiments, the regions of the sensory cortex connected with touch sensations from the monkeys' hands were localized. The "map" in the brain was found to be subdivided into regions for each of the five fingers and for other surfaces of the hand. After one or more of the fingers was amputated, it was found that sensory inputs from the remaining adjacent fingers gradually shifted over a period of weeks into the missing fingers' hitherto exclusive brain region. The increased areas of brain connected to the adjacent fingers were associated with an increase in the acuity of sensation in these fingers.[5]

The dynamism of the nervous system is also shown when the brain is damaged. For example, if a portion of the sensory cortex is injured, the appropriate sensory "map" in the injured region can shift to the region surrounding it, although with some loss in acuity. This movement of the "map" probably does not depend on growth or movement of nerve cells, but rather on a spatial shift of nerve-cell activity.[6]

This dynamism in the structure and functioning of the nervous system presents the theory of memory traces with great difficulties; and at the molecular level there is also a dynamism that makes long-term storage problematic, as Francis Crick has recently shown. The time span of human memory is often years or tens of years. Yet, says Crick,

> it is believed that almost all the molecules in our bodies, with the exception of DNA, turn over in a matter of days, weeks, or at the most a few months. How then is memory stored in the brain so that its trace is relatively immune to molecular turnover?

Crick has suggested a mechanism whereby "molecules in the synapse interact in such a way that they can be replaced by new material, one at a time, without altering the overall state of the structure." His ingenious hypothetical scheme involves protein molecules, which he endows with a number of unusual properties. There is as yet no evidence that such molecules exist.[7]

Thus, the trace theory of memory is very far from being well established; it is still essentially speculative. A number of contemporary philosophers have drawn attention to a further serious difficulty of a logical nature. If memories are somehow encoded and stored as traces within the brain, then there must be some way in which they are retrieved from the memory store. But for a retrieval system to function, it must somehow be able to recognize the appropriate memories. And to do so, it must itself have some sort of memory for what is to be retrieved. Hence, the very notion of a memory-retrieval system begs the question, because it presupposes what it seeks to explain.[8]

The Hypothesis of Formative Causation

An alternative approach to the problem of memory is provided by the hypothesis of formative causation, described in detail in my book *A New Science of Life*.[9] This hypothesis starts not from the phenomenon of memory itself, but with a consideration of the coming into being of form in plants and animals.

The mechanistic approach to biology, in spite of its successes at the molecular level, has failed to shed much light on the way in which embryos develop from relatively simple egg cells into organisms containing tissues and organs of great structural complexity. During this process, more complex structures come into being from less complex ones. What are the causes of the forms they take? Biologists wedded to the reductionist or mechanistic approach assume that these must somehow be entirely explicable in terms of complex physiochemical interactions between the parts. But others (including myself) are convinced that this mechanistic approach is too limited. There is, to say the least, an open possibility that the phenomena of life depend on laws or factors as yet unrecognized by the physical sciences. The problem is to discover what these factors are and how they work.

The most influential alternative to the mechanistic paradigm is provided by the holistic or organismic philosophy. Biologists working within this framework have developed a new kind of field concept to help account for the development and maintenance of form and order in living organisms. These fields, called *morphogenetic* fields, from the Greek *morphe* ("form") and *genesis* ("coming-into-being"), can be thought of by analogy with magnetic fields, which have a shape even though they are invisible. (In the case of a magnet, this shape can be revealed by the patterns taken up by iron filings scattered around it.) Morphogenetic fields, through their own structure, mold developing cells, tissues, and organisms. For example, in a human embryo, a developing ear is molded by an ear-shaped morphogenetic field, and a developing leg by a leg-shaped field.

But what are these fields, and where do they come from? For over 50 years their nature and even their existence has remained obscure. However, I believe that these fields are just as real as the electromagnetic and gravitational fields of physics, but that they are a kind of field with very remarkable properties. Like the known fields of physics, they connect similar things across space with seemingly nothing in between; but, in addition, they connect things across time.

The idea is that the morphogenetic fields that shape a growing animal or plant are derived from the forms of previous organisms of the same species. The embryo "tunes in," as it were, to the forms of past members of the species. The process by which this happens is called *morphic resonance*. Similarly, the fields that organize the activities of an animal's nervous system are derived from past animals of the same kind. In their instinctive behavior, animals draw on a sort of species "memory bank," or "pooled memory."

This new hypothesis leads to a range of surprising predictions which provide ways of testing it experimentally. It is in the chemical realm that the most unambiguous tests should be possible. The hypothesis of formative causation applies not only to living organisms but also to chemical systems such as crystals. It predicts that the patterns in which molecules arrange themselves when they crystallize should be influenced by the patterns taken up in previous crystals of the same substance. This influence should act directly through both space and time, with the result that substances should crystallize more readily all over the world the more often they have been crystallized before.

New chemicals synthesized for the first time are indeed usually difficult to crystallize and in fact tend to form crystals more readily as time passes. The conventional explanation is that tiny fragments of previous crystals get carried from laboratory to laboratory on the clothing or beards of migrant scientists and "infect" solutions of the substance in question. When no such carrier can be identified, crystal "seeds" are assumed to have traveled around the world as microscopic dust particles in the air. But according to the hypothesis of formative causation, crystallization should occur more readily with the prior frequency of crystallization, even if migrant scientists are kept well away and dust particles are filtered out of the air. This prediction could be tested fairly easily experimentally.

Another kind of experimental test is possible in the realm of animal behavior. If a number of animals—for example, rats—learn a new trick that rats have never before performed, then other rats of the same breed all over the world should be able to learn the same trick more easily, even in the absence of any known kind of connection or communication. The larger the number of rats that learn it, the easier it should become for subsequent rats everywhere else to learn it.

Remarkably enough, there is already evidence from a long series of experiments carried out with rats in the United States, Scotland, and Australia that this effect actually occurs. The rate of learning of the ability to escape from a water maze increased in successive batches of rats, whether or not they were descended from trained parents. This increased rate of learning was found in different laboratories separated by thousands of miles.[10]

In relation to human beings, this hypothesis suggests that on average it should be getting easier and easier for people to learn to ride bicycles, to type, swim, or program computers, just because more and more people have already learned to do these things. Such improvements do in fact seem to have occurred. However, it is not possible to separate any potential effects of morphic resonance from various cultural and environmental factors which have also changed with time. Specially designed experiments are necessary to test for the effects of morphic resonance. Some preliminary experiments have already been performed, with encouraging results.

Tuning In to the Past

According to the hypothesis of formative causation, organisms tune in to similar organisms in the past, and the more similar they are, the more specific is the tuning. In general, an organism resembles *itself* in the past more closely than it resembles any other organism. It will accordingly be strongly influenced by morphic resonance from its own past states. In the realm of form, this means that its form will tend to be stabilized and remain fairly constant in spite of changes in its chemical constituents and material components. When we consider the influence of past patterns of behavior, this self-resonance has even more interesting consequences.[11] Both habit memories and memories of particular past events may be given directly by morphic resonance from the organism's own past. *These memories need not be stored inside the brain.*

In order to see more clearly the difference between the morphic-resonance and trace theories of memory, consider the analogy of a transistor radio. The music coming out of the loudspeaker depends on the energy supplied by the battery, on the components of the set and the way they are wired together, *and* on the transmissions to which the set is tuned. Slight damage to the set may lead to distortions in the sound, while more severe damage leads to a loss of the ability to receive the transmissions altogether. But of course these facts do not mean that the music is actually produced or stored within the set. And brain damage resulting in memory loss does not prove that lost memories were stored inside the brain. The damage might simply prevent the brain from tuning in to its own past states.

The loss of memory associated with brain damage is of course usually taken to prove that memories are inside the brain. Another piece of evidence that is commonly assumed to support the trace theory of memory is Wilder Penfield's discovery that the electrical stimulation of the temporal lobes of the brains of epileptic patients can result in the evocation of vivid memories that are experienced consciously by the patients. But here again, this need not mean that the memories are actually stored inside the nervous tissue. If one stimulates the tuning circuit of a radio or a TV set, the tuning may be changed such that transmissions from a different station are picked up; but this would not of course mean that these new programs are stored inside the components of the tuning circuits that were stimulated. Interestingly, Penfield, on further reflection, abandoned his original conclusions:

> In 1951 I had proposed that certain parts of the temporal cortex should be called "memory cortex," and suggested that the neuronal record was located there in the cortex near points at which the stimulating electrode may call forth an experiential response. This was a mistake. . . . The record is not in the cortex.[12]

If we pick up our own memories by tuning in to our own past states, and if these memories are not stored inside our brains, why don't we tune in to other people's memories? Perhaps we do. If we tuned in to the memories of large numbers of people in the past, we would not be aware of all the specific memories of particular events in their lives, but rather a kind of composite or pooled memory which would contain the basic forms or patterns of their experience and thought. This idea closely corresponds with Jung's theory of the archetypes of the collective unconscious; and Jung's approach to psychology harmonizes well with the notion of morphic resonance.

It might also be possible to pick up particular people's memories which are very recent—only a few seconds old. In this case there might be a transference of thoughts, or in other words, a process that is equivalent to telepathy. In this way the hypothesis of formative causation might provide a bridge between science and at least some of the phenomena of parapsychology.

It might also be possible to tune in to the experience of particular people in the past who are now dead. If so, we might then gain access to "memories of past lives," a phenomenon for which there seems to be persuasive evidence.[13]

Implications for Survival

If this new approach to the phenomena of memory is supported by experimental evidence, it will lead to a major change in the scientific context for the question of whether consciousness can survive bodily death. If memories are not stored inside the brain, there is no reason why they should decay when the brain decays. They may remain potentially present, and it may still be possible to tune in to them.

This hypothesis, however, does not automatically lead to the conclusion that such survival occurs. From a theoretical point of view, survival depends on the way we think about the relation of the mind to the body. On the one hand, this hypothesis can be interpreted within the framework of a sophisticated and updated philosophy of materialism. If the conscious self is nothing but an aspect of the functioning of the brain and its associated fields, then the brain would still be essential for the process of tuning in to memories, even if they are not stored inside the brain but are instead given directly by morphic resonance with a person's own past. In this case, the decay of the brain would still result in the extinction of consciousness. The memories would not exactly be destroyed, but they would be lost because there would no longer be a way of recovering them: The decay of the brain would involve the dissolution of the tuning system.

On the other hand, if the conscious self is not identical with the functioning of the brain, but rather *interacts* with the brain through morphic fields, then it is possible that the conscious self could continue to be associated with these fields even after the death of the brain, and retain the ability to tune in to its own past states. Both the self and its memories could survive the death of the body.

Precisely *how* the conscious self could interact with the morphic fields associated with mental activity is of course obscure. But it does not seem inconceivable that a field theory of the mind may be developed which is compatible with both a new scientific understanding of memory and the possibility of a conscious survival of bodily death.

MARK B. WOODHOUSE

Beyond Dualism and Materialism: A New Model of Survival

Mark B. Woodhouse, Ph.D., is associate professor of philosophy at Georgia State University, where he teaches courses in metaphysics, parapsychology, and Eastern thought. Author of the widely used college text A Preface to Philosophy, *he also serves as an editorial board member of the* Journal of Near-Death Studies.

It is possible to address the question, What, if anything, survives the death of the body? independently of one's metaphysical leanings. But it is difficult, and the quest for an adequate paradigm in this regard is a perennial affair. To this end I propose to refine a model that avoids the pitfalls of classical dualism, materialism, and idealism and synthesizes their partial truths. I dub this model "Energy Monism."

Energy Monism is not a new position. It has strong affinities to the perennial wisdom, Taoism, the new physics and, to a lesser extent, systems theoretical holism. Energy Monism is a broadly based master paradigm that incorporates many insights from both classical sources and new-paradigm discussions. Those tenets of particular relevance for the survival question are as follows:

All things emerge from and remain fundamentally connected to a common divine source. From this it follows that the idea of a separate, surviving, and substantial self is illusory, even though we may carry the illusion for a long time. It also follows that, whatever the "stuff" of reality may be, it must be of a single kind.

All events and objects are of a common stuff, energy-consciousness, which transcends the historical distinction between mind and matter. From this it will follow that the distinction between one's body and whatever survives is essentially one of *degree*, not *principle*.

Reality is structured according to six (possibly more) primary levels or "planes" in a Great Chain of Being. These range from the lowest of gross matter up through the highest ultimate ground, which transcends all subject-object dualities. Each level is relatively autonomous—that is, not reducible to lower levels—and subject to some laws not operative at other levels.

All levels are interconnected via the principle of asymmetric hierarchical interpenetration.[1] This is to say that each level "contains" its lower-level neighbor—literally permeates it—and is in turn contained by its upper-level neighbor. This allows us to say, for example, that God (or the ground of being) is in all things, but not all things are equally in God.

The ontological priority of the Great Chain runs from the top down. This means, for example, that simple matter is precipitated out of higher-order fields of energy-consciousness. It also means that as we grow into the higher-order, or transpersonal, bands of existence we are closer to the core of our own being. Moreover, we originally came from the higher to the lower, and consequently the entire survival question is inverted. In this context, the question is not so much, How is it possible to survive physical death? as, Why did we ever take on bodies in the first place?

Change on all but the highest level is implemented vibrationally. This is not to say that a complete explanation of change can be given by appealing to vibrations. Much more is required. It is to say, however, that energy-consciousness vibrates at different frequencies, creating different interference patterns, density levels, and resonances that mark out the parameters of particular levels. To move from one level to the next is to experience a different vibrational matrix and, with it, a dramatically altered perspective that colors our interpretation of its contents. Adequate explanations of channeling, survival on other planes, local out-of-body experiences, astral travel, apparitions, and even Kirlian photography, despite other explanatory principles they may individually require, must all ultimately appeal to the interdimensional transduction of vibrating energy-consciousness.

Matter and the New Physics

At the core of the survival question is one of the deepest reality questions we can pose: What is the "stuff" that constitutes the Great Chain of Being? To answer this question is to make major headway in understanding what survives. I have proposed energy-consciousness. Initially, this proposal will please nobody. Dualists will see it sneaking in their prime distinction under different labels. Materialists will want to know what happened to the "physical" body. Idealists and defenders of some version of the perennial wisdom justifiably will resist any suggestion that higher states of consciousness could be identical with plain old physical energy. Zen Buddhists, phenomenologists, and Copenhagen-leaning physicists will urge us simply to describe or live through the appearances, not to worry about what is behind them or the stuff of which they are constituted. Let me begin to address these concerns.

Common sense distinguishes routinely between physical objects, energy (such as electricity), and conscious processes (thinking, feeling, etc.). Reflective common sense informed by developments in the new physics is still committed to the existence of physical objects, but it interprets them energetically. Matter *is* compressed energy. Materiality drops out of the picture as a fundamental metaphysical category, leaving us with energy and consciousness. Let us review briefly a few of the reasons for this shift.

Einstein's discovery that an object's energy is equivalent to its mass times the square of the speed of light is usually interpreted to mean simply that mass and energy are interconvertible. Under this interpretation, matter and energy are extensions or aspects of each other—"coequal realities," as it were. From an operational point of view, this is of course perfectly correct. We routinely convert one into the other. From a metaphysical standpoint, however, matter and energy lose their coequal status. Energy becomes the primary underlying reality and matter its derivative state. The conversion from matter to energy is essentially the conversion from one compressed field state to another.

Even the contemporary application of an older mechanistic line of reasoning supports this view. We might call it the "argument from divisibility." Atoms are divisible into their primary constituents—electrons, protons, and neutrons. Beneath this level are even more fundamental units with a menagerie of labels and properties. Finally, we come to quarks, which are by some accounts the most basic units. But quarks are purely energetic. They are not solid "things," but are more akin to flashes of energy. On the other hand, when we inquire into the deeper levels of physical energy, we find only more energy, not material particles. As David Bohm and others have urged, matter is simply "gravitationally trapped light."[2]

If matter were not already compressed energy, we could not conceive of how it could be convertible to energy, for example, in spontaneous radioactive decay. Nor could we conceive of creating it from kinetic energy in particle-collision experiments, since the classical properties of matter—namely, strict localizability, solidity, deterministic trajectories, and inertness—are logically incompatible with energy particle/fields. If so-called "empty space" were not fundamentally energetic, we could not account for the creation of virtual particles from such space. Put differently, we can conceive of how matter is a compressed section of field energy, a part within a larger whole, but we cannot conceive how a field might be a literal extension of material things without giving up our conception of rigidly delineated material particles in the first place.

Both relativity theory and quantum field theory present distinctively energetic interpretations of matter. According to the general theory of relativity, space, gravity, and matter are continuous with one another. Material objects represent curvatures of the gravitational field, which in turn is coextensive with space itself. In Einstein's words: "We therefore regard matter as being constituted by the regions of space in which the field is extremely intense. . . . There is no place in this new kind of physics both for field and matter, for the field is the only reality."[3] Herman Weyl summarizes the field theorist's vision:

> A material particle such as an electron is merely a small domain of the electrical field within which the field strength assumes enormously high values. . . . Such an energy knot, which by no means is clearly delineated against the remaining field, propagates through empty space like a water wave against the surface of a lake.[4]

Energy Monists are partial to fields, waves, and interference patterns. They view "particles" as derivative. Yet there is an apparently overwhelming array of experimental evidence in physics for making the properties of particles as fundamental in the total scheme of things as those of waves. Max Planck's constant, one of the absolute foundations of quantum mechanics, is a mathematical description of the smallest discrete absorption or emission of energy in the (known) physical universe. And most physicists, beginning with Einstein in 1905, interpret the photoelectric effect to mean that photons of light must possess the properties of particles in addition to those of waves. The physicist Nick Herbert effectively presents the corpuscular vision as follows:

> If we look at the world with fine probes, it breaks up into little dots; you don't see the whole anymore, but an array of what printers call "process dots." And that's the way the universe is, too. You may look closer and closer, trying to get down to the ultimate substance, but it breaks up into little dots—quantum jumps. The world is made of particles.[5]

The Energy Monist's vision stands in marked contrast. At a physical level in the Great Chain of Being the "ultimate substance" of which Herbert writes, for example, is field energy itself, not discrete particles. *This interpretation does not deny any experimental evidence for the existence of particles or for wave-particle duality.* For Energy Monism involves a metaphysical thesis about the *nature* of particles, not their existence. All arguments for particles or particlelike properties are perfectly consistent with understanding those particles to be compressions of field energy or the function of complex interference patterns. That we can measure something as discrete as a quantum of energy—Herbert's "process dot" conforming to Planck's constant—is simply to say that it is the smallest possible localizable expression of a field. It should not surprise us that the world of atomic physics appears to divide into discrete entities, because it is the very nature of measurement to make quantitative differentiations. We measure nature only as it is exposed to our method of questioning.

For the Energy Monist, the distinction between particles within a field fundamentally represents the distinction between several visible places within multiple underlying field vibrations where the action is, so to speak. Radiation energy, for example, is put out in the *form* of apparently discontinuous quanta because waves in any medium reflect distinct oscillation and interference patterns. Erwin Schroedinger even went so far as to urge that electrons "have no real existence" because they are essentially "standing waves."[6]

In summary, the Energy Monist stakes his case on the fact that it is possible to derive discontinuous functions from a larger continuum, but it is not possible to construct a continuum from a series of discontinuities. We can derive particles from interacting frequency patterns of compressed field energy, but we cannot derive waves from particles. We can divide a line into segments, but the sum total of those segments never constitutes a continuum. Matter is but a localized expression of complex matrices of vibrating field energy, which is itself suffused by higher levels within the Great Chain. By implication, the same is true of the human body. As far as the human body and whatever might survive its death are concerned, the only candidates remaining for a comprehensive paradigm are (a) energy, (b) consciousness, or (c) energy-consciousness—not material stuff.

Integrating Energy and Consciousness

Putting energy and consciousness together in a way that will advance discussion on the survival question is an extraordinarily difficult task. It ultimately may fail. For it represents a tenuous gestalt, the stability of which is easily undermined by the tendency to fall back into more traditional ways of thinking. Still, the potential rewards justify the undertaking. We shall proceed slowly, a step at a time.

By inserting the hyphen between the terms—energy-consciousness—I stress the irreducibility of either to the other. For each is both. In other words, I am not saying that energy is (really) just consciousness or that consciousness is (really) just energy. Neither one's full nature is captured by assuming that it is a subset of the other.

Energy Monism stipulates that energy and consciousness are indissolubly connected aspects of the same underlying Chain of Being. However, either may assume a primary or a peripheral significance depending on the context of discussion. For example, in the context of nuclear radiation or of plant physiology it is appropriate to speak in terms of changes of energy because the properties by which we identify such changes are more abundant. This does not mean that plants or minerals are without consciousness. It does not mean that, from our perspective of ordinary waking consciousness, the properties to which we would ascribe consciousness are significantly less abundant. As the literature of the perennial philosophy makes clear, however, a substantially altered perspective has led many enlightened beings to experience plants and even the earth itself as expressing consciousness.

We cannot conceptually push the reality question beyond energy-consciousness. For the ultimate ground of our being, the highest level of the Great Chain, the source of all things seen and unseen, is itself beyond form, beyond all distinctions, beyond all description, and beyond all names. It is what it is, and from it springs the only stuff for which we have barely adequate names—energy-consciousness. Stated differently, "beyond" energy-consciousness there is literally nothing to say, no words in any language that point to anything in particular. Our options at this point are either energy-consciousness or silence.

Energy and consciousness share each other's properties. And this is another reason to run them together. For example, consciousness expresses itself energetically, say, through intentional movement, and energy expresses itself consciously, say, through intelligent patterns of self-organization in biological systems.[7] Moreover, both energy and consciousness satisfy the same textbook definition as the "power to produce change." Also, both are expressed vibrationally, although in the case of consciousness, this is more directly acknowledged in Vedic spiritual traditions, e.g., Patanjali's Yoga Sutras, than in Buddhist traditions.[8]

Finally, both are most adequately understood as underlying *fields* that may express themselves in particular form, as thoughts, sensations, etc., in the case of consciousness, or as electrons in the case of quantum field theory. It should be stressed, however, that in citing these familiar examples I am *not* restricting consciousness only to ordinary consensual domains, nor am I restricting energy only to standard physical domains. In summary, their strong parallels suggest that we not distinguish too sharply in principle between energy and consciousness, and at most that we think of them as correlative aspects of the same stuff—that is, as energy-consciousness.

When all is said and done, proponents of the more spiritually based perennial wisdom will want to give an edge to consciousness such that the Great Chain of Being becomes the Great Chain of Consciousness. They are happy to see consciousness projected down to the lower levels, but do not want to see energy projected upward from more limiting ordinary physical contexts. Energy Monism, it should be stressed, does not pretend to do this. It does *not* pretend, for example, that the soul is merely electromagnetic energy. That is simply to fall back into an old inverted dualistic way of thinking.

On the other hand, proponents of holistic and systems-oriented models of human nature well might wish to give the edge to energy: "If we must have a Great Chain of Being, which many of us do not care for anyway, let's at least make it the Great Chain of Energy." This has the ring of being more "scientific." This kind of *projectio ad ignorantium* again inverts the priorities, mistaking the whole for one of its parts. Energy in the context of physics is *not* where we begin. It is a slice of a much larger spectrum. Energy in Energy Monism is no more physical than it is nonphysical.

That this philosophical divergence might even take root is a good reason for adopting Energy Monism, and with it the notion of energy-consciousness. In proper holistic fashion, it both allows for yet transcends the "spirit" camps and the (physical) "energy" camps. The drawback of each interpretation of the Great Chain becomes the strength of the other. To make consciousness primordial certainly captures more of our inward sense of residual *subjectivity*, our sense of what it is to be a feeling, living, self-aware being. On the other hand, to make energy the prime category captures more of our sense of *objectivity* as, for example, when we measure electrical fields or see auras "out there."

I would urge, therefore, that within the Great Chain, consciousness is the inner subjective aspect of energy and that energy, whether in physical or nonphysical forms, is the outward, objective aspect or expression of consciousness. Subjectivity and objectivity, however, are logical complements. The attempted reduction of either category to the other would be logically self-defeating. Therefore, if subjectivity and objectivity are logically complementary, and consciousness and energy are their respective reflections, then it is reasonable to think of consciousness and energy also as complementary aspects.

The ground of being transcends all subject-object polarities. But insofar as the Divine expresses itself in an evolutionary fashion, it must rely upon the capacity to draw contrasts. And this requires that it *appear* to split itself. The subject-object dichotomy is simply the price of drawing this contrast in infinitely marvelous and complex ways. In a sense, it is the price of anything's existing or any event's occurring whatsoever. So the tendency to split energy-consciousness into correspondingly distinct domains is a natural one, especially as long as we must have names for things and wish to *talk* about our experiences.

A useful metaphor is to think of consciousness as the "inside" of energy, and energy as the "outside" of consciousness. But "inside" and "outside" are correlative aspects of the same thing, not two names for two distinct and fundamentally different types of things. The same is true of "energy" and "consciousness." The ground of our being expresses itself both energetically and consciously in greater and lesser complementary proportions relative to our perspectives.

A proper understanding of the dynamics of the Great Chain should prompt us to ask not how we can get energy-consciousness back together again, but why we were ever inclined to take it apart. It cannot be done except, of course, in *thought*. Our practical scientific and spiritual endeavors may require that we focus just upon energy (while doing an experiment) or just upon consciousness (perhaps in meditation). There are no persuasive reasons, however, to project our practical needs or linguistic distinctions into the deep structure of the Great Chain of Being.

The Incompatibility of Dualism and Survival

The suggestion that survival of bodily death constitutes a good reason for *not* being a dualist looks at first as incoherent as suggesting that Baptists do not have to believe in a supreme being in order to be Baptists. Yet I hope to make good on this proposal. To do this, however, we shall need to determine more precisely what *dualism*, *survival*, and *nonphysical* each entail.

J. B. Rhine once defined parapsychology as "the science of the nonphysical." He may as well have said the same for psychical research, which historically is more directly linked to the survival question. Yet before, during, and since his time the concept of the nonphysical has harbored a critical ambiguity. In both popular and critical discussions of the survival question, this ambiguity often appears to be unacknowledged or unaddressed. Yet it is so important that, as soon as the topic of paradigms for survival is raised, the different meanings of *nonphysical* should receive some attention.

Accordingly, in an ontological sense *nonphysical* typically describes an entity (mind, spirit, etc.) that possesses properties not merely different from the properties of physical entities but, in at least some instances, fundamentally incompatible with them. Thus in classical dualism *mind* may be described as active (capable of agency), invisible, nonspatial, and even (substantially) immutable—as contrasted to matter, which is passive, visible, spatial, and mutable. In other words, minds are in principle qualitatively different and numerically distinct from bodies.

In a functional sense, however, *nonphysical* is a much more open-ended term. In this sense it simply describes "a kind of stuff, energy, etc., that is not measurable or accepted by current physics." In other words, the nonphysical is merely a domain that the science of the day does not understand very well. It is a domain that is suggested but yet goes beyond empirical inquiry—for example, Rhine's psi fields, Rupert Sheldrake's morphogenetic fields, and David Bohm's implicate order. It is a domain that functionally allows out-of-body experiences (OBEs) and survival without necessarily taking a stand on the nature of what survives. To be sure, its properties differ from those typically investigated by science, but in ways that suggest differences of degree rather than of principle.

Suppose the evidence for survival and OBEs is quite strong. Of course, an OBE is *not* the same thing as (long-term) survival, yet both do involve the departure of a personality from its physical body. It is natural to describe whatever leaves the body as nonphysical. But what sense of *nonphysical* is implied here, the metaphysical or the functional? In fact, both senses are compatible with the survival hypothesis. The mere existence of OBEs, for example, does not in itself entail classical dualism (Plato, Descartes, etc.) any more than it does some form of energy not now acknowledged by science. Someday, such experiences might fall within the purview of a greatly expanded paradigm, such as Energy Monism.

What we need, therefore, is some reason to choose between these alternatives, something that tips the scales in favor of an expanded-paradigm approach. I shall attempt to provide such a reason by bringing out a fundamental incoherence in the dualist interpretation of OBEs, because survival also minimally involves OBEs.[9]

At least one of the defining characteristics of mind, according to dualism, is its nonspatiality: It doesn't seem to be at any particular place when we go looking for it. This is even more true of the traditional "soul." But OBEs are spatially oriented experiences. The subject moves through space in a continuous manner, perceives the environs from a certain *point* in space, and may occasionally even be seen by others as occupying a certain trajectory (especially under conditions of terminal illness). The subject sometimes even perceives parts of a "double," such as an arm, while detached from the physical body. Even apparitions of the departed appear and move around in consensual space. They may move on to other dimensions involving queer space-time warps. But even there, we are given to believe, they can and do appear to one another as akin to distinct holograms of energy-consciousness.

My reason for stressing the importance of space is this: Whatever occupies space in principle is localizable; and whatever is localizable, whatever is located in some space or other, whether three- or n-dimensional, in principle falls within the purview of a greatly expanded scientific paradigm. None of this is compatible with classical dualism. In other words, no metaphysical dualist can admit that a spirit could occupy space *next to* one's (physical) body—and still be a dualist.

Where does Energy Monism fit vis-à-vis dualism and materialism? On the one hand, it grants the singularly most significant consequence of dualism—namely, the possibility of OBEs and, beyond that, some probability of survival of bodily death. But it denies that whatever leaves the body is intrinsically nonphysical. On the other hand, it also denies that the stuff of the human body is intrinsically physical, and it views the body as a more densely integrated locus of energy-consciousness. Whatever leaves the body is characterized by a difference in frequency pattern—a difference of degree, not principle. Of course, the materialist may consider the revelation that the spirit is not nonphysical a victory in words only, since the Energy Monist affirms what *all* materialists deny—viz., the possibility of OBEs.

Energy Monism does not originate merely as a "compromise candidate" between two major metaphysical systems. Under different labels it has been around for a long time. The net result, however, is that it borrows elements from each system and rejects others. It acknowledges that there are properties of human experience that we would not ascribe to simple material objects and vice versa. However, it does not view the differences between minds and bodies as, in principle, involving any greater distinctions of degree than those implicit in, say, the distinction between X rays and radio waves on the electromagnetic spectrum or between mass and energy in the new physics. In the end it resists all attempts to reduce it to some queer version of either dualism or materialism.

A final example may help to clarify its logical status. Energy Monism does not predict whether the technology of the future will enable us to take "pictures" of persons during intentional OBEs or at the time of physical expiration.[10] Many things affect the progress of science apart from interest in a particular goal. But I would not be surprised if, someday, such pictures were taken. They might take a variety of forms, ranging from moving "spheres of light" to mass-less hologramlike "doubles" of the original physical form. X rays, after all, have been undetectable for all but a fraction of the history of the human race. To accommodate such a state of affairs, both dualists and materialists would have to revise their position so fundamentally that the resulting theory would deserve a different name altogether. Classical dualists would deny that such a picture in principle could be taken, and classical materialists deny that there is anything in principle to take a picture of. Ergo: Energy Monism.

It should be stressed that I am *not* suggesting that one could ever "take a picture" of thoughts or feelings per se—no matter what the technology of the twenty-second century might be. As inwardly and directly apprehended, the cognitive content of a thought, for example, will remain forever invisible. But thoughts and feelings have energetic (vibrational) expressions that can appear under a variety of formats, whether in or out of our bodies. Especially in the case of strong emotional states, this is self-evident to sophisticated clair-voyants. And while it raises more issues than I can address here, it should also be noted that such states are "energetically repre-sented" in Kirlian photography—an area where Energy Monism gains still further plausibility by virture of incorporating the strengths and avoiding the weaknesses of both "auric" and "coro-nal discharge" interpretations.[11]

In summary, survival (insofar as it involves OBEs) appears incon-sistent with both dualism and materialism and strongly suggestive of Energy Monism. Both of these classical schools, along with mate-rialism's logical counterpart, idealism, suffer the fundamental defect of imposing overly restrictive "reality grids" upon the Great Chain of energy-consciousness.

The Consequences of Interdimensional Penetration for Survival

Per the perennial philosophy, Energy Monism holds that each pri-mary level in the Great Chain of Being penetrates its next-lowest neighbor and is in turn penetrated by the levels above it. Higher levels in the chain are not mere epiphenomenal accidents of lower-level material processes. Rather, the lower unfolds from the higher through successive stages of vibratory density. It remains for us to map out some of the more significant implications of this vision for survival.

The first consequence is that it helps us make sense of the notion of literally "occupying a body." For a dualist whose mind is nonspatial, the very idea of occupying a space must self-destruct. Per Energy Monism, however, we are asked to conceive of nothing more difficult than a certain vibratory density of energy-consciousness occupying the same (roughly coextensive) space as that of another level. Indeed, this is part of the meaning of interdimensional penetration. Conceptually, this should be no more difficult than acknowledging that gravitational and electromagnetic forces can occupy the same space, although, to repeat, this is not to suggest that the mind is just a chunk of gravitational or electrical energy. Human personality does not enter the picture until farther up the ladder, so to speak.

If we can conceive of two levels of vibratory density occupying the same space, it follows that we can conceive of them occupying different spaces, as when, for example, one undergoes an out-of-body experience. In itself, of course, this entails nothing about where the mind goes or for how long it persists. Those are different issues. However, on this modeling of matters, the very idea of survival itself should not strike us as especially problematic.

Nor should a host of related survival-related phenomena strike us as terribly problematic, at least insofar as their dynamics are concerned. For example, an apparition suddenly appearing as if from "out of nowhere" is not any more puzzling than a voice suddenly radiating from a radio as if from nowhere. Of course, the voice existed at a different level (radio-transmission waves) at the low end of the electromagnetic spectrum prior to being "transduced" to even lower spectra of sound frequencies at the point of reception. By analogy, this is what happens when an apparition makes it appearance. The wave forms of the energy-consciousness of at least some of the perceivers are sufficient to create a partial "phase lock" of frequencies with those of the disembodied energy-consciousness, giving us the appearance of form. Similarly, spirits "moving through walls" or allowing persons to move their (physical) hands through them is, on this view of matters, as unproblematic as radio waves passing through walls.

Another consequence of hierarchical interdimensional penetration is that, strictly speaking, there is no substantial self, no ego or "I," that survives death. There couldn't be, because whether we are in or out of our bodies, there is no such entity. Such a bold assertion, of course, requires some elaboration.

To begin, I am not suggesting that there are no differentiations to be made between persons. Clearly there are. Nor am I proposing that all persons in the world are really one. I am saying that, as we progress up the Great Chain of energy-consciousness to transpersonal bands, it becomes ever more apparent that there are no fundamental "gaps of nothingness" that separate one spirit from another. From out of a universal, multidimensional matrix of energy-consciousness an indefinitely large number of persons, processes, and objects are expressed. An apparition, for example, may look like a completely separate and distinct thing. But insofar as it, too, is interpenetrated with higher bands of energy-consciousness not typically visible to the naked eye, that appearance should not lead us to a metaphysics of fundamental discreteness.

Each of us, to be sure, carries a distinctive personality, set of memories, character traits, intelligence, skills, and (physical) form. When we die, it is this matrix of states, traits, and properties that collectively make up the empirical "me" that leaves the body. Through their evolution and dynamic interplay, whether over one life or many, they comprise our respective identities. Behind all this, however, there is for each of us no further self to bind it all together, no separate possessor of a personality, no "I." We may carry the illusion of "I-ness" to the next life. But insofar as it is assumed to refer to something over and above the empirical self or "me," it is just that—an illusion. Insofar as "I" refers to anything, it refers to me.

Although it has not been stressed, the principle of interdimensional penetration and its allied tenets embody a strong evolutionary dynamic. Unfolding and refolding from the one to the many and back again, or transformations from higher to lower or lower to higher, are a continuing fact of life. They are built into the Great Chain. Each of us is evolving in our own distinctive manner, in our own time, toward a greater understanding of, resonance with, and integration of the higher domains of the Great Chain that have been with us all along. The shifts themselves are often sudden, but they are a long time in coming.

At certain phases in the evolution of species, there is a convergence of cycles that makes for large-scale shifts in perspective over comparatively short periods of time. This brings us to the final implication of interdimensional penetration for the survival question. For it is an integral part of the larger paradigm of Energy Monism, though not necessarily of the more historically founded perennial philosophy, that we are now in such a convergence of cycles—a period of great transformation of consciousness.

This means that, for what may be the first time in modern recorded history, especially in the West, relatively large numbers of people are beginning to awaken to the very existence of interdimensional penetration with all of its attendant implications. Whether through widespread practices of meditation, (unintentional) NDEs, the renewed search for transcendence, some deeply buried evolutionary mechanism in our collective unconscious, psychical researchers making their case, or some combination of these and more, survival of physical death is going to become progressively less problematic in contexts where it previously has been.

Growing into resonance with interdimensional penetration involves more than just the area of survival. It means, among other things, that we shall witness greater numbers of children with telepathic and clairvoyant skills, and the unparalleled growth of energy medicine and seemingly miraculous healings. In survival-related contexts alone, we shall see growing numbers of persons intentionally "leaving their bodies" all out of proportion to what psychiatrists and sociologists can explain away in terms of mass hysteria or cults of irrationality. Psychical research, including reincarnation investigations, will enjoy increased support. Past-life emotional-release work will gradually be incorporated into mainstream psychotherapy. Apparitions will be less rare, and, more important, they will be less productive of fearful or negative reactions. The care of terminally ill patients will reflect a clear awareness of the dynamics of the impending transition.

The actual dynamics of survival will remain open to debate well into the future. But the question of *whether* we survive the death of our bodies will be taken by a majority to have been settled. The skeptical Committee for the Scientific Investigation of Claims of the Paranormal (CSICOP) will have lost one of its major substantive battles and will find its own agenda more aligned with *constructive* criticism.

Is all this simply wishful thinking? Speculation? On the one hand, it is clearly visionary. On the other, it is certainly falsifiable. But from the perspective of Energy Monism, the current abandonment or transformation of historically powerful paradigms, the evidence from psychical research, and the spontaneous cases that are fueling grass-roots trends collectively bestow upon such a vision more than a modicum of intellectual respectability. Under whatever labels it may evolve, this vision is, so to speak, one to watch.

CHARLES T. TART

Who Survives? Implications of Modern Consciousness Research

Charles T. Tart, Ph.D., is associate professor of psychology at the University of California at Davis. He is a pioneer in the field of consciousness research and the author of several books on altered states of consciousness and human potential, including States of Consciousness *and* Waking Up: Overcoming the Obstacles to Human Potential.

According to the materialistic view of human beings, so widespread today, any discussion of consciousness is essentially a discussion of computer circuits—biocomputer circuits, to be precise, but still *nothing more* than this. The materialist maintains that ordinary consciousness is like an actively running program in the biocomputer. Specific conscious processes such as memory, emotions, perception, and so forth are merely subprograms of ordinary consciousness. Altered states of consciousness, as occur in dreams, in psychedelic sessions, or spontaneously, are simply different programs. Although this interlocking system of programs and subprograms may produce all sorts of outputs and experiences, many of which are very useful to our pleasure and biological survival, many of them are also quite arbitrary or even nonsensical. In any case, my biological, material self is nothing but the totality of all these programs and subprograms running on the "hardware"—the brain and body—of the human biocomputer. Therefore, the materialist con-

This essay is based on a more extensive discussion in Tart's book *Open Mind, Discriminating Mind.*

cludes, when this hardware is destroyed, when the brain and body die, consciousness necessarily dies with them. No belief, no fervent religious faith, not even mystical experiences of being independent of the body, mean a thing in this view: When the brain/body dies, *you* die. Period.

To put it simply, the materialistic equation is:

$$mind = brain$$

and this is considered to be the complete story. Any apparent counterexamples, such as ostensible contacts with the spirits of deceased persons, out-of-body experiences, near-death experiences, and so forth are considered to be symptoms of pathology, hallucination, or imagination. They are seen as simulations of experience that have no basis in reality.

A totally materialistic philosophy, however, invalidates vital aspects of human nature and creates a dismal outlook on life, an outlook that is usually not explicitly acknowledged because of its dismalness. When hope, love, and joy, when intellect and the materialist philosophy itself, are reduced to their "ultimate reality"—nothing but electrochemical impulses in a biocomputer that originated by chance in a universe of dead, randomly moving material particles—what is left?

Flaws in the Materialistic Equation:
The Evidence of Parapsychology

If it did not claim to be all-embracing, if it merely claimed to be a specialized branch of knowledge, useful in its own area yet not especially relevant to things outside that area, materialistic science/philosophy would lose much of the influence it now commands. But, because the practical and intellectual results of modern science are so far-reaching and powerful, we (including almost all scientists) are overly impressed with the materialistic assumptions intermixed with it. We may consciously reject these assumptions because they lead to a loss of vital spirit, but it is still difficult for us, as Westerners, to effectively reject the cultural conditioning and emotional involvement produced in us by the worldview of materialistic science (scientism). Hence, it is important for us to be able to deal rationally with scientism's claim of comprehensiveness, rather than merely taking the position, "I don't like the way materialism feels. Therefore I'll reject it, even if I have to ignore my intellect."

Those who feel that the "mind = brain" equation is not the whole story need not despair, however. You don't have to be ignorant or unscientific in order to argue reasonably that the scientific position is far from complete and thus not an all-powerful set of reasons for rejecting the possibility of conscious survival beyond death.

This claim is based on the findings of scientific parapsychology, a body of research involving thousands of empirical observations and at least seven hundred laboratory experiments in the last six decades. To a growing number of members of the scientific community, including myself, parapsychology has conclusively established that there are aspects of human consciousness that simply cannot be reasonably reduced to materialistic explanations. Any unbiased reading of the parapsychological evidence must result in the conclusion that the "mind = brain" equation is woefully incomplete and should therefore not be used to rule out spiritual realities or the possibility of survival on an a priori basis.

Briefly, parapsychological research has firmly demonstrated the existence of four major psychic abilities. (*Psychic* refers to information transfer or physical effects on the world that are produced by no reasonably conceivable physical means.) These are *telepathy, clairvoyance, precognition,* and *psychokinesis*—collectively referred to as *psi phenomena*.

Telepathy is the transmission of information directly from one mind to another mind after we have ruled out ordinary physical means (like talking or sign language). Its existence has been firmly established by laboratory card-guessing studies in which a sender, isolated in a room, looks at one card after another from a thoroughly shuffled pack of cards, trying to send his or her thoughts of the cards, while a receiver, isolated in another room, writes down impressions of the cards. Although perfect scores are extremely rare, there are enough studies showing more hits than could be reasonably expected by chance to establish the reality of telepathy.

Clairvoyance is the direct extrasensory perception of information about the physical world without the intervention of another mind that already knows that information by ordinary sensory means. This ability, too, has been established by card-test studies, although of a different kind. In these studies, the test subject gives impressions of the order of a deck of cards that have been randomized in such a way that no one knows the order of the deck. Many such studies show enough hits to confirm the existence of clairvoyance.

Precognition is the ability to predict the future when the future is determined in a random way. This ability has been established by studies in which a subject is asked to predict the order of a target deck of cards that will be randomly shuffled at some date in the future. Precognition of this sort has been successful at intervals of up to a year.

Collectively, telepathy, clairvoyance, and precognition are known as *extrasensory perception* (ESP), because they all involve information gathering.

Psychokinesis (PK), the fourth well-established psychic phenomenon, is popularly called "mind over matter" and has been established by classic tests that involve wishing which way machine-thrown dice will turn up. (In more recent studies, the target object is usually an electronic random-number generator.)

These psi phenomena are important to the question of survival after death because they are manifestations of *mind* that have resisted all attempts to reduce them to known physical forces or to straightforward extensions of known physical forces. Thus, they are clear counterexamples to the materialistic "mind = brain" equation.

No doubt some aspects of mind and consciousness are partially or wholly dependent on the functioning of the brain and nervous system, as materialism claims. But psi phenomena seem independent of the physical limits of that functioning. Hence, they demonstrate the need to investigate mind on its own terms. These psi phenomena do not "prove" postmortem survival, of course, but they do at least refute the claim of materialistic science that survival of consciousness after death is impossible in principle.

Survival Research

At one time parapsychology (originally called *psychical research*) focused heavily on the question of survival after death. Today, however, survival research has become a very small part of parapsychology, which now focuses on aspects of the four psi phenomena mentioned above. From the central role it once had, survival research has fallen into almost complete abandonment for half a century. The reason for this abandonment is quite interesting.

The idea that living people have psychic abilities was not generally accepted when the first psychical researchers began investigating mediums (often referred to today as "channels"). If an ostensible surviving spirit transmitted information that agreed with what the researcher knew about the deceased, the researcher was inclined to accept it at face value, as evidence of survival: After all, who but the researcher and the deceased could have known the information? As studies gradually established that ordinary people sometimes had psi abilities, however, the picture became more complicated. The validating information *might* have come from the deceased, but it might also have come from a number of other sources—for example, from the medium's unconscious telepathic reading of the investigator's mind, from a telepathic reading of the mind of a friend or relative of the deceased, or from a clairvoyant transfer of information from surviving documents and records. Also, if *pre*cognition existed, then why not *retro*cognition, in which the medium used unconscious psychic abilities to go backward in time to retrieve information about the deceased during that person's lifetime?

New facts from the emerging studies of hypnosis and abnormal mental states such as multiple personality added further complications, because they showed that a person's subconscious mind could allow him or her to do incredible imitations of other people. And when it also became apparent that subconscious processes could distort a person's mental functioning and alter experience to support deeply held beliefs, the ground was laid for a powerful alternative explanation of the best data for survival—the *unconscious impersonation theory*.

According to this theory, the medium believes in survival and needs to have experiences that reinforce this belief system, so an unconscious part of his or her mind *imitates* deceased people. Because the medium's subconscious mind occasionally uses ESP abilities to obtain information about deceased persons that could not normally be known to the medium, these imitation personalities are very convincing. And because of the dissociation between the conscious and subconscious minds, the medium consciously feels as if he or she were indeed simply a channel for "external" personalities.

Because it became too difficult to decide between the survival hypothesis and the unconscious-impersonation theory, most parapsychologists abandoned survival research and concentrated on the psi abilities of the living. Today only a few parapsychologists are still actively working to invent better tests of survival that can distinguish between these two explanations.

Ordinary Consciousness and Survival

What little survival research has been done by parapsychologists has implicitly been about the survival of ordinary consciousness, our ordinary sense of "I." Modern consciousness research, however—as well as certain branches of the perennial philosophy, including Buddhism, Sufism, and the teachings of G. I. Gurdjieff—indicates that what we call "I" is actually quite changeable from minute to minute, rather than being as fixed as we like to think it is. Because certain forms of "I" occur quite often, it is useful, especially if we are interested in personal growth, to speak of our many "I"s, or *subselves*.[1] But it is important to note that many of these ordinary "I"s often do not long "survive"—that is, maintain their presence and integrity—through many of the small changes of ordinary life, such as intense emotions, sexual desire, hunger, fatigue, alcohol intoxication, and the effects of many other mind-altering drugs. If ordinary "I"s cannot survive even these relatively minor shocks, it seems quite unlikely they could survive the vastly greater changes of death.

What are the implications of these facts for the question of life after death? First, although it is not impossible that *some kind* of consciousness survives death, it would be unreasonable to expect that the state of consciousness we may regain after dying will be the same as the ordinary state of consciousness to which we are accustomed in life. In other words, we are not likely to awaken after death with our ordinary sense of "I" intact.

Second, the question, Will I survive death? cannot really be satisfactorily answered except as part of the larger question, Who and what am I? This is the central question I will consider as I examine the issue of survival after death in the remainder of this essay.

What Is Ordinary Consciousness?

I have written elsewhere that ordinary consciousness can be conceived as an interrelated network of processes or subsystems of the overall system of consciousness.[2] The following is a brief description of each of these processes or subsystems.

Exteroception is our sensing of the external world with the normal five senses. Your eyes and ears, for example, are exteroceptors, and hearing and seeing are instances of exteroception.

Interoception is perception of the internal state of one's body—for example, feeling "butterflies in your stomach" or noticing a pain in your back.

Input processing refers to the way we "construct" our reality from the raw data of our perceptions. It is a complex process of shaping, modifying, adding to, and subtracting from the immediate input from our sensory receptors, so that our sensations become organized into percepts of familiar, recognizable objects. The mechanisms of this reality-construction process have become fully automatic in the course of our enculturation; hence, we are generally unaware of its operation.

Memory refers to the storage of information about previous experiences, thoughts, and feelings. Memory is used extensively by input processing for direction of its construction process.

Awareness refers loosely to our ultimate ability to know that something exists or is happening. In ordinary consciousness, awareness is usually very closely bound up with words; what we usually mean by "thought" is a kind of internal talking to ourselves. But awareness is far more basic than words. To anticipate my later discussion, if something survives death, it seems likely that it will be more closely connected with basic awareness than with ordinary consciousness.

Sense of identity is a special feeling and cognitive quality of "This is me!" that is added to certain contents of awareness. This quality is what makes the perception "*He* is in pain" so much different from the perception "*I* am in pain." Interoception is normally an important part of one's sense of identity: The feeling of being "I" is usually associated with a whole set of internal bodily sensations.

Emotions are familiar psychophysical experiences such as fear, excitement, anger, love, joy, and so forth.

Space/time sense, like input processing, is part of the way in which we construct our perceptions of our self and our world. It provides a space and time reference for our experiences, which usually don't happen in a vacuum, beyond the space/time continuum, but happen *now*, at this *place*.

Evaluation refers to our various processes of assessing and weighing information: Given what I am perceiving and what I already know, what does this perception *mean*? What should I do? Evaluation consists of relatively formal, conventionally logical reasoning processes, as well as alogical and illogical processes. Emotional reactions are also evaluative processes, but they have been treated separately because of their special quality.

Subconscious processes are the ordinarily invisible intelligent processes we invoke to explain organized experiences and behavior that cannot be explained adequately in terms of what a person consciously experiences. When someone claims to be happy, for instance, yet shows classical signs of depression, we may surmise that subconscious mental processes are at work.

Finally, *motor output* refers to processes for controlling our muscles and our bodies (e.g., hormonal reactions) that allow us to act on the results of evaluations and decisions.

The fact that these processes can be described separately should not, of course, lead us to take a static view of what is actually an interlocking and mutually supportive collection of dynamic processes. Usually, the net result of this dynamically acting and interacting system is *me*, my ordinary state of consciousness. To the extent that some of these processes (motor output, for example) are primarily functions of the physical body and nervous system, rather than inherent qualities of the mind, they will not survive death. Hence, we can expect that the quality of what one might perceive as "I" after death will be quite different from what it is in the ordinary waking state.

An especially important quality of the system of functioning that makes up our state of consciousness is that it is *stabilized*. This means that it generally maintains its overall pattern, its integrity, in spite of constant changes in our external world and our body. For instance, I can see a bright light, I can have a mild headache, and so on, yet still remain *me*. Like any well-engineered system, the system that constitutes "me" can generally compensate for changes so they don't push it out of its range of optimal functioning.

Much of the stabilization of ordinary consciousness is produced through the load, or work, that all these processes impose on awareness. Because doing this work is almost completely automated, we ordinarily don't feel like we're working hard to maintain our ordinary state; we just seem to be in it. When much of that load is removed, however—as typically occurs in the induction of altered states of consciousness ("Relax, don't evaluate, just float along," etc.)—the nature of conscious experience can change drastically. To the extent that much of the loading stabilization of ordinary consciousness, our ordinary "I," depends on bodily and nervous-system processes, this loading will be removed at death, thus favoring the appearance of altered states.

In short, ordinary consciousness is a semiarbitrary construction. During our growth and enculturation, we have developed a great many habits: routine ways of perceiving, thinking, feeling, and acting. These habits function automatically in our ordinary environment to constitute a system—the pattern we call "ordinary consciousness"—that is stabilized, automatically maintaining its integrity through varying circumstances. Forgetting the work that went into constructing this system as children and the cultural relativity and arbitrariness of much of it, we take it for granted as "ordinary" or "normal" consciousness.

The question of survival after death is usually framed in terms of the survival of personality. It is important to recognize, however, that personality—the set of characteristic behaviors and expressions that distinguish us from others—manifests itself through our state of consciousness. In our ordinary state of consciousness, we will have our ordinary personality. If our state of consciousness is drastically altered, however, so is our personality. And if the after-death state is especially conducive to the appearance of altered states, then even if something survives death, it is not likely to be our ordinary personality, our familiar sense of "I."

Altered States of Consciousness

Each of the psychological processes described above can change radically under special circumstances. For example, an ordinary face can be seen as a god or demon; your blood, which is normally imperceptible, can be felt as a river or radiant energy pulsing through your veins; you can seem to merge into a state of dual identity with someone else; your consciousness can appear to go beyond the normal limits of space and time, as in mystical experiences of eternity. When many of these kinds of changes occur simultaneously, we refer to experiencing an "altered state of consciousness," which means that the state resulting from these simultaneous changes is too radical to be seen merely as a variation of one's ordinary state: It is qualitatively, as well as quantitatively, different.

Consider the following example of an altered state reported by Peter Stafford:

> At one point the world disappeared. I was no longer in my body. I didn't have a body. . . . Then I reached a point at which I felt ready to die. It wasn't a question of choice, it was just a wave that carried me higher and higher, at the same time that I was having what in my normal state I would call a horror of death. It became obvious to me that it was not at all what I had anticipated death to be, except it was death, that something was dying. I reached a point at which I gave it all away. I just yielded, and then I entered a space in which there aren't any words. The words that have been used have been used a thousand times—starting with Buddha. I mean at-one-with-the-universe, recognize your Godhead; all these words I later used to explore what I had experienced. The feeling was that I was "home". . . . It was a bliss state of a kind I never experienced before.[3]

We shall return to this kind of altered-state experience later, because it is particularly relevant to the question of survival.

Dreaming: The Most Common Altered State

Modern sleep research has shown that, whether we remember it or not, we all spend about 20 percent of our sleep time in a specific brain-wave state called *stage1*, which is associated with the mental activity of dreaming. In order to dream, we must fall, and remain, asleep—that is, we must induce an altered state of consciousness. Normally this involves reducing exteroception and interoception to very low levels: We turn out the lights and close our eyes, eliminating input from visual exteroception; we relax our bodies and remain still, eliminating input from kinesthetic interoception. If we survive death in some form, we will certainly not have the physical exteroceptors and interoceptors we had during life; hence, this customary input will be drastically reduced, as in dreaming.

We also now know that in dreaming there is a very active inhibition of the input that does reach our receptors. If a sleeper is deliberately stimulated, but not so intensely as to wake him, and if he is then awakened and asked for a dream report, his report will indicate that most of the time stimuli do not make it through into his dream world. The few stimuli that do get through are usually distorted in such a way that they fit in with the ongoing dream: Tapping with a pencil, for example, could become the sound of a woodpecker in the dream. Parapsychologists investigating reported communications with the dead would do well to remember this type of distortion, because similar distortions of our questions to the deceased would be likely to occur if the after-death state were indeed like a dream state. This hypothesis could explain the garbled and distorted nature of much ostensible communication with deceased persons received through mediums.

The function of memory, too, is quite different in the dream state. When we remember something in the waking state, we usually know that we are having a memory. The images in our mind have a nonverbal "This is a memory" quality attached to them. In dreams, however, this quality disappears. The conventional view of dreaming is that we construct all the objects in our dream world from memory images, yet dreaming is experienced as *perceiving*, not as *remembering.*

Our sense of identity, our emotions, and our evaluation processes can also operate quite differently while we are dreaming. Sometimes in dreams we seem to be having experiences that belong to another person—someone with different emotional, evaluative, and intellectual reactions to events. Things that make sense by dream standards may be completely absurd or incoherent by waking-state standards.

In dreams, our sense of space and time is radically different as well: Rather than placing your dream experiences in their "real" context—that is, realizing that you are asleep in your bed, dreaming—you may believe that you are flapping your arms and flying over the Himalayas. If we routinely experience such drastic alteration of the processing styles of emotion, evaluation, sense of identity, and space/time sense in dreams while we are alive, why couldn't such alterations—and perhaps even more radical ones—occur after death? Suppose you awake after death in something more like a dream state than your ordinary conscious state. Would someone who knew your personality in its ordinary state recognize your personality in something closer to its dream state?

Psychologists credit the subconscious mind with the intelligent and active creation of dreams. This psychological explanation is not terribly good, of course, but it is the best we have at this time—and an excellent reminder of how little we actually understand about our minds. If such a potent source of experience as dreams is controlled by mental processes of which we have practically no understanding, it reminds us of how careful we must be in extrapolating the characteristics of waking consciousness to a potential after-death state.

Instability of the After-Death State

We noted earlier that the body and brain are important as stabilizing mechanisms for both ordinary and altered states of consciousness, and that the absence of a body and brain in an after-death state might well indicate that such a state would be very unstable. Thus, in order to gain a better understanding of what an after-death state could be like, it might be well for us to investigate what happens to mental functioning in life when awareness of the body is greatly reduced or temporarily eliminated.

Dreaming, as we have seen, provides a useful analogue of the possible nature of after-death states, because in dreaming we have virtually no awareness of our physical bodies, but only of our mentally constructed dream bodies. Studies of sensory deprivation also seem pertinent to this question, as do studies of ketamine intoxication, which is another excellent analogue for studying the qualities of mind when no body is perceived in life. Ketamine hydrochloride, normally used as an analgesic in surgery, has also been used in much lower doses (about one-tenth the surgical dose) as a psychedelic drug, causing some users to have "out-of-body experiences" in which the physical body effectively disappears from consciousness. The experience cited earlier from Stafford was induced by ketamine.

It may, of course, still be possible for stable states of consciousness to develop in an after-death state, if there are other kinds of stabilization processes—that is, other than interoceptive input from our physical bodies—in such states. But in order to answer to this question, we need to wait and see.

Survival Research and the Problem of State-Specific Knowledge

One of the most important qualities of knowledge is that important aspects of it are state-specific: What you can know depends on the state of consciousness you are in.

The idea of state-specific knowledge can be understood by the simple analogy of using a fishing net to troll through the ocean: If your net has a one-inch mesh, it will not pick up anything smaller than one inch, thus excluding an enormous potential catch. If you understand this property of your net, your "data-collection system," there is no problem; if not, you are likely to think that all ocean life is bigger than one inch. You cannot study small life unless you change nets.

Research on altered states of consciousness shows that some kinds of human knowledge are *state-specific:* If you are not in a certain state of consciousness, certain things cannot be known. For example, in your ordinary state of consciousness you can read about merging into a state of dual identity with another person, but you will not really know what that expression means unless you are in the state of consciousness where you can actually experience your identity merging with that of another person.

Certain kinds of knowledge may be only partially state-specific—that is, they may be known in two or more states of consciousness. For example, if I ask you your name, you will probably be able to give me a correct answer in your ordinary state, while dreaming (assuming I am a dream character asking you the question), while in pain, or while under the influence of alcohol or LSD. But some things can be known *only* in an altered state; you cannot even remember them in your ordinary state, much less explain them adequately to others.

In order to enlarge the sphere of human knowledge, we must study some phenomena in the altered state(s) of consciousness appropriate for knowing those subjects. Unless we personally experience and work with the state(s) in question, we will never really know the answers. One of the great misfortunes of the modern era has been that we have forgotten about the state-specificity of many kinds of vital spiritual knowledge. Because we approach spiritual questions—for example, the question of our destiny after death—only from the perspective of ordinary states of consciousness, it is not surprising that the answers we get are only distorted, pale reflections of reality. We have become so blinded by abstract verbal statements about spiritual truths that we miss the chance to verify those truths for ourselves by direct experience. Hence the prevalent spiritual dissatisfaction of our times.

How is all of this relevant to the question of survival? In various altered states of consciousness, the direct experience of existing in some form that seems partially or fully independent of the physical body is relatively common, and such experience is the most direct knowledge of survival an individual may have.

Of course, indirect forms of evidence are useful too. But by rejecting the direct evidence of experience in altered states of consciousness, we force the issue of survival to be merely one of *indirect* experience, of abstraction and conceptualization. Such a rejection amounts to ignoring some of the most relevant evidence we have concerning survival, and may make it impossible ever to get a personally satisfactory answer.

Putting It All Together

To summarize, our ordinary personality, our ordinary sense of "I," does not seem to be a likely candidate for more than temporary survival, having little unity and being made of many "I"s, each of which often fails to "survive" for long the shocks of ordinary life. Thus, the much greater shock of dying could easily destroy many of these aspects of ordinary consciousness, either temporarily or permanently. Further, ordinary consciousness depends heavily for its stability on a number of body-based processes—for example, exteroceptive and interoceptive input. Lacking such processes, consciousness can change drastically, as it does in ordinary dreaming or under the influence of mind-altering drugs. Unless something very analogous to an external world and a body is provided in the after-death state, much of the ordinary "I" seems unlikely to survive.

Thus, although we should not be too surprised if we regain some sort of consciousness after death, by the same token we should not be too surprised if that consciousness is considerably—perhaps profoundly—different from the ordinary state of waking consciousness to which we were accustomed during life. In order to answer the question Will I survive death? we must first determine the range of possible expressions of "I." If, through profound meditation and self-investigation, we find that there is a basic awareness of "I" that survives the minor shocks of ordinary life as well as the greater shocks of altered states, then that awareness will be the most likely candidate for survival beyond death. And if we want to prepare for death by thinking about what the after-death state of consciousness might be like (and thus perhaps reduce our shock and confusion after death), we should not ignore the evidence from modern research on altered states of consciousness.

Death and Beyond in the Perennial Philosophy

In Part Three we turn to the perennial philosophy, to the insights of the world's great sages and seers, in our quest for more understanding of the fate of human consciousness after death. As we shall see, the perennial teachings corroborate the evidence for survival that we have just examined—that is, the transpersonal and mystical experiences reported from near-death studies, experiential psychotherapies, and modern consciousness research.

In "Thoughts at the Moment of Death," Ram Dass examines the foundation of his own certainty that something continues after death, reviewing his own personal encounters with after-death experiences while exploring altered states of consciousness, and giving us a distillation of his twenty-eight years of association with the teachings of the perennial philosophy on death and beyond.

Noting the importance in Eastern spiritual paths that is attached to the nature of one's thoughts at the moment of death, Ram Dass points out that in both ancient shamanism and modern Western psychedelic research it is also known that the quality of a person's thoughts at the beginning of a shamanic or psychedelic journey largely determines the quality of the visions subsequently encountered. So, he reasons, if we encounter altered states of consciousness after death, it seems likely that our state of mind at the moment of death will strongly influence the character of those states. This is why it is said to be so important to die with a clear mind—a mind free of attachments and aversions. Hence, Ram Dass concludes, the best way to prepare for death is to practice being fully present and mindful during life.

As Georg Feuerstein points out in "Immortality and Freedom:

India's Perspective," the Vedic sages of India began millennia ago to search for direct, experiential knowledge of the fate of the soul after death. At first they carried out this search in altered states of consciousness induced by soma, a powerful psychedelic brew that allowed its partakers to explore dimensions of reality interpreted by them as spiritual realms inhabited by invisible forces, including the souls of the dead, which influenced and guided the destiny of the living. Later, they developed the nonchemical techniques known as *yoga* to help them attain transcendent states of consciousness. In these states they came to the realization that the core of the human personality is transcendental, immortal, and identical with the ground of the universe.

The early yogis sought contact with the Immortal by practicing various forms of asceticism, which brought about dissociation from the conditional realm of space and time. Although Indian spirituality is still usually associated with asceticism, Feuerstein points out that the ascetic ideal was not the final flowering of Indian thought, which peaked in the movement known as Tantrism, a school founded on the realization that enlightenment—the realm of freedom and immortality—is not different from the conditional realm of space and time, but underlies and coexists with it. Hence, the Tantrists discovered that the Immortal can be realized here and now, in the human body, without an ascetic withdrawal from life.

In "Death, Rebirth, and Meditation," Ken Wilber gives us a detailed look at the Tantric teachings of Tibet concerning the states of consciousness encountered after death. "Unlike our own Western culture, traditional cultures like the Tibetan live with death constantly," Wilber writes. "People die in their homes, surrounded by family and friends. Hence, the actual stages of the dying process have been observed thousands, even millions of times." And when we add to these observations a sophisticated spiritual understanding, which the Tibetans have, "the result is an incredibly rich store of knowledge and wisdom about the actual dying process and how it relates to the spiritual dimension, to spiritual development, to karma and rebirth, and so on." Therefore, Wilber argues, it would be foolish for a serious investigator to ignore the massive data that the Tibetan tradition has accumulated.

Describing the Tibetan account of the subjective experiences that occur during the dying process, Wilber notes that, although we may quarrel with the Tibetan explanation of the *cause* of these phenomena, there is a tremendous amount of "contemplative evidence" to support the existence of the phenomena themselves. This contemplative evidence, he explains, involves the experiences of countless meditators in diverse spiritual traditions who have practiced forms of meditation that "mimic" actual physical death, thus allowing them to experience an "imitation" of the stages of the dying process. The point of these meditations, as Wilber observes, is to familiarize oneself with the states of consciousness that appear after death. Then, he says, we not only may avoid being confused or terrified by such states, but can actually use them to attain final liberation from the necessity of rebirth.

In "What Survives? The Teachings of Tibetan Buddhism," Sogyal Rinpoche, a Tibetan meditation master, also emphasizes our need to prepare for death now, in this life. By practicing mindfulness and letting go of attachments during life, the Tibetans believe that one can die with a clear mind, without regret or clinging, and thus gain liberation at the moment of death.

According to the Tibetan Book of the Dead, shortly after death consciousness "faints" into a dark, empty space. The mind, however, dies only for a moment, and when the person awakens, he or she experiences the "clear light void," the sheer luminosity of the true nature of mind. It is at this crucial point that enlightenment can most easily be realized. "Extremely adept practitioners can simply recognize [the luminosity] as the nature of their mind," Sogyal Rinpoche explains. "Connecting it to their own awakened state, they maintain full awareness and merge with it, thereby attaining liberation."

The after-death visions described by the Tibetan Book of the Dead are strikingly similar not only to reports of Western near-death experiences but also to descriptions of the visionary phenomena encountered in shamanic journeys, LSD experiences, and experiential psychotherapies. From this fact, one may conclude that the altered states of consciousness charted by shamans, yogis, Tibetan Buddhists, and other mystics point to a common "geography" of nonordinary reality and that by familiarizing oneself with this territory during life, through spiritual practice, it may indeed be possible to prepare for death in a way that reduces its shock and terror.

The "geography" of after-death states is also the topic of Kenneth Ring's essay, "Shamanic Initiation, Imaginal Worlds, and Light after Death." Ring notes that the realms visited by shamans and those who have had near-death experiences is not one that awaits us only after death: "It exists now and is in principle available *in life* to anyone who has learned the 'access code.'" This code, he says, is connected with the "imagination," but not imagination in the sense of something "made up" or unreal, but in the sense of an objectively existing dimension of reality—the "imaginal realm."

Normally, says Ring, the imaginal realm can be apprehended in certain altered states of consciousness in which we may learn to see with a shaman's eye, with imaginal vision. And what we see, he suggests, is the state of our own soul, which appears to us in the form of *images*—the "natural language of the soul." From this perspective, then, the uniformity of the geography of the after-death realm can be explained as due to the universality of the human soul. So, according to Ring, "it is not that we 'go to a place' after death; instead, we enter into a state of consciousness where *images* are our reality and where that reality, which is not entirely fixed, is responsive to the thoughts, expectations, and desires of our soul."

An important implication of Ring's approach is that we should not conclude from reports of near-death experiences that the after-death experience will necessarily be "uniformly blissful." Ring notes that there are "voices of history," such as those of Plato and William Blake, who remind us that "we are at this very moment writing the script for our own after-death imaginal drama and that we ourselves are the shapers of our soul's destiny."

RAM DASS

Thoughts at the Moment of Death

Ram Dass (Richard Alpert, Ph.D.) is renowned for his psychedelic research at Harvard University and for his subsequent investigation and popularization of yoga and Eastern philosophy in such books as Be Here Now *and* The Only Dance There Is. *He is the founder of the Seva Foundation and now devotes his life to helping patients afflicted with AIDS.*

The following story was told to me by an Indian man some years ago about my guru, Neem Karoli Baba:

"Once in Bhumiadhar, where Baba was staying the night, we had all taken our evening meal and had retired at 10:30 P.M. Around 1 A.M. Baba started yelling that he was very hungry and that he must have dal [lentils] and chapattis. I awoke and reminded him that he had already eaten. But he insisted that he must have dal and chapattis. Who can understand the ways of such a being? So I awoke Brahmachari Baba [the priest] and he built a fire and prepared the food. It was ready about 2 A.M., and we watched Baba consume the food with great appetite. Then we all retired again.

"At about 11 the next morning, a telegram arrived saying that one of Baba's old devotees had died in a village down on the plains (about 150 miles away) the previous night at 2 A.M. When the telegram was read to Baba, he said, 'You see, that's why I needed chapattis and dal.' This aroused our curiosity, because we didn't see at all. We pressed him, but he would say nothing more. Finally, after two or three days of our persistence, he said, 'Don't you see? He [the man who died] had been wishing for chapattis and dal, and I didn't want him to carry that desire on through death, for it would affect a future birth.'"

This story reflects a view of life and death that I have lived with for the past twenty-eight years. When I ask myself how I know that something continues after death, I recognize that my faith rests in three sources: my own experiences, the views expressed by people whom I know and trust (such as those in the story above), and extrapolation from the spiritual literature that I have read. It is some combination of all these that engenders such a strong conviction in me that all does not end at the moment of death.

My personal experiences concern moving in and out of various altered states of consciousness. In the course of exploring these states, I have from time to time experienced a shedding of my identity with body and personality, thus allowing me access to a state of awareness that appears to have little to do with birth or death, coming or going. Through intensive meditation practice and my work with psychedelic chemicals, I have witnessed the manner in which the mind creates realities, and have touched the domain that lies beyond thought. As a result, I have arrived at some intuitive understanding of the after-death states—an understanding that is then corroborated by the other two ways of knowing mentioned above.

It is obvious that the conclusions I am going to present about what happens after death I do not "know" in the usual scientific sense that prescribes the criteria for knowing that we know. In fact, it is only because I listen to and honor my intuitive heart-mind as a way of knowing, even though it is not open to the criteria of public reproducibility, that I have had available to me abundant information about after-death states.

I have noticed that because of these personal experiences, along with the opportunities I have taken to become familiar with wise people and literature that support such experiences, my own fears about death have been deeply allayed. Consequently, I have been able to work with the dying and bring to them qualities of equanimity and peace in the face of the unknown—qualities that seem to have served them well. At those moments when I have been with a person who is approaching death, I find that only truth works, and so I am forced to examine and reexamine my faith in life after death. This, then, is the crucible through which what I am going to share has passed.

It is said in Eastern spiritual traditions that the thought forms to which we are attached at the moment of death determine what happens next. As my guru once said, "If you even desire the next breath, you will take birth again." It is because of this immediate effect of one's thoughts and desires at the moment of death that in countries where belief in reincarnation is widespread, there is so much attention paid to preparing for the moment of death. The Tibetans, for example, describe ways to avoid getting stuck in the feeling of heaviness that arises when the "earth" element of the body dissolves, or in the feeling of dryness when the "water" element dissolves, or in the feeling of coldness when the "fire" element dissolves, or in the feeling that the out-breath is longer than the in-breath as the "air" element dissolves.

This Eastern emphasis on the importance of thought forms at the moment of death is supported by evidence from shamanic studies and consciousness research. Shamans, for example, know that the nature of one's thoughts at the outset of the shamanic "journey" through altered states of consciousness is crucially important in determining the nature of that journey—whether the visions encountered will be heavenly or hellish. (Hence the emphasis on "purification"—either through fasting, sweating, or other ascetic practices—before shamanic initiations.) Similarly, Western psychedelic researchers discovered early on that a person's mind-set at the beginning of the psychedelic experience is a key determinant of the quality of that experience. Thus, if the after-death states are indeed likely to be similar to altered states of consciousness, it seems probable that one's state of mind at the moment of death will strongly influence the nature of one's after-death experience.

We can refer to that part of the individual that passes through the veil of physical death as the "soul," even though we may understand that this "soul" is itself but a subtler thought form that eventually dissolves as the fullness of the Buddhist term *anatta* (no-self) is realized. What the soul ultimately dissolves into is no doubt beyond words to describe, as many enlightened beings have testified. There are, however, numerous symbols that point toward this ultimate truth. Many words like *God, Nirvana, the Formless,* and so forth are used to indicate the Mystery. But these are only "fingers pointing at the moon"; for the knowing human mind, with all its conceptual and symbolic crutches, must be left behind when one dies into the ultimate truth.

Intellectually we may grasp that from the point of view of ultimate truth, reincarnation itself is an illusion; yet we cannot extricate ourselves from the web of this illusion until the final clingings of the mind are stilled. Most of us on the evolutionary journey need not worry at the moment about dissolving into nothingness, because we have sufficient karma (inertia of past attachments) left that we can expect to transmigrate, as souls, across many births to come.

The great spiritual teachers maintain that what one experiences after death is also a function of one's evolution as a soul—an evolution that is most clearly reflected in the quality of the manifestation of the life one is completing. I like to think that human birth is a bit like enrolling in the fourth grade: We stay just as long as necessary to achieve what our soul needs from that specific grade, after which we are naturally ready to go on through further evolution by leaving that life. Thus the soul leaves the physical plane neither a moment too early nor a moment too late. How it leaves is a part of the soul's curriculum. And what it takes with it as it leaves is the essence of what that life has been about—an essence that the soul knows even though the brain that fosters thought has been left behind.

According to various schools of perennial philosophy, those "young souls" who are deeply entrenched in attachment to the physical body die into a subtle physical sheath in which they experience a type of confused "sleep." It is said that their identification with the gross materiality of the body makes them ill prepared to recognize that they still exist after they have died; thus their confusion and some feeble attempts to carry on as if they were alive. I suspect that they are quite surprised when nobody on the physical plane notices them. These beings are then quite unconsciously reprogrammed by the inertia of their karma (a sort of "psychic DNA") into their next birth. Those with extreme physical attachments, usually through greed or anger, often persist on or near the physical planes as what are sometimes experienced by others as ghosts or poltergeists.

As a soul evolves further, it succeeds by the end of its incarnation on earth in awakening sufficiently to its predicament to extricate itself from one or more of its "sheaths" or "veils"—that is, the various physical, astral, emotional, mental, and spiritual bodies or vehicles of consciousness described in Vedanta, yoga, and other meditative traditions. A soul at this level of evolution immediately realizes at the moment after death that it has died, and experiences itself expanding as it is freed from the container of incarnation. The soul may tarry for a period of time as it feels caught between its delight in release from incarnation and the pull of attached love toward those whom it has left behind. But after some time it understands the way things must be, and, either alone or with guidance, continues into another realm.

At this stage the soul may pass into a mental realm, if that is where its attachments lie, or into vital or emotional realms. These are often called *astral* realms, or, in Mahayana Buddhism, bardos, or "islands in between." In dying into these realms, the Tibetans say that the soul may retain consciousness and have experiences there in some detail—for example, passing through tunnels of light; being filled with immense joy and profound love; meeting beings in subtle light bodies who are familiar to the soul; experiencing realms of intense color, sound, and so forth.

After some time in such a realm, it is said that the soul—alone or with the help of guides—reflects upon its past karmic journey and, as a result of these reflections, prepares and programs itself for its next incarnation. Evidence of people who, during close encounters with death, have had "panoramic memories" in which they experienced a deep understanding of the significance of their entire lives seems to support the truth of this teaching.

In yoga and Vedanta, it is taught that a yet more evolved soul who, at the time of death, has broken its identification with its subtle bodies may pass with full consciousness through the doorway of death into the higher or "causal" realms (sometimes called the "Brahma fields") and remain in its subtlest essential form for some time in its journey.

It is believed in some schools that unless such a soul is enlightened, or completely liberated from the illusion of separateness, it must, after a greater or lesser period in the subtle realms, inevitably take another incarnation in a physical body. I am not certain in my own mind, however, whether a soul must be incarnated via a physical birth before its final liberation from the illusion of separateness. Perhaps the final work can be accomplished in other realms, perhaps not. At this stage of my development I simply do not know, and will have to wait and see. What I do know is that the moment of death (or "dropping the body," as they say in India) is the most exciting moment of life. And I believe that the best preparation for it—as well as the best way to live one's life—is to Be Here Now, fully present and mindful in this very moment.

As one practices mindfulness of this moment, bringing the mind back again and again to the present activity—whether it be washing the dish, lifting the foot in stepping, or simply inhaling the next breath—sooner or later the mind stops reacting with attachment or aversion to thoughts or sensations. This letting go allows one's awareness to move into each new moment with no baggage. Thus Christ said, "Look, I am making all things new."

Such practice involves allowing the past moment to die as the new moment emerges. One is then no longer time-binding the past with the present and the present with the future. While it is relatively easy to maintain this kind of practice in situations involving little or no stress, it is difficult not to get caught in attraction or aversion when the stimuli in the situation are intense. But with enough practice, it is possible. And then one is prepared to keep one's awareness steady and open to the next moment, even at the moment of physical death, when there are many strong stimuli occurring. Then one takes no baggage or "old karma" along when entering death's door. In fact, there is nobody entering death's door at all. For even the thought of self has been released.

When the Buddha was asked where he, a fully evolved being, would go at the moment of death, he answered, "Where does the fire go when the fuel is used up?" Ah, so!

GEORG FEUERSTEIN

Immortality and Freedom: India's Perspective

Georg Feuerstein, M. Litt., is a scholar of Eastern religions and translator of the Bhagavad Gita, the Yoga Sutras of Patanjali, and author of several books on yoga philosophy, including Yoga: The Technology of Ecstasy.

Nothing can intellectually convince me that we survive physical death. All the empirical evidence I have examined and all the evidence that could possibly be marshaled in favor of our postmortem survival cannot change my mind—that is, my sober, rational mind, trained extensively in academic skepticism and well exercised in agnosticism.

Luckily, however, my rational mind doesn't exhaust who I am. I have other cognitive capacities that I can bring into play when pondering my destiny after death. Yet, curiously enough, I remain intellectually uncoverted even by my own firsthand experiences of psychospiritual states in which I have apparently transcended the body-mind as I normally experience it. I believe that my situation is shared by a good many other people who cultivate doubt as an appropriate professional attitude. They, too, remain rationally unconvinced by the thousands of cases of near-death experiences, out-of-body experiences, and body-transcending mystical raptures. This is both fortunate and unfortunate. It is unfortunate because in most cases it means that their lives remain relatively closed. It is fortunate because in at least some cases it provokes the kind of curiosity that turns the searchlight of science to matters that are all too frequently dismissed as metaphysical nonsense.

As I said before, reason or intellect is only one aspect of what I know myself to be. It has its place, but when it comes to metaphysical matters, I have always employed it rather judiciously because I understood early on that, generally speaking, its competence lies more in the structuring of information than in the acquisition of knowledge. And so, for the past twenty-five years I have with great personal benefit studied the spiritual traditions of India.

While I find many, if not most, of the metaphysical systems spawned on the Indian peninsula quite inadequate as descriptions of reality, they have never failed to inspire me, precisely because I have never approached them solely with the rational, scholarly mind. Thus, the mystical intuitions of the Rig-Veda, the Upanishads, and the yoga scriptures, the animated wisdom of the saintly literature of medieval India, and even the works and biographies of modern sages have been almost daily nourishment for me—and for this I am deeply grateful.

But for these often quite "outlandish" Indian teachings to be communicative to me, I have always had to approach them with the kind of openness, or open-heartedness, that one would use when approaching one's spouse or a dear friend. What they teach me about myself—that is, my larger being—is of immeasurable value to me. Their communication has always baffled my mind, and continues to do so; but it has also always enriched that native wisdom we all possess—a wisdom that comes to the fore when we discipline the rational mind and prevent it from tyrannizing our grasp of reality. Rational thought has the formidable power of whittling into a million pieces what should be grasped intuitively, as a whole.

In this essay, I want to convey some of the great insights about freedom and immortality to which the Hindu genius has given birth over a period of three millennia and which have informed my own thinking and feeling about this perennial subject.

It is often said that curiosity is the beginning of philosophy. But curiosity, the need to know, has a deeper, emotional root: our fear of death. Though we may deny it or behave as if it were not true, the fact is that our existence is as limited in time as it is limited in space. We know that, like all things, our life is bound to end and that we have to leave everything that we now call "me" and "mine" behind. As we see our body-mind gradually succumb to the law of entropy, we become increasingly mindful of our own fragile mortality. Hence, we become increasingly interested in what may lie in store for us *after* the inevitable physical dissolution we see looming ahead.

We also turn to philosophy, metaphysics, and theology at times of crisis, when our lives are threatened, or even when we suffer from what Colin Wilson dubbed the "outsider" syndrome—that is, when we feel marginal and displaced, whether socially or in our beliefs. In each case, however, I suggest that what prompts us to philosophical inquiry is our confrontation with the fact that we are not absolute, infinite, endless, all-powerful, all-knowing, fulfilled, or perfect—attributes that we reserve for the supreme being, which we call "God" or "ultimate reality."

But allow me to travel back in time to the concluding centuries of the second millennium B.C. The early Indians had ample occasion for pondering the meaning and purpose of life. The originators of the Vedas, the earliest Indo-European literature, were outsiders who had come from the steppes of what is now Russia. They were conquerors who felt surrounded by enemies. They had been seminomadic cattle breeders, but now they had to learn to cultivate the land and live with the dangers of the jungle and seasonal flooding. Their central deity was Indra, a god of rainstorms, thunder, and war. They prayed to him for wealth and to avert calamity, as well as to gain victory over the newly won soil and the native inhabitants.

These Indo-Europeans worshiped Indra by means of an "intoxicating" brew referred to as soma—to such an extent that some readers of the Vedas arrived at the erroneous conclusion that the Vedic Indians were permanent drunks, the unfortunate victims of soma addiction. Indra, of course, was the soma quaffer par excellence, and the humble human worshiper saw himself or herself as merely imitating the great god. The soma draught, whatever it may have been (R. Gordon Wasson suggested it was the mushroom *Amanita muscaria*), was obviously potent, producing altered states of consciousness. While they were soma-intoxicated, worshipers experienced themselves as being in the company of Indra and even as matching the great god's splendor.

Some people may wonder whether the experiences in question were purely hallucinatory or whether they were genuine mystical elevations. In my view, they were most likely both, just as the LSD takers of the 1960s and 1970s experienced a mass of inconsequential fireworks and, occasionally, genuine spiritual breakthroughs that had a decidedly positive effect on their lives. But, in contrast to the acidheads of the modern counterculture, who grew up in a confused, secularized society, the Vedic people were far more likely to experience the sacred dimension of existence. Thus, even hallucinations were apt to have great personal and social significance.

To coin a phrase, pharmacology is not destiny. A drug may change a person's perception and self-perception, but this does not mean that it will inevitably determine—or even have any impact at all on—how that individual will think and behave after the effects have worn off. Alcohol is a good example. But even a powerful psychogenic drug like LSD need not, and demonstrably did not always, lead to significant changes in a person's values or lifestyle. Much depends on what people bring to the drug experience and whether they choose to integrate it with the rest of their lives.

The Vedic seers and sages, and even simple householders doing their daily soma sacrifices, were steeped in sacred values and religious beliefs, which undoubtedly informed their soma-induced peak experiences. Here, however, I am more interested in the philosophical distillate of their soma experiences: How did their pharmacological excursions find expression in their thoughts and lives? The simple answer is that, far from turning them into incompetent soma addicts, the sacred draught sensitized them to the numinous hidden dimensions of the cosmos and their own psyches. They *lived* in a world that we would debunk as mythological fancy. Indra, Agni, Rudra, and Surya were gods that had immediate reality for them. Prayers and ceremonial offerings had effective power, influencing the hidden world and the visible world around them. The breath was not mere oxygen, but an all-sustaining life force. And death was not the end of human life, but a threshold experience, opening up another realm of existence.

With the possible exception of professional thinkers—for instance, Greek sophists and modern university professors of philosophy for whom thinking is a livelihood—thoughtful people of all cultures and periods have always been provoked to thought by the contemplation of their own finitude. This is well illustrated in the hymns of the ancient Vedas. The soma-inspired visions and metaphysical flights of their composers reveal to us a culture that was down-to-earth but not crassly materialistic. Even when the Vedic people prayed for more rain, more cattle, or victory over the enemy, they never lost sight of the invisible forces that they believed were influencing or guiding their destiny. They believed in and conversed with gods, ancestral spirits, demons, goblins, elfs, and a host of other creatures that have been made homeless by scientific thought.

Above all, the early Indians believed that after a long, prosperous, and happy life on earth they could look forward to a joyous life in the hereafter. They did not doubt in the least that death is merely a transition, not an end. For them, if one's earthly life had been just and noble, the after-death state would be a world where milk and honey flow in abundance. Evildoers, however, were promised a plunge into bottomless darkness.

The more sensitive or mature souls, who realized that even the most wonderful life on earth is marred by change and death, translated their desire to escape the clutches of death into a higher spiritual impulse: They prayed and prepared themselves for immortality in the domain beyond even the heavenly paradise where the average faithful individual is reunited with his or her family and friends. They wanted to share the immortality of the disembodied gods themselves.

Here we have the seed of the later Hindu notion that the core of the human personality is transcendental and perfectly identical with the very ground of the universe, as formulated in the Upanishads: *aham brahma asmi* ("I am the Absolute"), *tat tvam asi* ("That art thou"), *sarvam idam brahma* ("All this is the Absolute"). These are the great utterances of the Upanishadic sages. The transcendental Self (*atman*), which is the subjective core of the human personality, is immortal, deathless. It is coessential with the deepest core, or the highest dimension, of the objective universe, which is known as *brahman*. All that can be said about the Absolute is that it exists and is singular, supremely conscious (rather than insentient), and utterly blissful. The Upanishadic sages therefore spoke of it as Being-Consciousness-Bliss (*sat-cid-ananda*).

What is the relationship between that transcendental Singularity and the space-time world, which is a theater of subjects and objects? The Hindu sages thought deeply about this question and came up with different answers, which testifies to their philosophical ingenuity. The authorities of the earliest Upanishads still regarded the world as an emanation of the One Being, though they suggested different versions of this belief. Later thinkers, notably the eminent propounder of Vedantic nondualism, Shankara (A.D. 788–820), moved toward a more sophisticated point of view, which looks upon the world as a product of spiritual ignorance (*avidya*) without being entirely illusory. Some authorities, like the composer of the tenth-century Yoga-Vasishtha, took a still more radical stance, suggesting that the phenomenal world is an outright hallucination and that only the ultimate Being-Consciousness exists. The same idealist view is shared by some schools of Mahayana Buddhism.

What is important to realize is that these metaphysical formulations were not mere speculation or book knowledge. Primarily they were founded in actual yogic realizations. The Upanishads are not so much philosophical discourses as testimonies to the mystical experiences of hundreds of sages and adepts of yoga. They did not content themselves with mere belief in an afterlife or pious hopes about future immortality. Their quest was to discover immortality in this very lifetime. Freedom was no slogan for them, nor did it have the narrow political connotations it tends to have today. Freedom meant to be radically free, in spirit.

The yogis hoped to free themselves not from political enslavement or the yoke of economic necessity, but from the chains of their own psychomental conditioning. Whatever circumstances they were confronting, they wanted to stand fearless—even blissful—and quite unconcerned about their past, present, and future. In their quest for freedom and immortality, they explored a great variety of means—severe asceticism (*tapas*), absolute renunciation (*vairagya*), and the more integrated disciplines of meditation and ecstasy, which are at the heart of what came to be known as *yoga*. The breakthrough came, however, when they discovered that in order to acquire immortality, a person did not have to lose the body, but that perfect spiritual freedom could be attained in the embodied form. Thus, the ideal of "living liberation" (*jivan-mukti*) was born and from then on existed side by side with the earlier ideal of "disembodied liberation" (*videha-mukti*).

In its significance for humanity, that discovery is more important than the invention of the wheel, the invention of agriculture, or the domestication of animals—yet most of humankind is utterly unaware of it. And so the great adepts and sages of Hinduism and other religiospiritual traditions continue to be ignored.

Why is the discovery of living liberation so significant? Because, once its implications are fully understood, it frees us *from* the necessity of the religious-moral quest for a paradisiacal life in the hereafter, as well as from the search for fulfillment in the conditional realms of existence. At the same time, it frees us *for* a realistic, rather than idealistic, attitude toward life. How so? Actors who take their theatrical roles offstage are in serious psychological trouble. Yet this state describes our ordinary condition: We generally forget that our roles as marriage partners, parents, householders, breadwinners, car drivers, taxpayers, good citizens, and so on, do not define us exhaustively. Instead, we usually behave as if those diverse roles were our very living cells, as if we amounted to nothing apart from them. We are burdened by this mistaken notion, and yet do not even know that there is an alternative to it.

When we understand, however, that we are not identical with any of the roles that we so skillfully animate in the course of our conventional lives, we also no longer suffer the limitations of our multiple and often complex roles. Suddenly we stand in a free relationship to them, able to respond to the social game around us without being swallowed up or diminished by it. We are our "own man" or woman, achieving an autonomy that is founded in our recognition of the primacy of immortal Consciousness (*cit*). That recognition leads to a growing certainty that culminates in the process of permanent ecstatic self-transcendence known as liberation, or full enlightenment.

The enlightened being does not look for fulfillment in and through any role that "it" may temporarily animate, because it is already blissful and immortal. Such a being has no fear of death and therefore no need for the countless "vision quests" by which the unenlightened individual tries to affirm his or her own existence and outwit the cosmic law of entropy. The enlightened being is, of course, aware that the body-mind, the psychobiological organism with which it happens to be mysteriously associated (at least from the perspective of unenlightenment), will inevitably grow old and die. But this dreaded fate does not perplex or disturb the enlightened being, because "it" also knows that the same Consciousness-Identity remains forever, regardless of whether the body-mind, or even the entire universe, is annihilated. In enlightenment there is no illusion of proprietorship. To adapt E. F. Schumacher's well-known phrase: In the economy of enlightenment, *infinite is beautiful.*

In the Upanishads and later works of Vedanta, the transcendental Reality is often characterized as the eternal "Witness." It is the ultimate watcher of the contents of consciousness—the fleeting states of mind, the ongoing swirl of sensations, emotions, thought fragments, hunches, insights, desires, attitudes, and so on. In *Yoga: Immortality and Freedom*, the late Mircea Eliade, perhaps our century's greatest historian of religion, observed:

It is impossible . . . to disregard one of India's greatest discoveries: that of consciousness as witness, of consciousness freed from its psychophysiological structures and their temporal conditioning, the consciousness of the "liberated" man, of him, that is, who has succeeded in emancipating himself from temporality and thereafter knows the true, inexpressible freedom.

The notion of the transcendental Witness was indeed an important conceptual innovation, which stood at the fountainhead of the entire ascetical tradition of Hinduism. And yet it proved to be a doubled-edged sword. On the one side, it cut through the conventional materialistic idealism that projects the empirical subject, or ego, into dimensions in which it has no place. Thus, it effectively undermined the archaic ideal of immortality in some postmortem Elysium in the delightful company of the gods. On the other side, however, it tended to lop off conventional life, which was regarded as having nothing to do with the Witness—because the recommendation of the Upanishadic seers to realize the transcendental Self-Identity beyond all roles involved progressively disowning everything that is generally considered to belong to normal human existence: family, social life, work, and, ultimately, the body-mind itself. When asked about the nature of the Self, the Upanishadic sages responded, "Neti neti," ("Not thus, not thus"). The spiritual practitioner was expected to apply this wisdom to everyday life, which was supposed to be simple and contemplative. The tradition of renunciation (samnyasa, tyaga) is characteristic of that attitude of negation.

Thus, the ideal of living liberation (jivan-mukti) was an important step in humanity's spiritual evolution. Yet, it was not a big enough stride. Even though people could dedicate themselves to attaining enlightenment in this lifetime, they still had a problematic relationship to embodiment. For them, the body-mind and the world at large were something to be left behind, at least emotionally. The key prescription was dissociation. As a result, they did not entirely escape the pull of the earlier archaic notion of immortality. While immortality was no longer viewed as a goal in the hereafter, it still involved a form of death: The spiritual aspirant had to voluntarily withdraw from the world and from his or her body-mind until the glorious moment of illumination was reached. The adept had to die a metaphorical death, involving an inner deadening to the world. Later, upon Self-realization, he or she could return to the world and live in it but not be of it—like the proverbial lotus floating on muddied water.

This tradition has become the style associated in our minds with India's spirituality. Indeed, it was the tradition that dominated both

Hindu and Buddhist cultures for centuries. People seldom realize that it was not the ultimate flower of the spiritual heritage of India. The Hindu and also the Buddhist genius has recognized the limitation inherent in the ideal of the transcendental Witness—a recognition expressed as a total reappraisal of the physical dimension of existence in the great (and unfortunately much-maligned) spiritual movement known as *Tantrism*.

At the heart of Tantrism is the equation *samsara* = *nirvana*, which means that the conditional world of space-time is coessential to—that is, it exists together with—the unconditional dimension of existence that transcends the spatiotemporal world. Because this will mean as little to most people as Einstein's famous formula $E = mc^2$, a brief explanation is in order. *Samsara* is the world of change, as we perceive it through our senses. According to the Tantric adepts, this finite world is only the outermost aspect of an infinitely complex field. Thus, to identify with only the outermost aspect of this field constitutes the "ignorance" (*avidya*) that keeps us bound to the suffering inherent in limitation. By yogic means, however, it is possible to identify with the total cosmic field. From the point of view of the unenlightened consciousness, that total field lies beyond the known and knowable world. But the Tantric masters discovered that this field is all there is: Hence, it does not *really* lie beyond the world of change. Rather, it *underlies* conditional existence and, in the last analysis, is not different from it.

This insight has profound implications for our human condition, as the Tantric adepts realized. Thus they came to regard the body, and bodily existence in general, as the "temple of the Divine." No longer was the body viewed as a "foul-smelling bag of skin." Instead, embodiment was seen as a unique opportunity to realize the body's potential—the potential of divinity.

This new attitude is pithily expressed in the Kularnava-Tantra, an important Hindu Tantric work, in the following way:

> Without the body, how can the [highest] human goal be realized? Therefore, having acquired a bodily abode, one should perform meritorious (*punya*) actions.

> Among the 840,000 [types of] bodies of embodied beings, the knowledge of Reality cannot be acquired except through a human [body].

The Tantric masters aspired to create a transubstantiated body, which they called adamantine (*vajra*) or divine (*daiva*)—a body made not of flesh but of immortal substance, of Light. Instead of regarding the body as a "meat tube" doomed to fall prey to sickness and death, they viewed it as a dwelling place for the Divine, and as the cauldron for the alchemical process of spiritual perfection. For them, enlightenment was a whole-body event. The embodiment of an enlightened master is only apparent. His or her body is really the Body of all, and therefore he or she can assume any form at will. The Tantric adept (*siddha*) possesses a transubstantiated body endowed with great paranormal powers (*siddhi*). Hence, throughout India's history, the spiritual adepts have been celebrated and feared as great magicians.

The magical element of Tantrism came to the fore in the tradition of body cultivation (*kaya-sadhana*), notably in the schools of hatha-yoga, which are products of the tenth century A.D. Coming mostly from the illiterate social strata of Hindu society, the hatha yogins often tended to misunderstand the body-positive teachings of Tantrism. Instead of realizing that the physical body cannot survive indefinitely and that the immortal Tantric body is of a spiritual rather than material order, they went to great lengths in attempting to immortalize their mortal frames. Thus, they invented an impressive range of techniques for controlling the bodily functions—from practices that effectively arrest breathing to methods of preventing seminal discharge. In hatha-yoga at its coarsest, we have the ancient Vedic hope for immortality transferred to the physical level.

I have always defended hatha-yoga against scholarly prejudice; but I believe it is nonetheless true that the ideal of bodily immortality is no more than a pipe dream—a dream that can, in fact, be dangerous to the dreamer. The legends of Babaji, the immortal master of the Himalaya, are just that—legends. This is not to deny that there may well be adepts with extraordinary life spans. (In fact, I have written an introduction to a biography of one of them: Tapasviji Maharaj, whose life is as well documented as we can expect in India's timeless culture.) We can learn something from these exceptional ascetics—among other things that they, like the rest of us, are destined to die in the end. No ideology and no technology can prevent this fate. Everything that is born must die. More precisely, everything that *experiences* itself to be born (i.e., the ego-self) must die. Hence, the "deathless" (*anrita*) transcendental Self is traditionally said to be "unborn" (*aja*).

Our modern culture is apt to become fascinated with long-lived individuals like Tapasviji Maharaj or Shivapuri Baba, and with the ideal of physical immortality. The emergent medical discipline of genetic engineering is our contemporary secular answer to the ancient method of *kaya-kalpa* ("body fashioning"), a naturopathic way of rejuvenating the body through prolonged fasting, meditation, and special herbal remedies. For what is it that genetic engineers ultimately hope to accomplish if not the extension of life? While they may succeed in adding years and perhaps even well-being to our lives, they cannot teach the spiritual lessons that each person must learn for himself or herself. And those lessons will be in the future, as they are now, bound up with the inescapable fact that physical existence is finite, very finite, and that to give human life deep and lasting meaning, we must include in its purview the glorious dimension of what the sages and mystics of India have anciently called Being-Consciousness-Bliss.

We are today in the thick of a sweeping cultural transition. As Friedrich Nietzsche boldly declared a century ago, the parental Creator-God of our forebears has died for most of us. We can no longer believe in paradise and the resurrection of the flesh. But we are still mourning this loss, and we are certainly perplexed. Some of us have become sensitive to a new possibility—a possibility long realized on Indian soil, namely that Reality is immanent and transcendental and that we can discover this truth existentially, not merely intellectually, precisely because it *is* us.

Of course, the rational mind wonders at all of this. This is how it should be, for doubt is the province of reason. But then there is also the heart, which rejoices at such a possibility. Together, head and heart will aid our spiritual quest. We can feel free to listen to the whispers of immortality.

KEN WILBER

Death, Rebirth, and Meditation

Ken Wilber, the founder of "spectrum psychology," has written over one hundred articles and is the author or editor of ten books, including The Atman Project *and* Up from Eden.

Some type of reincarnation doctrine is found in virtually every mystical religious tradition the world over. Even Christianity accepted it until around the fourth century A.D., when, for largely political reasons, it was made anathema. Many Christian mystics today, however, accept the idea. As the Christian theologian John Hick pointed out in his important work *Death and Eternal Life*, the consensus of the world's religions, including Christianity, is that some sort of reincarnation occurs.

Of course, the fact that many people *believe* something does not make it true. And it is very difficult to support the idea of reincarnation by appealing to "evidence" in the form of alleged past-life memories, because in most cases these can be shown to be only a revival of subconscious memory trace from *this* life.

Yet this problem is not as serious as it might at first appear, because the doctrine of reincarnation, as used by the great mystical traditions, is a very specific notion: It does *not* mean that the *mind* travels through successive lives and therefore that under special conditions—for example, hypnosis—the mind can recall all of its past lives. On the contrary, it is the *soul*, not the mind, that transmigrates. Hence, the fact that reincarnation cannot be proven by appeal to memories of past lives is exactly what we should expect: Specific memories, ideas, knowledge, and so on belong to the mind and do not transmigrate. All of that is left behind, with the body, at death. Perhaps a few specific memories can sneak through every now and then, as in the cases recorded by Professor Ian Stevenson and others, but these would be the exception rather than the rule. What transmigrates is the soul, and the soul is not a set of memories or ideas or beliefs.

Now, according to most branches of the perennial philosophy, the soul has two basic defining characteristics: First, it is the respository of one's "virtue" (or lack thereof)—that is, of one's karma, both good and bad; second, it is one's "strength" of awareness, or one's capacity to "witness" the phenomenal world without attachment or aversion. This second capacity is also known as "wisdom." The accumulation of these two—virtue and wisdom—constitutes the soul, which is the only thing that transmigrates. So, when people claim to be "remembering" a past life—where they lived, what they did for a living, and so on—they are not, according to any major religion or branch of the perennial philosophy, remembering any actual past lives. Only Buddhas (or tulkus), it is said, can remember past lives— the exception to the rule.

Reincarnation as a Spiritual Hypothesis

But if ostensible past-life memories are not good evidence for reincarnation, what other type of evidence could there be to support the doctrine? Here we should remember that the perennial philosophy in general allows three major and different types of knowledge and its verification: sensory or empirical knowledge; mental or logical knowledge; and spiritual or contemplative knowledge. Reincarnation is not a sensory or a mental hypothesis; it cannot be explained or verified using sensory data or logical deduction. It is a spiritual hypothesis, which is to be tested with the eye of contemplation, not with the eye of flesh or the eye of mind. So, although we will not find any sort of ordinary evidence to convince us about reincarnation, once we take up contemplation and become fairly proficient at it, we will start to notice certain obvious facts—for example, that the witnessing position, the soul position, begins to partake of eternity, of infinity.

There is a timeless nature about the soul that becomes perfectly obvious and unmistakable: One actually begins to "taste" the immortality of the soul, to intuit that the soul is to some extent above time, above history, above life and death. In this way one becomes gradually certain that the soul does not die with the body or the mind, that the soul has existed before and will exist again. But this certainty has nothing to do with specific memories of past lives. Rather, it is a recollection of that aspect of the soul that touches spirit and is therefore radically and perfectly eternal. In fact, from this angle it becomes obvious that, as the great Vedantic seer Shankara put it, "the one and only transmigrant is the Lord," or Absolute Spirit itself. It is ultimately Buddha-mind itself, the One and Only, that is appearing as all these forms, manifesting itself as all these appearances, transmigrating as all these souls. In the deeper stages of contemplation, this realization of eternity, of spirit as undying and indestructible, becomes quite palpable.

Yet, according to the perennial teachings, it is not *merely* the Absolute that transmigrates: The individual soul itself, if not enlightened, also transmigrates. If the soul awakens, or dissolves in spirit, then it no longer transmigrates; it is "liberated," or it realizes that, as spirit, it is reincarnated everywhere, as all things. But, if the soul does not awaken to spirit, if it is not enlightened, then it is reincarnated, taking with it the accumulation of its virtue and wisdom, rather than specific recollections of its mind. And this chain of rebirths continues until these two accumulations—virtue and wisdom—finally reach a critical point, whereupon the soul becomes enlightened, or dissolved and released in spirit, thus bringing individual transmigration to an end.

Even Buddhism, which denies the absolute existence of the soul, acknowledges that the soul has a relative, or conventional, existence, and that this relatively or conventionally existing soul does transmigrate. When the Absolute, or *shunyata*, is directly experienced, the relative transmigration—and the separate soul—comes to an end. One might think, however, that a Buddhist would object to our use of the word *soul* in this context, since this term generally has the connotation of something that is indestructible or everlasting—a connotation that seems to be incompatible with the Buddhist idea that the soul has only a relative and temporary existence. A closer look at the teachings of the perennial philosophy, however, will resolve this apparent contradiction.

According to the perennial tradition, the soul is indeed indestructible, but when it fully discovers spirit, its own sense of separateness is dissolved or transcended. The soul still remains as the individuality, or expression of the particular person, but its being or center shifts to spirit, thus dissolving its illusion of separateness. And this doctrine accords almost exactly with the highest teachings of

Buddhism—the *anuttaratantra yoga,* or "highest Tantra teaching"—according to which there exists at the very center of the heart chakra, in each and every individual, what is technically called "the indestructible drop" (or luminosity). As the Vajrayana teaches, it is this indestructible drop that transmigrates. Further, it *is* indestructible; even Buddhas are said to possess it. The indestructible drop is said to be the seat of the very subtle "wind" (*rLung*) that supports the "very subtle [or causal] mind," the mind of enlightenment, or one's spiritual essence. Hence, Buddhism agrees with the perennial philosophy: The indestructible drop is the soul, the continuum, as I have defined it.

Stages of the Dying Process: Dissolution of the Great Chain of Being

The various branches of the perennial philosophy agree, in a general way, about the stages of the dying process and the experiences that accompany these stages: Death is a process in which the Great Chain of Being "dissolves," for the individual, "from the bottom up," so to speak. That is, upon death, the body dissolves into mind, then mind dissolves into soul, then soul dissolves into spirit, with each of these dissolutions marked by a specific set of events. For example, body dissolving into mind is the actual process of physical death. Mind dissolving into soul is experienced as a review and "judgment" of one's life. Soul dissolving into spirit is a radical release and transcendence. Then the process "reverses," so to speak, and based upon one's accumulated karmic tendencies, one generates a soul out of spirit, then a mind out of soul, then a body out of mind—whereupon one forgets all the previous steps and finds oneself reborn in a physical body. According to the Tibetans, the whole process takes about forty-nine days.

The Tibetan tradition contains the richest, most detailed description of the stages of the dissolution of the Great Chain during the dying process. According to the Tibetans, the subjective experiences that accompany each of the eight stages of the dissolution are known technically as "mirage," "smokelike," "fireflies," "butter lamp," "white appearance," "red increase," "black near-attainment," and "clear light." In order to understand these terms, we need a somewhat more precise and detailed version of the Great Chain. So, instead of our simplified version of body, mind, soul, and spirit, we will use a slightly expanded version: matter, sensation, perception, impulse, psychic, subtle, causal (or unmanifest), and spirit (or ultimate).

The first stage of the dying process occurs when the aggregate of form, or matter—the lowest level of the great chain—dissolves. There are five *external* signs of this: The body loses its physical power; one's vision becomes unclear and blurred; the body becomes heavy and feels like it is "sinking"; life goes out of the eyes; and the body's complexion loses its luster. The *internal* sign, which occurs spontaneously with these outer signs, is a "miragelike appearance," a type of shimmering, watery image, such as appears in a desert on a hot day. This is said to occur because, technically, the "wind" (*prana*) of the "earth" element has dissolved in the "central channel" and the "water" element thus predominates—hence, the watery or miragelike appearance.

Next, the second aggregate, that of sensation, dissolves. Again there are five external signs: One ceases to have bodily sensations, pleasant or unpleasant; mental sensations cease; bodily fluids dry up (the tongue becomes very dry, for example); one no longer perceives external sounds; and inner sounds (buzzing in the ears, for example) also cease. The internal sign associated with this second dissolution is a "smokelike appearance," which is like a fog. Technically, this is said to occur because the "water" element, which caused the miragelike appearance, is dissolving into the "fire" element—hence the smoky appearance.

The third stage is the dissolution of the third level or aggregate, that of perception or discernment. The five external signs: One can no longer recognize or discern objects; one can no longer recognize friends or family; the warmth of the body is lost (the body becomes cold); one's inhalation becomes very weak and shallow; and one can no longer detect smells. The internal sign spontaneously accompanying this stage is called "fireflies," which is described as an appearance like a bunch of fireflies or cinder sparks from a fire. Technically, this is said to occur because the "fire" element has dissolved and the "wind" element now predominates.

The fourth stage is the dissolution of the fourth level or aggregate, that of impulse (or "intentional formations"). The five external signs of this dissolution: One can no longer move (because there are no impulses); one can no longer recollect actions or their purposes; all breathing stops; the tongue becomes thick and blue and one can no longer speak clearly; and one can no longer experience tastes.

The internal sign of this is a "butter-lamp appearance," described as looking like a steady, clear, bright light. (At this point we can start to see similarities with the near-death experience, which I will discuss further below.)

To understand the fifth and subsequent stages of the dissolution process, it is necessary to know a little Tantric physiology. According to Vajrayana, all mental states—gross, subtle, and very subtle— are supported by corresponding "winds," or energies, or life forces, (prana in Sanskrit, rLung in Tibetan). When these winds dissolve, their corresponding minds also dissolve. Stage five is the dissolution of the fifth level or aggregate, that of cognition, or consciousness itself. As the Vajrayana teachings make clear, however, there are many levels of consciousness. These levels are divided into what are called the gross mind, the subtle mind, and the very subtle mind, each of which dissolves in order, producing specific signs and experiences. So, stage five is the dissolution of the gross mind, along with the "wind," or prana (life force), that supports it. There is then no gross conceptualization, no ordinary mind, left.

During this fifth stage, after the last of the gross mind dies away and the first of the subtle mind emerges, one experiences a state called "white appearance." This is said to be a very bright, very clear white light, like a clear autumn night brilliantly lit by a shimmering full moon. To understand the cause of this white appearance, however, we have to introduce the Tibetan notion of thig.le, which means, roughly, "drops" or "essence." According to Vajrayana, there are four drops, or essences, that are particularly important. One, the white drop, is said to be located at the crown of the head; one receives it from one's father, and it is said to represent (or to actually be) bodhicitta, or enlightenment-mind. The second, the red drop, one receives from one's mother; it is located at the naval center. (The white drop is also said to be connected with semen, the red drop with [menstrual] blood, but the point is that men and women have both, equally.) The third, which is called "the drop that is indestructible for this life," is located at the very center of the heart chakra. This drop is, so to speak, the essence of this particular lifetime of the individual; it is one's "continuum," which stores all the impressions and understandings of this particular life. And inside this "drop that is indestructible for life" is the fourth drop, "the drop that is eternally indestructible or forever indestructible." This is the indestructible drop that remains forever—that is, it is indestructible through this life, indestructible through death and the dying process, indestructible through the *bardo,* or intermediate state between death and rebirth, and through rebirth itself. This drop even remains through enlightenment and is, in fact, the very subtle wind that serves as the "mount," or basis, of enlightenment being. As mentioned before, even Buddhas are said to possess this eternally indestructible drop.

So, what we have seen so far is the dissolution of all the gross winds and the gross minds associated with them. The first subtle mind has thus emerged—that of "white appearance"—and it is "riding" a correspondingly subtle wind, or subtle energy. Now, the actual cause of this mind of white appearance is said to be the descent of the white drop, or *bodhicitta,* from the crown to the heart chakra. Usually, it is said, the white drop is held at the crown chakra by constricting knots and winds of ignorance and gross-level clinging and grasping. But at this stage of the dying process, the gross mind has dissolved, so the knots around the crown chakra naturally loosen, and the white drop descends to the indestructible drop at the heart chakra. When it reaches it, the mind of white appearance spontaneously arises.

Incidentally, if these Tibetan explanations of the phenomena in question sound a bit farfetched, we should remember that there is a tremendous amount of contemplative evidence supporting the existence of the various experiences said to occur during the dying process. The experiences themselves are real and seem largely incontrovertible, but there is plenty of room to argue with the traditional Tibetan account of what actually causes them. (I'll return to this point shortly.) Here I am merely describing the straight Tibetan version as a point of departure.

Nevertheless, we should also keep in mind that, unlike our own Western culture, traditional cultures like the Tibetan live with death constantly; people die in their homes, surrounded by family and friends. The actual stages of the dying process have thus been observed thousands, even millions of times. And when we add the further fact that the Tibetans possess a rather sophisticated understanding of the spiritual dimension and its development, the result is an incredibly rich store of knowledge and wisdom about the actual dying process *and* how it relates to the spiritual dimension, to spiritual development, to karma and rebirth, and so on. Clearly, it would be foolish for an investigator to toss out the massive data that this tradition has accumulated.

But, to continue with the stages of the dying process. At stage six, the subtle mind and its wind dissolve, and an even subtler mind, called "red increase," emerges. Red increase is also an experience of brilliant light; but in this case, it is an experience like a clear autumn day pervaded by bright sunlight. Technically, this is said to occur because the gross life-supporting winds have dissolved, and thus all the knots and constrictions around the navel, which were holding the red *bodhicitta*, or red drop at the navel, are released or un-loosened, and the red drop rises up to the indestructible drop at the heart. When it reaches it, the mind of red increase spontaneously arises.

Stage seven is said to be the dissolution of the subtle mind of red increase and the emergence of an even subtler mind and wind, called "the mind of black near-attainment." In this state, all con-sciousness ceases, all manifestation dissolves. Further, there is a cessation of all of the specific consciousnesses and energies that were developed in this life. The experience is said to be one of a completely black night, with no stars, no light. It is called "near-attainment" because it is "nearing" the final attainment, so to speak; it is nearing the clear light void. This level, in other words, can be thought of as the highest of the subtle or the lowest of the causal, or as the unmanifest dimension of spirit itself. Technically, this "blackness" is said to occur because the white drop from above and the red drop from below now surround the indestructible drop, thus cutting off all awareness.

In the next and final stage, however—in stage eight—the white drop continues downward and the red drop continues upward, thus freeing or opening the indestructible drop. Then, it is said, a period of extraordinary clarity and brilliant awareness results, which is experienced like an extremely clear, bright, and radiant sky, free from any type of blemish, any clouds, any obstructions. This is the clear light.

Now, the mind of clear light is said to be not a subtle mind, but a very subtle mind, and it mounts a correspondingly very subtle wind or energy. This very subtle or "causal" mind and energy are, in fact, the mind and energy of the eternally indestructible drop. This is the causal body, or the ultimate spiritual mind and energy, the *Dhar-makaya*. At this point, the eternally indestructible drop sheds the lifetime indestructible drop, all consciousness ceases, and the soul, the eternally indestructible drop, commences the bardo experience, or the intermediate states that will eventually lead to rebirth. The white drop continues downward and appears as a drop of semen on the sexual organ, and the red drop continues upward and appears as a drop of blood at the nostrils. Death, finally, has occurred, and the body can be disposed of. To do so before this has occurred makes one karmically guilty of murder, because the body is still alive.

Stages of the Rebirth Process

What we have seen so far is the progressive dissolution of the Great Chain, in an individual's case, starting at the bottom and working up. Matter, or form, dissolved into body (or into sensation, then perception, then impulse), and body dissolved into mind, into the gross mind. The gross mind then dissolved into the subtle mind, or soul realms, and the soul then reverted to causal or spiritual essence. Now, at this point, the process will be reversed, depending entirely on the karma of the soul—on the accumulation of virtue and wisdom that the soul takes with it. Thus, the bardo experience is divided into three basic realms, or stages, and these stages are simply the realms of spirit, then mind, then body and matter. The soul, according to its virtue and wisdom, will either recognize, and thus remain in, the higher dimensions, or it will not recognize them—indeed, will actually flee from them—and thus will end up running "down" the Great Chain of Being until it is forced to adopt a gross physical body and hence be reborn.

At the point of actual or final death—which is what we have been calling the eighth stage of the overall dying process—the soul, or the eternally indestructible drop, enters what is called the *chikhai bardo,* which is nothing other than spirit itself, the *Dharmakaya.* As the Tibetan Book of the Dead states, "At this moment, the first glimpsing of the Bardo of the Clear Light of Reality, which is the infallible Mind of the Dharmakaya, is experienced by all sentient beings."

This is the point where meditation and spiritual work become so important. Most people, according to the Tibetan Book of the Dead, cannot recognize this state for what it is. In Christian terms, they do not know God and thus they do not know when God stares them in the face. In fact, they are at this point one with God, entirely and totally in a supreme identity with Godhead. But unless they recognize this identity, unless they have been contemplatively trained to recognize that state of divine Oneness, they will actually flee from it, driven by their lower desires and karmic propensities. As W. Y. Evans-Wentz, the first translator of the Tibetan Book of the Dead, put it: "Owing to unfamiliarity with such a state, which is an ecstatic state of non-ego, of [causal] consciousness, the average human being lacks the power to function in it; karmic propensities becloud the consciousness-principle with thoughts of personality, of individualized being, of dualism, and, losing equilibrium, the consciousness-principle falls away from the Clear Light."

So, the soul contracts away from Godhead, away from *Dharmakaya*, away from the causal. Indeed, it is said that the soul actually seeks to escape from the realization of divine Oneness and "blacks out," so to speak, until it awakens in the next lower realm, which is called the *chonyid bardo*, the subtle dimension, the *Sambhogakaya*, the archetypal dimension. This experience is marked by all sorts of psychic and subtle visions, visions of gods and goddesses, *dakas* and *dakinis*, all accompanied by dazzling and almost painfully brilliant lights and illuminations and colors. But again, most people are not used to this state and have no idea about transcendental light and divine illumination, so they actually flee these phenomena and are attracted by the lesser or impure lights that also appear.

Thus, the soul again contracts inwardly, tries to get away from these divine visions, blacks out again, and wakes up in what is called the *sidpa bardo*, the gross-reflecting realm. Here the soul eventually has a vision of its future parents making love, and—in good old-fashioned Freudian style—if it is going to be a boy it feels desire for the mother and hatred for the father, and if it is going to be a girl, it feels hatred for the mother and attraction to the father. (So far as I can tell, this is the first detailed explanation of the Oedipal/Electra complex—about a thousand years ahead of Freud, as Jung himself pointed out.)

At this stage, it is said, the soul—because of its jealousy and envy—"steps in" in its imagination to separate the father and mother, to come between them; but the result is simply that it really does come between them—that is, it ends up being reborn to them. It now has desire, aversion, attachment, hatred, and a gross body: In other words, it is a human being. It is at the lowest stage of the Great Chain, and its own growth and development will be a climb back up the stages that it has just denied and fled from; its evolution is, so to speak, a reversal of the "fall." How far it gets back up the Great Chain of Being will determine how it handles the dying process and the bardo states when it is again time to shed its physical body.

Interpretation of the Subjective Death and Rebirth Experiences

The contemplative evidence strongly suggests that the data, the actual experiences that accompany the dying process—for example, the "white appearance," the "red increase," the "black near-attainment," or whatever terms we want to use—exist and are very real. Further evidence of their reality is found in the fact that they have actual ontological referents in the higher dimensions of the Great Chain of Being. The three experiences just mentioned, for instance, refer respectively to what I have called the psychic, the subtle, and the causal structures or levels of consciousness. Indeed, they refer very precisely to those levels, despite the various different and legitimate explanations that might also be given for them. In my opinion, then, the levels are real, they have actual and definite ontological status, and thus the experiences of those levels are themselves real. But this does not mean that individuals' experiences of these levels cannot be quite different.

For example, a Buddhist would probably experience the "white appearance" as a type of emptiness or *shunyata* experience, whereas a Christian mystic might see it in the form of a saintly presence, possibly Christ himself, or a great being of light. But this is as it should be. For, until the "lifetime indestructible drop"—the accumulated impressions and beliefs gathered throughout this lifetime—actually dissolves (at what we have called stage seven), it will color and mold all of one's experiences. A Buddhist will therefore have a Buddhist experience, a Christian will have a Christian experience, a Hindu will have a Hindu experience, and an atheist will probably be extremely confused. All this is what we should expect. It is only at stage eight, at the clear light void, or pure Godhead, that one's personal interpretations and subtle beliefs are shed and a direct realization of pure reality itself, as clear light, is given. Hence, the Tibetan explanation of the data is not the only account possible. It is, however, one among several very important reflections or perspectives on the process of dying, death, and rebirth, rooted in a profound grasp of the Great Chain of Being, both going "up" (meditation and death) and going "down" (bardo and rebirth).

Near-Death Experience and the Stages of the Dying Process

The most common phenomenon in Western reports of the near-death experience (NDE) is the experience of passing through a tunnel and then seeing a brilliant light, or meeting a great being of light—a being that has incredible wisdom and intelligence and bliss. The particular individual's religious belief does not matter here; atheists have this experience as often as true believers. This fact, in itself, tends to corroborate the idea that, in the dying process, one does contact some of the subtler dimensions of existence.

From the standpoint of the Tibetan model we have been discussing, the "light" reported in NDEs, depending on its intensity or its clarity, could be the level of the butter lamp, the white appearance, or the red increase. The point is that, at this point in the death process, the gross mind and body, or the gross winds and energies, have dissolved, and thus the subtler dimensions of mind and energy begin to emerge, which are characterized by brilliant illumination and mental clarity and wisdom. So it is not surprising that people universally, regardless of belief, report the experience of light at this point. Many people who report NDEs believe that the light they have seen is absolute spirit. If the Tibetan model is accurate, however, then what people see during the NDE is not exactly the highest level. Beyond white appearance or red increase is black near-attainment, then clear light, then the bardo states.

The experience of the subtle-level light is very pleasant—in fact, amazingly blissful. And the next level, the very subtle or causal, is even more so. Indeed, people who have had NDEs report that they have never experienced anything as peaceful, as profound, as blissful. But we need to keep in mind that all of the experiences up to this point are molded by the "lifetime indestructible drop"; hence, as we have already noted, Christians might see Christ, Buddhists see Buddha, and so on. All this makes sense, because the experiences of these realms are conditioned by one's present life experiences. But then, at stage eight, the "lifetime indestructible drop" is shed, along with all the personal memories and impressions and specifics of this particular life, and the "eternally indestructible drop" moves out of the body and into the bardo state. And thereupon commences the bardo ordeal—a real nightmare unless one is very familiar with these states through meditation.

The dying experience and the NDE are actually a lot of fun, in a sense: It is universally reported that, after one gets over the terror of dying, the process is blissful, peaceful, extraordinary. But when the "ascent" is completed, the "descent," or bardo, begins—and there's the rub. Because at that point, all of one's karmic propensities, all of one's attachments, desires, and fears, actually appear right before one's eyes, so to speak, just as in a dream, because the bardo is a purely mental or subtle dimension, like a dream, where everything one thinks immediately appears as a reality.

Thus, one does not hear about this "downside" to the death process from the NDE people. They are just tasting the early stages of the overall process. Nevertheless, their testimony is powerful evidence that this process does in fact occur. It all fits with a remarkable and unmistakable precision. Moreover, it is not possible to explain away their testimony by claiming that all of them have studied Tibetan Buddhism; in fact, most of them have not even heard of it. But they have essentially similar experiences as the Tibetans because these experiences reflect the universal and cross-cultural reality of the Great Chain of Being. It now appears that there is simply no other way to read the really extensive data gathered on this subject.

Meditation as Rehearsal for Death

Where does meditation fit into all of this? Every form of meditation is basically a way to transcend the ego, or die to the ego. In that sense, it mimics death—that is, death of the ego. If one progresses fairly well in *any* meditation system, one eventually comes to a point of having so exhaustively "witnessed" the mind and body that one actually rises above, or transcends, the mind and body, thus "dying" to them, to the ego, and awakening as subtle soul or even spirit. And this is actually experienced as a death. In Zen it is called the Great Death. It can be a fairly easy experience, a relatively peaceful transcendence of subject-object dualism, or—because it is a real death of sorts—it can also be terrifying. But subtly or dramatically, quickly or slowly, the sense of being a separate self dies, or is dissolved, and one finds a prior and higher identity in and as universal spirit.

But meditation can also be a rehearsal of actual death. According to Zen teachings, if you die before you die, then when you die you won't die. Some meditation systems, particularly the Sikh (the Radhasoami saints) and the Tantric (Hindu and Buddhist), contain very precise meditations that mimic or induce the various stages of the dying process very closely—including stopping the breath, the body becoming cold, the heart slowing and sometimes stopping, and so forth. Actual physical death is then not much of a surprise, and one can then much more easily use the intermediate states of consciousness that appear after death—the bardos—to gain enlightened understanding. The point of such meditations is to be able to recognize spirit, so that when the body, mind, and soul dissolve during the actual dying process, one will recognize spirit, or *Dharmakaya*, and abide as that, rather than flee from it and end up back in samsara again, back in the illusion of a separate soul, mind, and body; or, to be able, if one does choose to reenter a body, to do so deliberately—that is, as a bodhisattva.

These death-mimicking meditations are not actually life threatening; the body is not really dying, or going through the concrete death stages themselves. Rather, it is like holding one's breath to see what it is like: One does not stop breathing forever. But some of the states that can be induced by these meditations are really powerful imitations of the real thing. One's heartbeat, for example, can actually stop for an extended period, as can the breath. This, for example, is how it is possible to tell that the "winds" have entered and are remaining in the central channel. One is "imitating" death, but doing so by actually—if temporarily—dissolving the same winds that are dissolved in death. Thus it is a very concrete and very real imitation.

How exactly do the various winds, or energies, described in Tantra relate to meditation? The central idea of all Tantra, whether Hindu, Buddhist, Gnostic, or Sikh, is that every mental state, or every state of consciousness—in other words, every level in the Great Chain of Being—also has a specific supporting energy, or *prana*, or wind. (We have already examined the Tibetan version of this doctrine.) Thus, if one dissolves that particular wind, one will dissolve the mind that is supported by it. Hence, if one can gain control over these winds or energies, one can transcend the minds that "ride" them. This is the general notion of *pranayama*, "breath" or "wind" control. But also, since mind rides wind, wherever one puts the mind, its winds tend to gather. So, for example, if a meditator concentrates very intensely on the crown chakra, then wind, or energy, will tend to gather there and then dissolve there.

This means that mind, at whatever level, has a measure of control over the winds associated with it. Hence, by mental training and concentration, one can learn to gather winds or energies at particular places, then dissolve them there. And that dissolution is exactly the same type of process that occurs at death. So one is actually experiencing, in a very concrete way, what happens when all the various winds dissolve at death—beginning with the gross winds, then continuing as the subtle winds dissolve, leaving the very subtle or causal wind and the mind of clear light that rides it. By inducing these experiences of the dying process by one's own free will, then, when actual death comes, one knows exactly what the dissolution of the winds is going to produce.

This type of practice also gives one the ability to prolong each state, particularly the subtler states, such as those of white appearance, red increase, black near-attainment, and clear light, because one has already more or less mastered them. Then, at the actual final point of death, at what we have been calling the eighth stage—as one enters the *chikhai bardo*, the *Dharmakaya*—one can remain there if one chooses. That clear-light state is very clear and obvious and easy to recognize, because one has seen it many times in meditation and in the mind of one's guru; hence, one cleaves to that and is thus released from the necessity of rebirth. One might, however, still choose to be reborn in a physical body in order to help others reach this understanding and freedom.

A common technique for gathering and dissolving winds at a particular spot in the body is to concentrate on the "red drop" at the navel center (the source of what is called the *tummo* fire). One simply concentrates on that object—visualized as a fiery red drop, the size of a small pea—until one can remain concentrated, with unbroken attention, for thirty or forty minutes or so. At that point, the energies of the body will be so concentrated in that area that breathing will subside and become very soft, almost imperceptible. All of the winds or energies of the body are being withdrawn from their ordinary work and concentrated there. Hence, it is very similar to these winds dissolving, or being withdrawn, as occurs in actual death. So if one continues to meditatively concentrate, one will begin to experience all the signs of the dying process, in order, including the miragelike appearance, the smoke appearance, the fireflies appearance, and the butter-lamp appearance.

At this point, as the winds or energies of the body begin to gather and dissolve at the heart, as in actual death, one will experience the levels of the subtle mind, the mind of white appearance, then red increase, then black near-attainment. Then, through the power of one's meditation and spiritual blessings, all winds or energies will finally dissolve in the indestructible drop at the heart, and one will experience the clear-light void, the ultimate spiritual dimension and realization. In short, this type of meditation is a perfect mimicking of the dying process. And again, the whole point is that by familiarizing oneself with the clear light, by developing meditative wisdom and virtue, then upon actual death, one can remain as the clear light and thus recognize final liberation.

What Survives? The Teachings of Tibetan Buddhism

Sogyal Rinpoche is an incarnate lama, scholar, and meditation master. He has participated in a number of major conferences on healing, psychology, and care of the dying, and has founded Rigpa meditation centers worldwide.

Each one of us, deep down, cherishes a desire to live and to continue living, which in itself perhaps indicates that we all have some basic intuition of a continuation of life after death. If life, or consciousness, failed to survive death, there would be neither any meaning to life nor any ultimate justice. Nevertheless, many people believe that life does not continue after death. Yet, as we often discover in life, what we believe may have little or nothing to do with reality.

Sometimes people argue that since they do not remember their past lives, they could not have had any. Their lack of memory, however, does not necessarily prove that they have not lived before. For example, earlier in this very life you may have undergone an experience of tremendous suffering. In the midst of its intensity, all the details will have seemed very close and real; but now that it has been over for so long, not only do you hardly remember it, but it even feels like it happened to someone else. Yet you are that very same person. In the same way, whether you have any memory of it or not, consciousness goes through various transitions and lapses of memory. Although you lose your identity when you die, you are still the same person. Losing your passport does not mean that you cease to exist!

If there is survival after death, the question that really needs to be answered is, What survives? Or, What kind of consciousness survives? The most important issue here—that of understanding the nature of mind or consciousness—has not been investigated scientifically in the West. Most investigators have limited themselves to looking at the projections of mind, rather than at the mind that projects. Yet the one who suffers and the one who enjoys happiness are both the mind. The one who dies is the mind and the one who survives is the mind. This is why the whole Buddhist teaching, particularly on death and dying, centers around understanding the true nature of our mind.

The Tibetan Book of the Dead is now quite familiar in the West, but without understanding the background of its teachings, it can be more than a little confusing. It forms only one part of a complete cycle of teachings given by the remarkable teacher Padmasambhava, who is regarded by Tibetans as a "second Buddha" who brought Buddhism to Tibet and the Himalayan region. These particular teachings demonstrate how, by realizing the nature of consciousness, the confused mind can be "liberated into the original nature of the Buddha mind."

The actual title of the so-called Tibetan Book of the Dead (a title coined by the late W. Y. Evans-Wentz for the first English translation) is *The Great Liberation through Hearing in the Bardo*. The Tibetan word *bardo* simply means the transition, or gap, between two realities. Padmasambhava expressed the whole spectrum of life and death within the context of six of these bardos, three of life and three of death. Each bardo has a set of teachings and meditation practices related to it. In these gaps, the possibility of the nature of mind being revealed is particularly present.

Actually, bardo experiences are happening to us all the time. The objective of the teachings of Tibetan Buddhism is to show us how to make use of these opportunities for awakening that are presented continually in both life and death.

The three Bardos of Life outlined by Padmasambhava are:

1. ordinary consciousness from the moment we are born until we die—this lifetime;
2. the sleep and dream state; and
3. the meditative state, or higher state of consciousness.

The three Bardos of Death are:

1. the moment of death, which is the time between the onset of the process of dying and its culmination in death;
2. *dharmata*—the "essence of things as they are," when the nature of consciousness manifests itself in the form of visions; and
3. becoming, from the time when the consciousness leaves the body until the next birth.

The message continually spelled out in the Tibetan Book of the Dead is the need to prepare for death now, in this life. Buddhist training places special emphasis on two factors—the realization of the nature of mind on an absolute level, and the need to observe and value the working of karma on a relative level.

From the Buddhist perspective, mind has two aspects: the "ordinary mind," known in Tibetan as *sem,* and the "fundamental consciousness," or clarity of mind, known as *rigpa.* The ordinary mind, *sem,* includes our sense of self, which we would like to continue. Because we want ourselves to continue, we mistakenly wish the ordinary mind to endure, because it is the only indication we have of our existence. In reality, however, there is another aspect of ourselves that we have not realized. This aspect is beyond the ordinary mind. It is our real nature, and it survives beyond the death of the body and ordinary mind. The whole point of Buddhist teaching, meditation, and practice is to realize our true nature, which is beyond birth and death. Those who master these teachings and practices and can recognize the nature of this mind are prepared when transition occurs. Then, at death, they can let go of this life more confidently, in the realization that they are not really losing anything at all, but only gaining.

In all religions, one finds the idea that every person has an inherent quality of essential goodness. Buddhists call this essential goodness "Buddha nature" and maintain that the whole process of our evolution is aimed at uncovering, or freeing, that basic goodness. Whenever we perform a positive action, it moves us toward that goal; whereas our negative actions further inhibit or obscure it. Thus, the reason we suffer in this life is that we are not true to our essential nature. Yet, at the same time, suffering is a teaching, which points to this fact. Sometimes it seems that the very reason for our suffering in this life is to free our essential goodness. Otherwise, we can see no purpose for evolution. That is, if there were no purpose for our suffering, we would be forced to regard life as meaningless or as some kind of joke.

At the heart of understanding reincarnation is the principle of karma. Karma and reincarnation are not simply theories of pre-destination. Actually, the future is in our own hands and in our own actions. As Buddha himself said, "If you want to know your past life, look into your present condition. If you want to know your future life, look into your present actions." In other words, the way in which we conduct this present life is the key to the future. The word *karma* in fact means "action." Our every action is powerful and already pregnant with its consequences. We fail to see the natural evolution of karma, however, because the results do not mature immediately. Instead, whenever happiness or difficulties crop up, we simply call them "good luck" or "bad luck."

In the East, home of the greater part of the world's population, karma and reincarnation are regarded as realities. Yet Eastern spiritual traditions do not teach that our salvation lies in reincarnation alone. Much more to the point is how a person uses his or her understanding of karma and reincarnation as a basis for leading a positive life. A good Buddhist actually *lives* karma rather than simply *believing* in it.

In Buddhism, we explain the confusion of the mind by reference to what are called in Tibetan *digpa* and *dribpa*. Both digpa and dribpa are rooted in the unawareness caused by our stubbornness and ignorance. *Digpa* means "negative actions" or "neurotic crimes" and is the closest Buddhist equivalent to the Western concept of sin. *Dribpa*, obscuration or defilement, is created when we perform a negative action, just as a cloud of smoke is given off by a fire. These obscurations of the mind then create further unawareness and mindlessness. By becoming more unaware, we also become more prone to negative actions, with the result that, mindlessly and unconsciously, we again create negative karma or *digpa*, which in turn produces more obscurations, and so on, thus generating a vicious cycle, samsara. In short, karma affects our minds, which in turn affects our actions and our life.

As the great Tibetan master Longchenpa said, the only way to end this cycle is to cut it. Right where you cut it is the beginning and the end. If only we were to recognize the true nature of mind in this very moment, we could end confusion here and now. In this moment we can do it, beginning with ourselves and with our own mind.

The first step in cutting through the cycle of samsara is to become more mindful and peaceful. When you are mindful, obscuration will effectively be less. Mindfully you try to avoid negative actions, and at the same time you develop mindfulness by disciplining the mind in meditation—for example, by practices like simply watching the breath, and developing concentration through focusing on one simple action. Once developed, mindfulness itself clarifies one's awareness and banishes obscuration.

Another important element in the Buddhist training and preparation for death is working toward an emotional acceptance of death through contemplation and meditation, as well as learning how to make use of the crises, upheavals, and changes of life. The changes, or "small deaths," that occur so frequently in our lives are a living link with real death, prompting us to let go. They reveal the possibility of seeing, in the gap they open up, the skylike, empty, open space of the true nature of our mind. Thus, in the transition and uncertainty of change lies the opportunity for awakening.

In the Tibetan tradition, the complete training in meditation and purification culminates when the student is introduced directly to the nature of mind by the teacher. This direct knowing is then integrated and stabilized through practice, thus giving rise to confidence and skill in liberating all thoughts and emotions. When we have mastered these teachings, we are able at death to remain in the recognition of our true nature. Our ultimate aim is, over the course of many lives, to discover our fundamental mind. It is revealed slowly; when it is completely realized, that is enlightenment.

So, more important for an individual than a scientific proof of survival after death is the question of what survival really means to an individual. From deep understanding, a personal conviction is born, and to all intents and purposes that conviction is a scientific discovery. If we actually realize the continuity and meaning of life, as well as the effects of our actions, then leading a good life will have a point. When we really pay attention to our own actions, the future is in our hands. Hence, the very best way to help yourself prepare for the time of death is to begin with attention to what you do now.

The main emphasis of practice in the Buddhist tradition is to let go of the attachments, conditioning, and habits that make up the cloudy level of mind. Buddhism teaches that when we die, whatever memories we have gathered in this life die utterly, and that when we are reborn, we develop a fresh memory. But, at a deeper level than conscious memory, karma is registered as a person's basic character or disposition, affecting his or her whole being.

Regardless of whether we remember our past lives or not, our true nature exists and survives. The moment of death is the moment in which we can break through the shell of the ordinary mind and gain liberation. If we fail, it is because we do not let go: We hold on to our habits, which then become the nucleus of our new life. Our future birth is dictated by our old ways. We may not be able to surrender completely; there may be some karmic residues; yet however much we are able to surrender, to that extent our karma becomes free or purified, thereby determining a better rebirth.

We mentioned earlier the three Bardos of Life: ordinary consciousness from birth until death, sleep and dreams, and the meditative state. All three, if used well, are opportunities for realizing the nature of mind. Through becoming more sensitive to the gaps or transitions that occur in these three states, we are more prepared for the gap that occurs in a more powerful way at death.

Through meditation we arrive at a clearer understanding of mind and familiarize ourselves with its true nature. The dream state can also help us to understand better the awakened state and develop a more detached and humorous attitude to life. A spiritual practitioner can work with sleep, because maintaining awareness during sleep is a way of rehearsing for death. Likewise, the dream state is analogous to the bardo state after death. Sleep and the dream state can also be used by a meditator to reflect whether his or her practice is working.

During the day we experience different levels of consciousness: Our waking state is the grossest, the dream state less so, and deep sleep the most subtle. Similarly in life and death, our ordinary life represents the grossest level of consciousness, the intermediate state between death and rebirth is subtler, and death itself is the most subtle.

Mind has many levels. Tibetan Buddhism teaches that at the moment of death, the important thing is whether you can hang on to the aspect of mind that survives and let go of the one that dies—like backing the right horse. What dies at death is the grasping that dilutes the pure energy of our mind and clouds its natural space. When that grasping habit dies at the moment of death, then, if we let go, the possibility of awakening presents itself most prominently, just as when clouds evaporate and reveal the clear sky. To the Buddhist, eternity is the space where even discontinuity is part of a fundamental continuity.

At death, when all the gross aspects of our body die, our ego, memory, and many outer levels of consciousness peel off and die as well. We then die into our essence, our true nature, and from there we are born again. Knowing the nature of mind affords us the courage at death to let go of all the smaller aspects of ourselves.

Although the fundamental mind, or *rigpa*, is always present, usually it is hidden behind the cloudlike screen of our thinking mind. Occasionally, though, inspired by meditation or certain situations, we are awakened to a deep knowledge of the fundamental essence of mind. At the moment of death, when the ordinary mind dies completely, we experience complete enlightenment. That is the birth of *rigpa* in its fullness. Though this experience happens to all of us when we die, the point is *how* we die, depending on whether we have practiced or not. If we are spiritual practitioners, the moment of death is the crowning spiritual moment: Because we have been practicing, when we experience the essence of the mind, it is familiar and we can unite with it, thereby attaining enlightenment.

The Tibetan Book of the Dead describes many opportunities for liberation in the three Bardos of Death. It is designed to be read to a dying person who has practiced in and is acquainted with this tradition so as to awaken his or her recognition and introduce the nature of mind at each juncture.

According to this teaching, entering the Bardo of the Moment of Death, when the signs indicate that death is inevitable, a person should gather together all his or her strength and, instead of worrying or thinking too much, focus on the essence of spiritual practice. The individual's state of mind is of paramount importance at the moment of death, and it is essential that he or she is not distraught or disturbed. Hence, a peaceful and loving atmosphere, an opportunity to make this last period of life really meaningful, a chance for forgiveness and clearing up unfinished business, and, above all, abandoning attachment all contribute toward a person's ability to surrender at the moment of death.

To help a dying person is to help that person toward understanding the nature of mind. When practitioners approach death, their practice makes them self-sufficient, although obviously they can benefit from loving support. But when we come to help those who have no spiritual experience in their life to support them, we find that it is our love itself, and our spiritual confidence and strength, that can draw out the confidence in them and bring out their spiritual essence. Love can help people come to terms with dying. The more they accept, the more they can understand.

It is also very important for people who are dying to maintain their awareness at the moment of death. If they fail to do so, their consciousness will be interrupted and they will have no memory, because they will have moved on to a different dimension of being, a domain where their previous consciousness has no way of recalling its past or feeling familiar. This is why most of us are afraid of what will happen after death: Since we have not worked with mind, we have no idea of what we will experience.

The process of dying itself begins with the "stages of dissolution." This dissolution is actually the reverse process of the conception and formation of a new child. According to Tibetan Buddhist teachings, at the moment of conception, when the sperm and ovum unite, the consciousness of the would-be child is sucked in, and the elements within the father's and mother's essence provide the basic constituents for the body. The father's essence subsequently rises to the level of the head, whereas the mother's descends to reside below the navel, at the level of the womb.

The process of death, then, begins with the dissolution of the bodily elements into one another, along with the simultaneous dissolution of the psychological components, or "aggregates," of ego: form, feeling, perception, intellect, and consciousness. The stages of this dissolution are each marked by identifiable external, physical signs as well as inner experiences. Thus, the earth element dissolves into water, water into fire, and fire into air. When air dissolves, the person breathes out and can hardly breathe in. Finally, even the out-breath ceases. At that time, the "inner air," or life force, dissolves into the "central channel," whereupon the father's essence descends, producing a vision of whiteness likened to looking through a window and seeing the autumn moon, and the mother's essence rises, producing a vision like a red sunset. As these essences meet at the heart and fuse, the consciousness faints into a dark, empty space. The mind, however, dies only for a moment, and when the person awakens, he or she experiences the sheer luminosity of the nature of mind, the subtlest level of consciousness, which is compared to an immaculate dawn sky in autumn.

The crucial issue from the Tibetan perspective is how well we are prepared for the moment of death, and consequently, how we react to these experiences. A person whose energies are very closed because of karma or who has not done much spiritual practice can remain in the state of darkness after fainting for quite a while. Then the luminosity, the experience of the enlightened mind, appears for only a second or two. For a practitioner, in contrast, the consciousness faints for only a short period, after which it awakens to the vision of the enlightened mind.

As the nature of mind and its energy of tremendous luminosity dawns, extremely adept practitioners can simply recognize it as the nature of their mind. Connecting it to their own awakened state, they maintain full awareness and merge with it, thereby attaining liberation. For others, the point when the outer breath is ceasing but the inner breath is continuing is the time when someone who is assisting the dying person should begin reading from the Tibetan Book of the Dead. Or, if the person has been trained in the meditation practice of *phowa*, a method of direct transference of consciousness into the enlightened state, he or she should be assisted in effecting this practice.

At the moment of death, all the conditioning—everything that has clouded the enlightened mind—has fallen apart and the consciousness enters the Bardo of Dharmata, where the "as-it-isness," or true nature of reality, presents itself nakedly. When one fails to recognize this first vision of luminosity, it dissolves and disappears. Then, as the mind begins to free itself of its projections and blockages, pure energy is released and explodes as visions of color, sound, and light, depicted in the tradition of the Tibetan Book of the Dead as the forty-two peaceful and fifty-eight wrathful deities.

This energy has the quality of the subtle elements: earth, water, fire, air, and space. The consciousness experiences all the various aspects of the mind—anger, desire, ignorance, and so on—which are the blocked energies of our inherent nature. As these are unleashed and opened up, they emerge in their own "wisdom form," with tremendous light and brilliance. All depends on whether we can recognize these visions as projections of our own mind, as nothing but our inherent wisdom. If we can take refuge in the brilliant light of wisdom that dawns when these energies are freed, we have another opportunity for liberation.

This is difficult, however, for a person who does not have the experience of practice and the trust and stability that come from understanding the nature of mind. We are prone to take refuge in our old habits, rather than simply let go; we are more inclined toward anger, for instance, than to its pure and liberated counterpart. This is because our basic tendency toward grasping, which is built up during life, gives rise to a range of instincts such as aggression, greed, stubborn stupidity, passion, jealousy, arrogance, and self-intoxication. These energies manifest themselves as a soft, cozy light that is less challenging and overwhelming than the light of wisdom. If our reaction is instinctive, we accordingly progress to a rebirth determined by the confused and diluted energy with which we identify.

For most Westerners, the forms of the visions detailed in the Tibetan Book of the Dead may seem quite strange and unfamiliar. Everybody, being composed of the same psychological components and elements, will experience visions of one form or another. Western people, however, will probably experience them in forms that are more familiar to them, according to their cultural conditioning. The important point about these visions is not what particular form they may take, but how a person *relates* to them. Their form merely provides a reference point for the practitioner, who is able to attune himself or herself to the energy, luminosity, and quality of the vision.

If a person fails to gain liberation by recognizing these phenomena as his or her own projections, the visions dissolve. It is at this point that consciousness leaves the body and continues its journey into the Bardo of Becoming. It now possesses a "mental body" that has a number of characteristics: It is very light and lucid, the consciousness is nine times clearer than in earthly life, and it possesses clairvoyance and other miraculous powers. This body is similar to the body of the previous existence, but perfectly complete and in the prime of life. It can move unobstructed almost anywhere and can travel just by thinking, although its only light is a dim glow that illuminates the space immediately in front of it.

The consciousness of the deceased undergoes various experiences in the Bardo of Becoming—for example, repeating all the experiences it had in life; returning to places where it even spat just once; suffering all kinds of terrors; and having precognitive visions of where it is to be reborn. At first, not realizing that it is dead, the consciousness of the deceased tries to converse with its family, only to be tremendously distressed when it receives no response. Finally, however, when it sees its relatives weeping, disposing of its possessions, and not laying its place at the table, it realizes that it is dead. Moreover, it finds that it can see and converse with the many other travelers it meets in the bardo world.

Many of the qualities of the mental body—heightened clarity of consciousness, mobility, paranormal perception, increased susceptibility to subtle influences, ability to concentrate and meditate when instructed, and keenness of attention due to the intensity of fear in the bardo—in fact render it more accessible to help from the living. This help may take the form of spiritual practices, of charity dedicated in the name of the deceased, or even of good thoughts directed toward the person who has died. Such assistance is said to be especially effective during the first twenty-one days after death. The whole bardo experience associated with death is said to have an average duration of forty-nine "days," of which the first twenty-one are more involved with the life just lived, and the remainder more involved with the life to come.

Because consciousness is so extremely light and mobile in the bardo experience, whatever thoughts arise, whether good or bad, are very powerful. Hence, a negative reaction—for example, anger on observing rituals being carelessly performed on its behalf or greedy relatives squabbling over its possessions—can be very potent and dangerous. The Tibetan Book of the Dead therefore urges the consciousness of the deceased to guard against impure thoughts such as feelings of aggression, fear, and attachment to former possessions. At the same time, the text seeks to awaken the dead person's connection with any spiritual experience that he or she might have had, and once again gives instructions on using this opportunity to recognize the nature of mind and be liberated. "Do not be distracted," the text advises. "This is the dividing line where Buddhas and sentient beings are separated. It is said of this moment:

> In an instant, they are separated,
> In an instant, complete enlightenment."

The text then gives instructions on how to recognize signs of the next rebirth (and thereby avoid an unfavorable one), as well as how to select a birth in the human world where one may once again encounter the teaching.

Here we have taken a brief glance at the Buddhist view of what survives beyond biological death, tracing the passage of consciousness through life and death. What emerges from this discussion is the emphasis placed in Tibetan Buddhist teachings on understanding the nature of consciousness, or mind—an understanding regarded as the ultimate goal of life and as essential preparation for dying free of regret at the moment of death. The whole point of the Buddhist teachings is, in a sense, summed up by the great Tibetan yogi Milarepa: "not to be ashamed of myself when I die." An ordinary person who had the Tibetan Buddhist perspective of the continuity of consciousness throughout a series of lives would certainly never despair in life, nor be reduced to the point of suicide.

How consciousness will survive after death depends on its immediate condition, what state it is in at this very moment. To take care of the future, we need to attend to the present, to the consciousness we have now. We are usually overly concerned about the consciousness that will survive; but, as we have seen, the mind we have now is the whole basis for our evolution and our preparation for death. Our response to the question, What survives? should therefore be to cultivate a deeper awareness and understanding of ourselves in this life. An understanding of the fundamental consciousness that we all share, even now, can inspire in us a more caring attitude and a more positive, responsible approach to life, furthering a more enlightened outlook in the world and encouraging that peace and harmony for which we all yearn.

KENNETH RING

Shamanic Initiation, Imaginal Worlds, and Light after Death

Kenneth Ring, Ph.D., is professor of psychology at the University of Connecticut. He is the author of Life at Death *and* Heading toward Omega *and is the founder and first president of the International Association for Near-Death Studies.*

> The belief, the knowledge, and even the experience that our physical world of the senses is a mere illusion, a world of shadows, and that the three-dimensional tool we call our body serves only as a container or dwelling place for Something infinitely greater and more comprehensive than the body and which constitutes the matrix of real life—this surely is the most powerful idea man has ever conceived.
>
> *Holger Kalweit*

Anyone who becomes familiar with the phenomenon of near-death experiences (NDEs) must inevitably think about life after death. No matter that we NDE researchers have been virtually unanimous in insisting that these experiences do not and cannot prove the existence of an afterlife. Despite our careful disclaimers, to say nothing of the cold water of skeptics' outright denials, the implied promise of the NDE continues to exert a pervasive and powerful appeal. Indeed, everyone, critics included, understands that the reason many moderns have become fascinated with NDEs is not simply that they suggest that the moment of death is one of stupendous splendor and joy beyond reckoning. No—it is rather the unmistakable implication that this kind of experience *continues*, that there really is a life after death and that, furthermore, it will be wonderful.

Surely, underneath it all, this is why the NDE, as soon as it was publicized through the work of Elisabeth Kübler-Ross and Raymond Moody, stirred the public imagination through the Western world and why the NDE persists as a topic of widespread interest today. Clearly, reports of NDEs paint an enormously attractive picture of the entrance hall into the house of death, making people hopeful that they, too, will dwell in its luminous and loving interior for all time, surrounded by those whom they cherish and revere. Regardless of how justifiable such hopes may seem, no one can deny that they are what sells books and tabloids that feature guests describing their encounters with death.

Of course, we in the West have traditionally nurtured such hopes—or at least we long did so until the ascent of science and the corresponding decline of religious sensibility made them appear to be unfashionable and insupportable anachronisms. Obviously, the idea of life after death no longer fits with our postmodern, secular view of things. And yet, ironically enough, we now find that right out of the womb of medical science itself, with its power to restore seemingly lost lives, these hopes have been born anew with the emergence of the NDE as a subject of serious scientific research. No wonder people are simultaneously disturbed and enthralled by this phenomenon, which is reviving thoughts about life after death that most of us had assumed were *themselves* dead for keeps.

Thus, the NDE is not only an experience of riveting fascination; it is also potentially an extremely *subversive* one, threatening to undermine our hard-won secular and scientific worldview. Hence, the urgency in some quarters either to explain away or lampoon this phenomenon: Either way, we won't have to take it seriously and we can go back to our more or less materialistic view of life. Of course, in other quarters there is exactly the *opposite* tendency—that is, to embrace the NDE and accept its implications for life after death quite literally.

My own approach to this matter, however, is to advocate a third response. Suppose for the moment that we take neither the side of the skeptic nor that of the partisan. Instead, let us examine the NDE in a context that doesn't require us to either accept *or* reject it, but only to try to see it clearly for what it is. To do so, we need to view the NDE in a light that will for the time being strip from it all connotations of life after death. In this pursuit, we will be well guided, I think, by following the shaman's torch.

A Shamanic Approach to the NDE

In traditional tribal societies, the shaman is what we might call "a doctor of the soul." He or she typically comes to this calling either because of some unusual personal characteristics or by virtue of having survived an ordeal of some kind. So, for example, many shamans as youths are marked by psychic sensitivities or by a history of epilepsy. They tend from the start to be odd, eccentric, or different from others in some way. Or, not infrequently, they have survived a life-threatening illness that has profoundly transformed them. The Lakota medicine man Black Elk is a famous instance of someone who took this route to a shamanic career.[1]

In any event, through either inadvertent personal experience or deliberate shamanic training, shamans normally go through an initiation that ritually confirms them in their societal role. Ordinarily, such an initiation begins by separating the apprentice shaman from his community so that he can be put into the hands of his shamanic teachers. The initiate is then required to undergo various ordeals, both physical and psychological, as the training progresses. Often, as is well known, these rites involved powerful motifs of dismemberment and reconstitution as the candidate endures the ultimate trial of death and rebirth—a necessary component for all true initiations, as well as the experiential foundation for a new sense of identity as a shaman. And from the candidate's point of view, his continued *physical* existence is by no means assured, as the following passage makes clear:

> The shaman's is an ego death that may miss real death by no more than a hair's breadth. We are not referring here to a mytho-poetic imagination of death in the form of allegories and archetypes. The death experience of the shaman is a dangerous walk on a tightrope between this world and the Beyond. It is not a hallucinatory pseudovision of death.[2]

Sacred mysteries are vouchsafed to the individual as he learns to enter into otherworldly realms and acquires his particular shamanic skills, power animals, sacred songs, secret languages, and so forth. After his initiation is complete, he returns, following a period of readjustment and assimilation, to his community. He is now prepared to become a healer, a psychopomp, a "master of ecstasy" (the phrase is Mircea Eliade's), a mystic, and a visionary. In brief, the shaman is a man (or woman) who now knows how to live in *two worlds:* the world of the soul and the world of the body. And though

indispensable to the welfare of his tribe, he often remains somewhat apart from it, precisely because of his special knowledge and
his sometimes disturbing presence.

To see how these initiatory strands are woven together into the
fabric of an actual shamanic ritual, consider the procedure followed
by the Arunta—an aboriginal people of Australia made familiar to
generations of anthropologists through the work of Baldwin Spencer and F. Gillen—around the turn of the century.[3]

> Among the Australian Arunta the person destined to become a medi-
> cine man seeks out a cave inhabited by the Iruntarinia, the spirits of the
> ancestors who lived in Alcheringa, the Dreamtime. He lies down at the
> mouth of the cave and sleeps until one of the spirits appears, piercing
> him with a spear through the back of the neck until the spear emerges
> at the mouth, perforating the tongue. The perforation of the tongue
> does not heal and is accepted as a physical sign of a medicine man. How
> the hole in the tongue comes about is unclear, but in any case it is big
> enough to put one's little finger through it. The spirit ancestor then
> pierces the head of the initiate with a second spear, sideways from ear
> to ear.
>
> The initiate is taken into the cave, where the Iruntarinia operate on
> his body, taking out the organs and replacing them with new ones. He
> awakens in a state of madness, but this disturbed state does not last
> very long. He is returned to his tribe by the ancestors and thereafter has
> the gift of seeing the spirits. . . .
>
> During the sacred Dreamtime, the material limitations and physical
> restrictions of ordinary people do not exist. The novice returns to his
> primordial state by contacting the spirits of the ancestors. He thus gets a
> taste of the sacred nature of being, of a timeless age, accessible to
> anyone who knows how to open himself to it. To be in the company of
> these ancestral spirits is an experience of such transcendental force that
> it could be said to be tantamount to death or self-annihilation.
>
> Upon his return to this world, the novice is mentally disturbed and
> has difficulty readjusting to his human environment. Catapulted out of
> sacred space, he gets the standards of earthly life all muddled up and
> only gradually succeeds in reassembling this nonsensical mosaic. He
> enters our world from the timeless world of the "eternal now" where
> the space/time continuum is [again] magically present. He is therefore
> unsure of himself and behaves in a socially and mentally abnormal
> manner. Yet this is the way a medicine man is born. The sacred Dream-
> time has turned a man into a healer.[4]

During his initiation—and of course many times thereafter—the
shaman goes on a journey in which he enters into a transcendental

world beyond time and space and returns to his physical world transformed and imbued with new knowledge. As students of shamanism and religion have already begun to observe,[5] such shamanic journeys often have substantial phenomenological overlap with NDEs. Indeed, I submit that no one acquainted with the literature of both shamanism and NDEs could fail to see that there are many connections between these two categories of experience.[6]

Hence, the implication is clear: By coming close to death, the NDEer has inadvertently and involuntarily been initiated into a shamanic journey. According to this view, then, NDEers are modern shamans, and the NDE itself may be understood to be a classic form of shamanic initiation.[7] In summary, the NDE *is*, in its form and dynamics, essentially a *shamanic experience*—whether the NDEer realizes it or not.

But having pointed out the commonalities between these two types of experiences, it is also crucial to note their differences. Whereas the effect of the NDE is to introduce the individual to the mysteries of death, the shaman, as a result of his training, has become, in Kalweit's words, "a *master* of death." That is, he is someone who, unlike the NDEer, can enter into—and leave—the world of death at will and can therefore provide us with something of a map of the postmortem terrain whose contours can be only briefly glimpsed by the NDEer. For this supreme accomplishment, shamans, everywhere their kind is recognized, are accorded the highest stature among men:

> As a Chosen One, as someone who, during his own lifetime, succeeds in penetrating the frontiers of transcendence, the shaman moves as a messenger between two worlds—the world of living humanity and the world of the dead or of nonmaterial existence. He is a hero who overcomes supernatural dangers and, as such, is celebrated in the tradition of the people, immortalized in their myths and epic poems. The shaman transcends the profane order of existence, leaves the world of the banal and travels to an etheric subtle sphere, *accessible to ordinary people only in death or as a result of serious illness, accident, shock, violent emotions, and in dreams.* This conscious and controlled penetration into such a closed realm must be counted among the greatest achievements of Man. This is the reason why shamans are respected and honored wherever they practice their art.[8]

Thus, it is the shaman, rather than the NDEer, whose torch illuminates most revealingly the realm beyond death. And therefore, to peer into it we must not only continue to follow in the light of this torch, but learn to see with a shaman's eye—with the true "vision not of this world."

Imaginal Vision

By taking this shamanic perspective, we can appreciate that the plane of experience NDEers enter into during their near-death crisis is the same one that shamans learn to access freely during the course of their training. Therefore, strictly speaking, this realm is not one that awaits us only after death. It exists now and is in principle available *in life* to anyone who has learned the "access code."

And here is the second important lesson we can derive from this shamanic perspective: how to enter this world at will. The key to such entrance is surprisingly simple to state in words, although certainly not always easy to effect in practice. It all turns out to hinge on the *imagination*—though what I mean by this term is *not* what is commonly understood by it. Accordingly, let us take a moment to look at this familiar idea, the imagination, more closely in order to see how it actually holds the key to the door of the so-called afterlife.

In the West, with the notable exception of certain champions of the imagination such as Coleridge, we have tended to use this term in a somewhat pejorative way to signify something "made up," or, in short, a *fantasy* of some kind. Certainly, there is usually the implication that the realm of the imagination is not truly real, as in the common phrase "That's just your imagination." In part, this view is a direct legacy of an outmoded Cartesian dualism that forces us to choose between the conceptual categories of mind and matter and has, with the rise of science, given ontological priority to the latter.

But perhaps there is, after all, a *third realm*—the realm of the imagination sui generis, not as something unreal, but as something *objectively self-existent*, the cumulative product of imaginative thought itself. Indeed, this is a point of view that has been advanced within the past fifteen years by many scholars representing such fields as religious studies, mythology, psychology, shamanic studies, ufology, and NDE research.[9] Much of this work has been predicated on a now-classic distinction between the *imaginary* and the *imaginal*, originally proposed by the great French Islamic scholar

Henri Corbin in 1972. This distinction is not only important; it is, I believe, absolutely fundamental to any formulation that seeks to shed light on the nature of the NDE and on what kind of a "life" we may expect after death. To follow Corbin's argument, we need to start with his concept of the imaginal.

First of all, in dealing with things of the imaginal realm, we are *not* talking about the stuff of fantasy, or even of imagination, as these terms are generally used today. Specifically, we are not concerned here with fictive matters or with what is "made up" through creative invention. Instead, the imaginal refers to a *third kingdom*, access to which is dependent neither on sensory perception nor on ordinary cognition (including fantasy). Normally hidden, it can be apprehended in what we would today call certain altered states of consciousness that destabilize ordinary perceptual modalities and cognitive systems. When these are sufficiently disturbed, the imaginal realm, like the night sky that can be discerned only when sunlight is absent, stands revealed.

The most important attribute of the imaginal realm, however, is that it is ontologically real. According to Corbin, who was a deep student of mystical and especially visionary experience,

> it must be understood that the world into which these [visionaries] probed is perfectly *real*. Its reality is more irrefutable and more coherent than that of the empirical world, where *reality* is perceived by the senses. Upon returning, the beholders of this world are perfectly aware of having been "elsewhere"; they are not mere schizophrenics. This world is hidden behind the very act of sense perception and has to be sought underneath its apparent objective certainty. For this reason we definitely cannot qualify it as being *imaginary* in the current sense of the word, i.e., as unreal, or nonexistent. . . . [The imaginal] world . . . is ontologically as real as the world of the senses and that of the intellect. . . . We must be careful not to confuse it with the imagination identified by so-called modern man with "fantasy."[10]

Not only is the imaginal realm ontologically real, it is also a world that has form, dimension, and, most important for us, *persons*. Corbin suggests this when he writes:

> [This is] a world possessing extension and dimension, figures and colors; but these features cannot be perceived by the senses in the same manner as if they were properties of physical bodies. No, these dimensions, figures, and colors are the object of imaginative perception, or of the "psychospiritual senses."[11]

In summary, imagination in Corbin's sense is actually, as Coleridge claimed, a creative power and should be understood as a kind of "organ of perception" in its own right—what the alchemists called *imaginatio vera* (true imagination). And the world that it discloses is, as Blake knew, a supersensible reality that can be directly apprehended.

We are beginning to see now with a shaman's eye, with *imaginal* vision. But before we can understand what it is we are seeing, we need to pause to consider and examine the next step—a pivotal one—in the logic of this imaginal journey.

Just what is seen when one views with the eye of the imagination? What Corbin suggests is that we see *our own inner spiritual state*, transformed and projected outward into a seemingly objective external vision. In other words, what we are looking at—as well as with—is our soul.

Indeed, soul and imagination are indissolubly bound to each other in this kind of formulation. Virtually all scholars who have come to view imagination in Corbinesque terms have found themselves back, as it were, with Heraclitus, having to give primacy to the soul and having to acknowledge, with Aristotle, that the natural language of the soul *is* the image. Robert Avens, for instance, concluded his brilliant essay on imagination with the assertion that soul *is* imagination and that it is, in the end, our absolute ontological bedrock: "Only soul (the imaginal realm) is not reducible to anything else and so constitutes our true, ontological reality."[12]

Corbin's argument leads us to the threshold of death itself, for he goes on to tell us that imagination is ultimately a purely spiritual faculty, independent of the physical body, and is accordingly

> able to exist after the latter has disappeared. . . . The soul is also independent as to its *imaginative capacity* and its *imaginative activity*. Moreover, when it is separated from this world it can continue to avail itself of active imagination. . . . After this separation all the soul's powers are assembled and concentrated in the sole faculty of active imagination.[13]

Light after Death

At death, then, we are *released* into the imagination, the creative expression of our soul no longer yoked to our physical body. And what we see—as though external to us—is the soul's own image.

What we see is light. Light, the soul's own effulgence, incomparably radiant, splendid, primordial, and unconditioned. This light is both symbol and apogee of the NDE, as we know, and it is the universally recognized expression of our divine core manifesting itself in spiritual experience. The light is one's pure soul essence, undefiled by human character, though the *way* in which the light presents itself (its hue, brightness, etc.) does seem to reflect the state of one's soul—the "real you inside," as NDEers tend to put it.

This primordial light is then refracted through the prism of the soul so that it yields a world of images—an imaginal world.[14]

> The environment of the life between life is a reflection of each person's thought forms and expectations. The Tibetan Book of the Dead asserts repeatedly that the *bardo* dweller produces his own surroundings from the contents of his mind. Rudolf Steiner maintained that thoughts and mental images of our inner realm appear to us after death as our external world. "After death," he said, "all our thoughts and mental representations appear as a mighty panorama before the soul."[15]

And here unfolds that familiar succession of hyperreal images that collectively defines "the otherworld journey," the first stages of which NDEers have described so often, consistently, and convincingly. These accounts, which at least in their broad outlines (and allowing for local variations from culture to culture) seem remarkably congruent, might naively be thought to represent some kind of uniformity of postmortem geography. But from an imaginal understanding, this apparent consistency has less to do with any actual topological uniformity of an after-death realm than with the universality of the human soul. Clearly, if there is any merit to this perspective, it is not that we "go to a place" after death; instead, we enter a state of consciousness where *images* are our reality and where that reality, which is not entirely fixed, is responsive to the thoughts, expectations, and desires of our souls.

To see this from another angle, let us return to our earlier context of shamanism, for it is the shaman, once again, who sees most penetratingly here. Compare, for example, this passage from our chief expositor of shamanic vision, Holger Kalweit, with what we have already heard from Corbin:

> The geography of the Beyond portrayed [here] should not be seen as a naive description of other landscapes . . . but as an attempt to make the Surviving consciousness aware of the fact that *it itself* constitutes the world of the Beyond. . . . *There is no realm of death as such.* Instead the

Beyond consists of all those properties particular to our consciousness once it is independent from the body.[16]

The shaman, whom modern research has shown to be a person extraordinarily gifted in his imaginative proclivities and whose training further strengthens those talents, is someone who has learned to see with the eyes of the soul. Thus, while fully alive, he has already entered into what most ordinary persons will encounter only when their mortality is upon them. This is precisely because the imagination of the shaman—his *imaginatio vera*—has been completely awakened.

Of course, the soul's journey after death eventually must depart from the common story line we know so well from our NDE narratives. That story begins, as we have seen, with the pure light of the soul's unconditioned divine splendor, follows the lineaments of its universal form, and must of necessity devolve into the particularities of each soul's perfectly appropriate but highly individualized imaginal world. In the face of such imaginal diversity, we must turn our attention elsewhere.

I suggest that we return it to *this* world, because though we *meet* our soul in "the next world," we *make* it in this one. And "making soul" (the phrase comes from Keats), as opposed to seeing the soul's essence after death, is after all what life requires of us.

In contemplating this task, however, it will behoove us to realize that what the shaman has achieved through the ordeals of his own training, we too may learn through other means.

Implications for the Question of Survival

Paracelsus wrote: "Everyone may educate and regulate his imagination so as to come thereby into contact with spirits, and be taught by them."

Having acknowledged that the subtextual appeal of near-death narratives is their implied promise of a glorious afterlife, I cannot refrain from observing that in my personal opinion this lure of the NDE may also prove to be a dangerous distraction. The enormous publicity that these reports have received, and the hope they inspire about a life to come, may well seduce many persons into an attitude of comfortable complacency. The light appears to shine on all with its unconditionally accepting radiance, and everyone seems to enter eternity in an atmosphere of all-pervasive pure love that reveals the soul in its blessed immanent divinity—or so these accounts of what awaits us at death tempt us to believe. And I, for one, *do* believe it. Still, we must not, I think, allow the light of the NDE to blind us to the rest of the imaginal journey to follow. To emphasize only the light, or to suppose that it will, in itself, make all things well after death, regardless of how we have lived, is in my judgment a naive and fallacious reading of the implications of NDE research.

Even Blake, who is perhaps the preeminent poet of the NDE and certainly the still-towering seer of the visionary imagination,[17] held that it was possible to fall off "the golden track" into true death. And likewise, we remember Plato's assertion that the whole purpose of philosophy was to provide "a rehearsal for death"—that is, a means by which to engage in a form of soul training whose consummate value would be fully evident only after death.

These are the voices from history that rise above the noisy clamor of today's NDE enthusiasts and critics alike, reminding us that we are at this very moment writing the script for our own after-death imaginal drama and that we ourselves are the shapers of our soul's destiny. The light may indeed reflect our true nature and dissolve our personal sense of sin, but it can never absolve us of the responsibility for our own lives. Not just what we are in our essence, but how we have in fact lived will be evident—perhaps painfully so—after death. For there, what was subjective becomes imaginally objective: What we see is a representation of what we have been in the depths of our psyche.

This may sound like a sermon on the virtues of the moral life, but I have something very different in mind in making these remarks. Everything I've said here points to the primacy of the soul as the vehicle of the *imaginative life*. Soul and imagination are inseparable. To "build soul" is to cultivate the imagination. And, as Terence McKenna, Blake's space-age successor and an ardent advocate and practitioner of modern shamanism, has observed, "the imagination is everything. . . . This is where we came from. This is where we are going."[18] Thus, to enter into the imagination before we die is to know both our source and our destiny. It is also to practice the shaman's art and Plato's philosophy so as to see with imaginal vision while still alive.

For me, the true promise of the NDE is not what it suggests about life after death, but what it says about how to live *now* and how to wake up to the divine imagination now by following the soul's passionate yearning to experience its boundless depths *before* death. Who better than Kabir to remind us how?

> Friend, hope for the Guest while you are alive.
> Jump into experience while you are alive!
> Think . . . and think . . . while you are alive.
> What you call "salvation" belongs to the time before death.
>
> If you don't break your ropes while you're alive,
> do you think
> ghosts will do it after?
>
> The idea that the soul will join with the ecstatic
> just because the body is rotten—
> that is all fantasy.
>
> What is found now is found then.
> If you find nothing now,
> you will simply end up with an apartment
> in the City of Death.
>
> If you make love with the divine now, in the next life
> you will have the face of satisfied desire.
> So plunge into the truth, find out who the Teacher is,
> Believe in the Great Sound!
>
> Kabir say this: When the Guest is being searched for,
> it is the intensity of the longing that does all the work.
> Look at me, and you will see a slave of that intensity.[19]

PART FOUR

Transcendence of Death

The authors in this final section share an interest in the question of how we can go beyond our habitual negative reactions about death and an afterlife—the pessimism, despair, and fear these thoughts usually engender—to develop more positive attitudes. Here, for example, we will discuss such issues as dying with dignity, the psychological roots of our fear of death, how belief in survival after death affects the quality of one's personal mythologies of death, and whether we are justified in believing in a life after death, even if it cannot be proven by scientific standards.

In "What Survives?" Stephen Levine offers insights gained from his many years of working with those who are in the process of dying. In a moving personal account of his work with one such patient, Robin, he tells of experiencing, during a meditation retreat, a "transference" of the death process in which the actual symptoms of Robin's death were reproduced in his own body, including a sense of being "evicted" from his body by an overwhelming pressure in the chest, thus allowing him a glimpse of what it is like to die. "This experience [of being evicted from the body] was very satisfying," Levine writes. "I was no longer contracted around my life, but felt myself expanding beyond my body. I thought, 'Ah, this is just right, it's all happening perfectly.' "

Levine then analyzes his experience from the standpoint of Buddhist teachings on "mindfulness," suggesting that if the after-death state is projected by the mind, as Buddhism teaches, then our work at the moment of death—as in the present moment—must be "to acknowledge what is happening, to remain open to it, without clinging or resistance, and to let it go in order to see beyond the mind's imaginings, goals, and fears." Then, he says, we will be able to "go beyond the relative and conditional to the truth; to merge with the Ever-shining."

In "Where Children Are Crying: A Shaman's Work in the Afterlife," Lisa Ann Mertz and Lorin W. Smith shed further light on the shamanic attitude toward death and beyond. In this firsthand account, we are offered a glimpse of Smith, a California Indian shaman, in his traditional role as psychopomp—one who helps in the transition of a deceased person's spirit from this world to the next—and as a retriever of lost souls. Here, too, we see how a shaman works with his guardian spirits in his journeys to the "land of the dead," and how, with the help of these spirits, he is permitted to choose the "vocation" he will pursue in the next world after he dies.

As Mertz makes clear, Smith's extensive exploration of the geography of the "other world," and knowledge of where he will go after he dies, give him a more expansive view of things. "His experiences in this life become invested with wider significance," she writes. "Experiencing losses and other hardships become, for him, preparation for what lies ahead." Thus, Smith's attitude toward death and survival after death, gained through his intensive spiritual work, directly affect the quality of his present life, adding an extra dimension of meaning and giving him the ability to face difficulties and setbacks with more strength and endurance than would otherwise be the case.

Given that faith in a life after death can have these positive benefits, why are some people so resistant to any evidence for the reality of an afterlife? In "Fear of Life after Death," Michael Grosso explores this phenomenon of resistance to the evidence, especially as demonstrated by educated believers in modern scientific materialism. "It's as if there were a conspiracy against this information," writes Grosso, "a need to make it harmless, irrelevant, nonexistent." The key to this need, he proposes, can be found by looking at the beliefs of tribal peoples about the spirits of the dead.

Grosso says, "Tribal peoples everywhere believe that the spirits of the dead are capable of inflicting all kinds of mischief on the living, and this primordial fear of the dead, along with the enormous paranoia it presupposes, is probably still part of our collective psychic heritage." From this standpoint, he proposes that the invention of scientific materialism can be seen as a powerful fetish for banishing, at least from our conscious mind, the fear of hostile spirits. In other words, by *de-animating* nature and reducing mind, soul, and consciousness to highly perishable by-products of biochemical reactions, scientific materialism helps to reassure us that "there's nothing in the dark to frighten us."

After considering other motives for disbelieving in a life after death, Grosso goes on to develop a new paradigm for discussion of the survival question, based on an examination of the issue from an evolutionary perspective—a perspective in which it is possible that human beings are only beginning to develop an ability to survive death. "The conditions for an 'afterlife' may be in the process of emerging," he suggests. If so, the incompleteness of the evidence for survival would merely reflect the uncompleted evolution of afterlife mechanisms. "We do not yet know the evolutionary implications of such things as mediumistic transports, near-death visions, out-of-body travels, anomalous time perceptions, apparitions, poltergeists, miracles of saints and avatars, and a good deal more," he notes. "Such phenomena may be only the beginning of a vast evolution of the species mind."

David Feinstein takes a somewhat different perspective on our attitudes toward death in "Personal Mythologies of Death and Their Evolution." Defining a personal mythology as the "deep, largely unconscious, and often internally inconsistent complex of images, emotions, and concepts by which an individual interprets the past, understands the present, and finds guidance for the future," Feinstein argues that at some level we are all continually dealing with issues involved with our understanding of life and death. "Making the process more conscious," he writes, "can ultimately lead one toward a more viable and empowering personal mythology of death."

To this end, Feinstein describes a five-step program for making the process of personal myth making more conscious, involving the construction of personal rituals and the use of techniques based on imagery and contemplation. "Taking yourself on an inner journey in which you confront your deepest fears about death and excavate archetypal impulses toward death transcendence can have a number of benefits," he writes. "By squarely facing your mortality, you bring a new intensity to the life you have."

Facing death squarely is also the topic of my essay "Journeys to the Land of the Dead: Shamanism and Samadhi," in which I draw parallels between the otherworldly "journeys" undertaken by shamans, yogis, and near-death experiencers, and suggest that it is appropriate today that mystical knowledge of the after-death realms is being "democratized"—made available to large numbers of people, rather than limited (as in the past) to a small clique of mystical specialists. This is because, in the present situation of global crisis, the world can ill afford to be populated by masses of people driven by an unconscious fear of death. The ideal of global healing demands widespread access to the previously secret knowledge of after-death states and the mystical "death-rebirth" experience, thus pointing to the need for a new Western mystical tradition with its own appropriate initiations and rites of passage.

Finally, in the Epilogue, I consider the consequences of belief in survival after death for the quality of one's present life. Given that the evidence and arguments both for and against the survival hypothesis are inconclusive, are we nevertheless justified in *believing* in a life after death? I suggest that if faith in an afterlife enables one to live more meaningfully; if it allows one to overcome hardships and difficulties with more strength and endurance; if it gives one more energy and enthusiasm for moral and spiritual pursuits—then such consequences in themselves provide a justification for believing, not as a dogmatic assumption, but as a "working hypothesis" on the basis of which to conduct one's life.

What Survives?

Stephen Levine is a former editor of the San Francisco Oracle *and a former director of the Hanuman Foundation Dying Project. He is widely known for his work with those confronting death and grief. His books include* Grist for the Mill *(coauthored with Ram Dass),* Who Dies?, Meetings at the Edge, *and* Healing into Life and Death.

Many years ago, sitting on a high mesa in Arizona watching the red sun set, a Zen monk friend turned to me and said, "What need survival?"

We think that we depend on the body for our existence, but it is really just the other way around: The body depends on us—who we really are—for its existence. And when we leave this body behind, it instantly becomes trash and a disposal problem.

Many of the dying patients that my wife, Ondrea, and I have worked with over the past twelve years, upon experiencing some sense of themselves as being independent of the body, through either near-death experiences (NDEs), out-of-body experiences (OBEs), or other meditative inner workings, have found that letting go of the body is a natural part of the continuum of conscious experience. Personally, I have never had an NDE or an OBE; yet I have occasionally had "other-than-the-body" experiences.

In the silent tasting of deeper flows within, one may come to directly experience the state of "the Deathless"—the boundaryless vastness of being in which floats the continuum out of which thoughts of a separate self arise and into which they disappear. The Deathless is the shared heart in which all seemingly separate mental experience floats—the "beingness" that is beyond all dualities such as being and nonbeing. In this indefinable yet directly experienceable state, birth and death disappear like bubbles on water or thoughts in the mind, leaving one with a quiet confidence that one will indeed survive beyond the death of this perishable body, which is merely a classroom for the spirit.

It is with some delight and considerable ignorance that I approach the title of this work, "What Survives?" To answer such a question, one would clearly need to know the truth. But to "know" essential truth, we must fully be. It cannot be known with the mind, only experienced in the heart. It exists beyond language and the mind. The answer to the question, What survives? is in fact the answer to the inquiry, Who am I? Although words can never express the reality of who we are, by exploring our own consciousness deeply, we can surpass death and impermanence by discovering the ever-present beingness that existed before birth and continues on to look back at death.

The answers that have been proposed to the universal inquiry, What survives? almost define the various religions of the world. According to some schools of thought (e.g., the Christian), that which survives is the soul, an individual entity created by but ultimately separate from God because it is somehow different in essence. According to other schools, in which nothing is seen as separate from our true nature (e.g., the Buddhist), the answer might be directed toward the constant unfolding of the process (continuum): After this candle (the body) has melted away, the flame that lit it passes on, lighting another wick and continuing to burn. Elsewhere in the Orient, a shaved-headed, orange-robed monk might answer the question, What survives? by posing the counterquestion, Who is asking? Discover that by self-inquiry and you will know what survives.

Perhaps the best answer I have heard to the survival question came from one of the great Laotian meditation masters who, at eighty years of age, came to visit a meditation center in the United States where I was on retreat. After this honored elder of the Theravada Buddhist school had asked the assembled group of meditators, "What survives when an enlightened being dies?" a man who had once been a monk in the same school replied, "When an enlightened being dies, nothing remains." Although this was the standard view of his sect, the teacher smiled and, quite to our surprise, replied "No, the truth remains!"

From my own experience, it appears that the answer to this question cannot be uncovered by intellectual inquiry, but can only be directly experienced as an aspect of our being that is available to us in deep, direct inquiry. Thus it is said, "What we are looking for is that which is looking." Yet "that which sees" cannot itself be seen; it can only be entered into beyond the mind, at the very center of oneself.

Working with those who are in the process of dying, I have sometimes had the opportunity to accompany a dying patient to the very threshold of death. Although unable to cross that threshold with them, I have nevertheless been able to see a bit beyond the doorway into the unfolding that follows. In the course of many years of working with those who are approaching death, I have occasionally "merged consciousness," for lack of a better term, with those to whom I had a particularly strong heart connection.

Perhaps the most extraordinary of these experiences was with a patient named Robin, with whom I had been working for many months. Robin was in extreme pain from bone cancer and had worked long and hard to meet herself in a merciful and awakened way. Her dying was a teaching to us all. After staying at her bedside for nearly three weeks, she encouraged me, with a wink of her eye, to keep my commitment to attend a retreat at a meditation center several hundred miles away. Leaving with the final good-byes of a long relationship of mutual growth, I went to the retreat. Arriving at the meditation center and calling Robin to see how things were going, I found that her dying process continued on its own natural course and that all was well. Each day I called her from the retreat, it was clear that there was little she needed from anyone.

One day about a week into the retreat, during the first group sitting for meditation at five in the morning, I started to feel a pain in my chest. I noticed the sensations getting hotter and deeper, and after a few minutes began to think that perhaps I was having some sort of dying hallucination. "Not surprising," I thought, "considering all the people I've been with as they die." I did not know where the pain originated, and all I could do was stay open to it and see what the next moment held. It felt like some kind of pressure was displacing my lung capacity. I had to concentrate on each breath, and it began to seem as if I had to consciously draw in air, almost at the molecular level, to keep from fainting. It became more and more difficult to breathe, and the pain in my chest spread. I could feel my body tightening with each breath; but as long as I could stay open to it, I had room for the experience. So, I just sat with whatever seemed to be happening, not labeling or even trying to understand it, but just attempting to stay open to it.

Then, about ten minutes into the experience, I suddenly heard

Robin's voice saying, "We've been so close, we've shared so much, and there is really nothing I can give you. But I know you want to know what it's like to die, so I am sharing my death with you."

I mused to myself, "Well, that's an interesting thought. True or not, whatever it is, it's just a thought. Who knows?"

I was suspending judgment, not knowing what was really happening. But I did feel as though I was in the process of dying, whatever the reason. The effort to breathe was becoming even more difficult, and I watched my body starting to vibrate with a sense of emergency. The "red light" was definitely on. There was something happening that the physical form was treating as a threat. I felt fear arising as I watched the body trying to hold on, contracting almost as if it were involuntarily trying to encapsulate or contain the "fire," the life force inside itself, trying not to let it out. Yet the fire was burning its way through, in spite of the effort. I was trying just to breathe, not thinking of anything else, because I sensed that if my attention wavered, I was going to pass out. In my body there was only the pain and the slow hiss of my breath, drawn in and released under pressure.

Perhaps twenty-five minutes into the experience, I felt as though I was being evicted from my body by the pressure in my lungs. I continued to watch the body trying to hold on, even more on "alert" than before, with the mind trying to think its way out of the situation. But there was no room for control. I sensed that I must just give the body space, because any control would cause it to burst. I felt like a tube of toothpaste being squeezed with its top still on. Finally, however, the mind said, "Stay in? Why?" No answer came. And suddenly there was great peace. My priorities had instantly changed: Leaving the body now seemed entirely appropriate; there was no reason to resist or hold on. It was as though I had remembered something that I had forgotten a long time before, perhaps since birth. Then the pressure in my chest seemed perfectly natural: It was doing exactly what it should to eject me. Right! Death was no longer a threat, but became just another inconsequential bubble in the flow of change and the sense of joyous expectancy of the next moment. I thought again, "Yes, why stay in the body? How could I have been so foolish as to hold on to this thing? Everything is perfect." I felt a pervasive sense of knowing that everything was as it should be, and the certainty of this knowing converted the pain and pressure ejecting me from my body into an ally, instead of an enemy.

This experience was very satisfying. I still felt pain, but also an immense expansiveness. I was no longer contracted around my life, but felt myself expanding beyond my body. I thought, "Ah, this is just right, it's all happening perfectly." And again I heard Robin's voice, this time saying, "It's time to stop being Robin and become Christ dying." Then I no longer identified even with "someone" dying—with "my" dying or "her" dying—and just experienced the process itself in its perfect unfolding. I no longer related to myself as a body, but more as a process of consciousness in its next perfect stage, the stage of dying out of its vessel. And I knew that dying was just another part of living. Silence.

As the bell rang to end the meditation period, my mind wondered, "What was that all about? An interesting hallucination, to be sure—but was it anything more?" Then I got up to go to breakfast, my chest still aching. But just as I was about to begin eating, I was called to the phone. It was Robin's brother. Robin had just died.

Some time ago, we received a letter from a woman in New York City who said that she was thinking of visiting her mother, who was dying in the Brooklyn Convalescent Hospital, and that she wanted to sit by her mother's bed and read her the Tibetan Book of the Dead. I called that day to suggest to this woman that she might be making an error of judgment. I asked her to consider the likely reaction of an eighty-five-year-old Jewish woman, in considerable pain and fear and dying in a strange environment, who is forced to lie helplessly and hear how she will soon have to confront overpowering lights and thunderous roars coming from strange gods and demons in circumstances that she has never experienced in life. Death is frightening enough as it is. To put it in terms so unfamiliar, I said, would be likely to cause her mother yet more anxiety and fear. The Tibetan Book of the Dead was intended for Tibetan monks, not for old Jewish ladies dying in Brooklyn. Since Tibetans and Westerners do not share the same cultural conditioning in life, why should we expect a Western mind to project Tibetan conditioning after dropping the body? Instead, we suggested to the woman that she sing old Yiddish love songs to her mother.

The Tibetan Book of the Dead (also known as the Bardo Thodol) is a text written by Tibetan monks for other Tibetan monks and devout lay people to help them incorporate a lifetime of spiritual practice into the moment of transition we call "death." It is meant to make the unfamiliar familiar and to reinforce visualization techniques that the dying person may have been practicing for years. It is perhaps the best-known example of a type of literature found in almost every culture in the world—the "postmortem guidebook" that seeks to help dying people chart a wise course of navigation through the states of consciousness experience encountered after death. The book is part of a long spiritual practice intended to keep spiritual practitioners on the mark, even under the most bizarre circumstances. It counsels the dying person to constantly recognize and affirm that all the visionary phenomena perceived in the after-death state are projections of one's own mind; that the observer and the observed are one and the same. Thus, the text attempts to liberate practitioners from clinging to old desires and feelings of separation, which cause fear and self-protection, and encourages them to merge with their original nature by surrendering the false and uniting with the real.

To this end, the Tibetan Book of the Dead personifies states of consciousness as celestial beings, angelic and demonic entities recognizable by their garments, colors, ornamentation, and costume. Thus, compassion personified becomes the shimmering figure of the bodhisattva Avalokiteshvara; fear becomes a six-armed blood-soaked warrior demon; and discriminating wisdom—the faculty of cutting through the attachments that bind us—becomes the sword-wielding bodhisattva Manjushri. Such personifications are a means of demagnetizing the power of heavy emotions. But we in the West have not been raised with a long familiarity with such ornate personifications. Hence, they are not likely to represent the same things to us that they do to a Tibetan monk. Perhaps for the Western mind, the states of consciousness in question are better described simply as love, fear, jealousy, envy, or unconscious tendencies—those energies that have always caused clinging and confusion and have always reinforced fear and self-doubt.

The Buddhist practice of "mindfulness," or "bare attention"—the moment-to-moment acknowledgment of one's inner states, the noting of feelings and thoughts as they occur—accomplishes much the same goal as the Tibetan personifications, and does so perhaps more directly for the Western mind. Just being open to one's inner states, not closing around them or becoming identified with them, allows one to go beyond them.

If, after leaving the body, the mind does continue to create its own world; if we are indeed confronted after death by everything to which we were attached in life—projected by a mind whose con-

centration is greatly increased because distractions from bodily input are eliminated—then perhaps we will see compassion not as
Avalokiteshvara but as Mother Teresa or some kind of friend who
has helped us at one time. Rather than appearing as a wrathful
deity arising in our path, anger may well be personified as some
enemy we made while alive. Similarly, wisdom may appear to us as
a spiritual teacher we have known; jealousy or envy may take the
form of the fierce green-eyed lover we jilted years before, whereas
fear might become a great serpent threatening to swallow us. Yet
whether clothed in Tibetan garb or in the more familiar images of
our own cultural conditioning, we would still feel attraction or re-
pulsion to whatever images our imagination projects.

And if the after-death state is projected by the mind, the work
will be the same for the Tibetan monk as for us: to acknowledge
what is happening, to remain open to it without clinging or resistance, and to let it go in order to see beyond the mind's imaginings,
goals, and fears. Indeed, at this moment or at the moment of death
the work is always the same: to go beyond the relative and conditional to the truth, to merge with the Ever-shining.

It is your self-image that continues after death. If you have related
to yourself as a body during life, why should you imagine that your
fear of death, your fear of the dissolution of that body, should cease
in the afterlife? It is interesting to note that in the postmortem
"navigational" instructions of various texts in widely divergent cultures, even after leaving the body one is said to be still motivated by
fear of death. For instance, if a demon or tiger approaches, the souls
of the departed find themselves attempting to escape as though the
body still needed to be protected. For what other reason would the
deceased pull back from a red-eyed demon appearing with a broad
ax? It is because they still identify with the body, regarding it as the
essence of their self-identity, even when they no longer have a body.
Those who think of themselves as a body have much to protect,
whereas those who identify with the spirit cannot be assaulted by a
tiger or even by a red-eyed demon. Being cannot be threatened;
only one's self-image causes fear and creates something to protect.

The poet Kabir says, "What is found now is found then." The way
we relate to states of mind in the present moment gives the best
clue as to how we are likely to relate to those same states in the
future—a future that may consist of the usual routine at work tomorrow, or may consist of floating out of the body after the screech-
ing of brakes and the crumpling of steel. In either case, our uncon-

scious tendencies and mental accumulations continue from moment to moment. Death is not a barrier to this continuance. To the degree that we identify with states of mind and regard them as who we are now, to that degree we may be frightened or attracted by what the mind projects in the next moment, whenever that moment may occur.

The unknown quantity, x, that departs the body upon what we call "death" is called by some people "soul," by others "the karmic bundle," and by still others "the consciousness element." It doesn't matter what you call it, only that you investigate it directly and recognize, without creating holy wars of interpretation, that there seems to be some type of continuing on—not of "someone," but of the energy with which that "someoneness" was mentally constructed. According to the spiritual traditions of the Orient, as long as there is any attachment left to take incarnation, it will. To the degree that the illusion of separate existence seems real, it may well appear again in a new physical form in order to continue mirroring itself.

Even those who have spoken of their experiences of approaching "the Light" during NDEs seldom seem to have recognized that it was their own true nature, their essential being, that they were approaching. They either were frightened by it or supplicated to it. Few say that they sought to merge with it and let go of all that was separate. Instead, they somehow still held on to much that seemed so precious as "individuality." The "experiencer" seldom dissolves into the experience—not unlike the ego wanting to be present at its own funeral or like the dandy living life before a mirror. Yet the healing we took birth for, which is available moment to moment in life, is also particularly available at the moment of death—a profound insight into the illusion of separateness. Entering fully and wholeheartedly into boundless being, we simply return to who and what we have always been. Then, all the superficial "becoming" of the past dissolves into the Light of the underlying reality that we share with all there is and all there ever will be.

Question: I have read so much in the works of Raymond Moody, Elisabeth Kübler-Ross, and others about the near-death experiences of people leaving their bodies and meeting a Being of Great Light. Does everyone meet Buddha or Jesus or whomever they personify as "the Soul" after death?

Answer: Please remember that all these so-called near-death experiences are only of the early stages of death, of what might be called the "first bardo" after death. Experiencing the luminosity of being during the primary stages of dying is the basis of hundreds of cosmologies and writings on the after-death experience. The Tibetan Book of the Dead and many other such texts indicate that if we are unable, after meeting the primary light, to surrender wholly into it and become one with it, the light breaks up into its individual components, as if passed through a prism, allowing the various inclinations that create duality and a sense of separation to reassert themselves. The shimmering silence is disturbed by old tendencies that agitate the mind, just as the mirror-smooth surface of a quiet pond is rippled by submerged creatures swimming to the surface. Then, if the eschatological texts are correct, one may go through a process of purification, a meeting of one's mind in a way that allows surrender and conversion of obstacles into allies. Such a process, it is said, provides an opportunity to meet one's conditioning and imprinting with wisdom and love and to enter into the essence shared by all.

Some years ago I spent time with a teen-age boy who was dying of a brain tumor. We hadn't talked much until he asked, "What is it going to be like when I die? What do you think death is like?" I told him that I didn't know what death is like, but that there seem to be certain kinds of experiences, referred to in the writings of various sages as well as in modern research on reports of those who had been clinically dead and then resuscitated. Raymond Moody's book *Life after Life* had just been published, so I related to the boy some of the experiences mentioned by those who had "died"—for example, how they had viewed their body as if from above and had recognized themselves as not being identical with that body. Sharing with him some possibilities of how to stay open to this process, we went through the whole scenario. Occasionally an "Ah!" would escape his lips. "They speak of being outside their body," I told him, "and able to move as fast as thought."

He frowned and asked, "Could I create thunderstorms and lightning?"

"I don't know if you could or not," I said, "but I sense that once you are outside this body, which has been giving you so much trouble, you might have a different perspective on all this. You might have a different view of how these troubles that anger you so much now have actually brought you a kind of compassion and maturity. You might not be so angry. It might not even occur to you to create thunder and lightning."

He wasn't so sure about that. "You know," I continued, "a few minutes after you die, you are going to know more about death than any of the so-called experts like me. Many people speak of moving down a corridor or across some barrier like a river and coming into the presence of a great loving light. And there may be a being of great wisdom there to guide you—a being whom some have seen as Jesus and others as Buddha."

"Wow!" he said. "It will be like meeting Spock!"

I wonder how many young people, upon leaving their bodies, meet Spock. It doesn't matter what form the personification of wisdom takes. What matters is one's relationship to wisdom itself, to the shimmering silence that is disguised in form.

As one person put it, "Death is just a change in lifestyles." It is an opportunity to see the cause of suffering—our clinging—and to discover the surrender that opens the way to our essential wholeness. Death puts life in perspective; it is a great gift that, if received in mercy and wisdom, allows the clinging mind to dissolve so that nothing remains but the truth, letting us become just the light entering the light.

As Walt Whitman wrote:

> All goes onward and outward
> Nothing collapses
> And to die is different from
> What anyone supposes
> and luckier.

The Buddha, when dying, was asked by his followers what they should do to maintain their practice after he was gone. He said, "Be a lamp unto yourself." In the Lotus Sutra he suggests, "Thus shall ye think of all this fleeting world: a star at dawn, a bubble in the stream, a flash of lightning in a summer cloud, a flickering lamp, a phantom, and a dream."

Referring to the idea that after death we are reborn to continue learning until we have become one with our true nature, a Buddhist friend once said, "You know, it's not hard to die, it's just hard to stay dead!"

LISA ANN MERTZ
LORIN W. SMITH

Where Children Are Crying: A Shaman's Work in the Afterlife

Lisa Ann Mertz is a doctoral candidate in shamanic studies and a research assistant for Michael Harner at the Foundation for Shamanic Studies, where she also designs and edits the foundation's quarterly newsletter. Lorin W. Smith is a healer, prophet, and "dreamer" (shaman) among the Kashaya Pomo in Northern California, where he is also an employee of the state park service. Called by Michael Harner "one of the foremost California Indian shamans," Smith has been sharing the stories of his life and spiritual practices with Lisa Mertz to "keep the culture going" for future generations of Indian people.

From Northern California's Highway 1, Skagg's Spring Road climbs through a forest of redwoods and ferns, dips to cross the Gualala River, and winds its way flanked by thistles and lilacs up to the ridge top, where the forty-acre Kashaya Rancheria lies nestled among live oaks, bay laurel, hazel, and huckleberry. It is here at Kashaya Rancheria (a *rancheria* is a nontreaty tribal reserve) that Lorin Smith carries on the traditional spiritual practices of the Kashaya Pomo Indian people together with his sisters and other tribal members who are dedicated to nurturing their culture.

The family has been organizing sacred dancing and seasonal festivals for many years in the ceremonial roundhouse in which healings are also performed by various healers within Kashaya. It is important to note that like most Native Americans, Lorin Smith and his family have been influenced by missionary activity, and hence are bicultural. Modern Christian beliefs and prayers are interwoven with ancient tribal ways.

In the Pomo language, Lorin Smith is called *yomta*, a healer, prophet, and "dreamer," also known as a shaman—one whose "soul can safely abandon his body and roam at vast distances, can penetrate the underworld and rise to the sky."[1] The shaman is "a man [or a woman] who has immediate, concrete experiences with gods and spirits; he sees them face to face, he talks with them, prays to them, implores them. . . ."[2] In a recent article, Ake Hultkrantz defines the shaman as "an inspired visionary who, on behalf of the society he serves, and with the assistance of his guardian spirits, enters into a deep trance in which his dreaming ego establishes relations with spiritual powers."[3]

In this article, while occasionally offering interpretive remarks, I will for the most part let Lorin Smith speak for himself (in italicized text) about the afterlife. Although certain details of this particular conception of the afterlife may be unique to the Pomo—or, indeed, to Lorin Smith himself—in broad outline the idea of a "land of the dead" where the spirits of deceased members of the tribe may be contacted is found in virtually all shamanic cultures worldwide. Hence, Lorin Smith's firsthand account may serve as an example of the shamanic attitude in general to the question, What survives?

By means of songs, prayers, and the use of herbs, Lorin Smith enters the "dream," an altered state that Michael Harner calls a "shamanic state of consciousness" to distinguish it from other altered states.[4] While "dreaming," Lorin Smith may be in a waking state, even during the day, but he is also capable of leaving his body while asleep at night and flying to other worlds. It is often in this world, however, that he contacts his spiritual teacher, Tom Smith, the California Coast Miwok prophet of the 1870 Ghost Dance whose house used to be located in Bodega Bay. Of his teacher, Lorin Smith says:

For me he's the seed, he's the starter of things. He's the person that can make things happen in my life. . . . When I want his guidance, I hear his voice, but most of the time, I see him. He appears to me; nobody else sees. If they want this kind of proof, then he'll appear. See, sometimes, they want to know who am I working with. They'll hear voices, they feel his presence. I let them feel his presence in the roundhouse. I can do that, because I'm the main channel to him. I worked with him for a lot of years, so I can let them really feel that there is a higher source that I talk to, make contact with. His body's gone, so no one could see him, but if you need him anytime, day or night, he's here [in Bodega Bay]. *He had to go to another world first, then after so many years, I feel that they* [spiritual teachers like Tom Smith] *. . . know how to come back again. But you know, they go through teaching* [in the other world], *same as we do* [in this world].

I think if there's someone here in the younger generation that wants to work with and hear about me when they grow up, like I did Tom Smith, then I can come back and work with that person.

Since the shaman knows how to follow the path from this world to the next and back at will, one of the traditional roles of the shaman throughout the world is that of psychopomp—that is, one who can facilitate the transition of a deceased person's spirit from this world to the next.

Rutherford Lone Man, a Native American shaman who taught spiritual practices at a center near Kashaya, died in an automobile accident on one of the twisting roads among the ridges of nearby Cazadero. Lorin Smith was called on to act as psychopomp for Rutherford's disoriented spirit.

The last time I saw Rutherford [in this life] *he was so tired. His students told him not to do anything for a while, but he didn't rest.*

During the day, I started seeing somebody walking by, you know, and I put it together who it was after I heard that Rutherford died in a car accident. I told a friend I was going to do something about it, because I knew what was going on. I could see that he was still here.

A belief found in many shamanic societies is that people who die suddenly and violently need special help in crossing over to the other world.

I did something in the roundhouse for him [Rutherford], *showing him which way to go—because when you die that fast, you're un-decided. . . . You don't really know which way to go, because you're try-ing to figure out what happened to you. Maybe the last thing he knew he was driving and, all at once. . . . He was too tired; he just killed himself.*

Even during the day I'd see him walking by—I'd see a glimpse of a person. After a while, when I put it together, I had an idea of who it was. He was looking to let me know that he needed my help. He had to go away from the place he died. All the spirit of him had to be lifted, you know, so he wouldn't disturb people he worked with. Maybe they'd start seeing him, too, and maybe they'd get scared because they didn't under-stand who it was. He started coming to me closer and closer, like he was confused, and I picked it up that he didn't know where he was supposed to go.

[A shaman] *can help the deceased to go where they're supposed to go. All I do is I'm giving him a ride or I'm giving him a helping hand to let him know that he can't come back here anymore. He has to go a different direction.*

I burned bay leaves and did a prayer, and after that you could feel that there was nobody there anymore, that Rutherford found his way. I use prayer, use song, and burn bay leaves—this shows him the way where he's supposed to go instead of trying to come back here and get in contact with people on this earth. I didn't know where he was going to go. Usually a spiritual teacher, a person like Rutherford, knows where he's supposed to go, since he's been dealing with the other world all these years. It really comes back to him where he should go, what trail, where he walked before. I'm just a reminder; I'm clearing his head to let him know. When you die fast you don't know what's happening to you. . . . So I just helped him on his way. All the years he'd been helping people, he learned where the trail is—or whatever way he reaches the other world. He has his contacts [his helping spirits], too, you know. He knows how to get there. I just helped him open up his mind to what he knew already.

The shaman, through repeated journeys to the land of the dead, becomes familiar with its "geography."

Some places [in the afterworld] I've been. There were three people [spirits] that were giving me a tour to work with a lot of the younger generation that died when they were on drugs and other things—that's where I want to go after death. I want to work with the younger generation. I chose to do that, so I was given the opportunity to do that. That word choice *doesn't mean you're chosen to go there. You have to work for it.*

Through interaction with the spirits, Lorin Smith was permitted to choose the vocation that he will practice in the afterlife. For him, his present existence—not an easy one—is in part a preparation for what lies ahead. The opportunity to be a productive member of a community in the next world comes with hard work in this world.

I'm still working for it, but I had to see what I was working for, why I'm so tired, trying to get the right sleep, and where all that's gonna go. I was wondering why I'm going through all this hardship—for what? So they showed me what I'm working for, what I want to do. That's what I want to do. They showed me the place where I'm gonna go. Where kids were crying.

See, my question was, What happens to these younger people that I see that always die off here in this land from drugs or whatever—murder— early in their teens? So they [these three spirits] said, "We'll show you, we'll take you there."

After certain preparations, including prayer, Lorin Smith "channels in," as he calls the process of contacting his teacher, Tom Smith. Tom Smith, in turn, "channels in" to his own spiritual guidance—for example, the three spirits whom Lorin describes as "tour guides" in the other world. In order to find guidance concerning his question about drug-related deaths of young people, Lorin had to "go through channels."

Well, I had to contact my teacher Tom Smith first. Then he has to go to a higher source. Those three, I believe, are higher than he is. During my sleep, my dream was to have somebody come to me and take me. I left from the house.

I went between two golden bars that lie to the west where you see the sun go down in the evening. They're not short; the golden bars are long. I believe that's the entrance they call the Pearly Gates.

When I reached that place, that two-golden-bars entrance—that's where they picked me up, those three. They didn't give their names, because the names alone can bring them. There I met them, and from there it's like I went on a carriage that moved so smoothly. From there I went so far, then we started walking.

Sometimes, Lorin says, it happens early in the morning that he leaves his body and finds his way to another place. Two golden bars mark the entrance to another world. The landscape in the particular part of this world where these children live differs somewhat from that of Northern California.

It's kind of not like this land, and there weren't many trees—where these young people were. The surroundings were like . . . they wouldn't be comfortable there. I mean, you know, it's a prison. Yeah, there were buildings, there was no fence around it, but the surroundings looked like they were separate from the beauty part of the whole land itself up there. So they were free to come up to me when I came there, even though I wasn't dead, but I was limited. My time had a limit to being there. I came there to see how they lived, that's what I asked for. So the three men were showing me that.

The kids came up to me and they asked me, "Are you going to be our teacher?" And I said, "Yeah, but I'm not here to stay today." Even so, they were so happy that they would be able to get another chance to better themselves with my teachings.

A lot of them were Indians from different tribes, but there were other people who in this world we'd call different races. They were all there. I guess their ages ranged from twelve to about seventeen or eighteen.

Apparently, the three spirits had told the teenagers prior to Lorin Smith's visit that a new teacher would be coming to meet them.

From their point of view, Lorin's commitment to teaching them represents an opportunity for them to improve themselves.

They were full of questions. They all ran up around me and greeted me and they wondered when it was going to start, and I just said my time is limited right now, that I had to . . . I just came to see who they were and what people I had to work with, what ages, and most of all, I just wanted to see how they would accept me. You have to want to be accepted, too, to take the job.

They were boys and girls. In life, they were out for good times and stuff all over the city. You know, died young. Mostly they talked about things like what happened to them. That's mostly what they know, because that's the way they died. They need somebody else to turn them around and teach them that they could be useful. See, when you die like that, you think there is no other thing for you. You don't hear anything else from somebody else—they never heard it here, they didn't want to. They always want to improve themselves, but they don't know how. So teachers are there teaching them; it's a school, already going.

There are a lot of others that are helping, too. I won't be alone, but they needed an Indian person like me for guidance with the old medicine. I'd be the only medicine man there. The rest of them would be other healers that deal with herbs, know what herbs can do for the body that's been wasted away with drugs and stuff, and especially the mind.

I think, far as my interest is, I'd like to stay there long as I can help these younger people, because from there, the ones I'll teach will move on to a better place. And meanwhile, there'll be other kids coming in mainly with the same problem or maybe a little different, but coming to the same place. I could have gone somewhere else, too, if I wanted to. But I didn't, I just went to that place. That was where I wanted to go. Then when you go beyond that, all that pain's taken away from you. There's a lot of other places you can go, and that was the first place I went to, and that's the one I chose. I mean there was no doubt in my mind. I didn't want to go anywhere else, because it seemed like they really wanted me, and it seemed like I could help them with what they need.

Being so well acquainted with the geography of other worlds and knowing where he will go after he dies gives Lorin Smith a more expansive view of things. His experiences in this life become invested with wider significance. Experiencing losses and other hardships become, for him, preparation for what lies ahead.

I guess I try to learn more here of how much pressure I'm going to stand. I don't feel sad that my work here is almost gone, because I know my next work is going to be where people really need me even more than here. So, to see that more and more people are fading away from my work here brings me closer to the group that's waiting for me. Then I wonder, Is there a date set for me to be there?

I don't want to know really, though. I kinda want to let things happen casually. That way I could accept it better if it happened all at once, you know, like I'm sitting here—next day or two days or three days from now I'm gone.

I mean there's fear of dying, too. You know, people say they're not scared to die, but they are. Some of them die before they tell somebody they're scared to die. They say, "Oh, we can accept that," but they can't; there's fear there. It's kind of like you're being smothered, death is. It's kind of like you don't breathe anymore: Somebody's got a hand over your mouth and you can't get . . . you're losing oxygen, and that's scary, you know? And you go beyond that and you start living in a better place. That's how I look at dying: You stop breathing all at once.

I experienced death more than once—I mean what they call death. The pain goes so far and then you go past that. There is no pain after you go past the golden bars. There is no more pain, you know, but you hurt as far as you go to the golden bars if you're in bad condition. Then when you go beyond that, all that pain's taken away from you. There's a lot of things that happened to me early in life before I turned to be a healer, too, where a lot of accidents happened to me and it seemed like my life was taken away all at once. Even when I went home after an accident, I felt like I was not all there. I mean, you're not fully—your whole spirit's not with you.

The concept of soul loss, or becoming dis-spirited, is widespread cross-culturally, and it is a role of the shaman in many cultures to bring back the soul or part of the soul that has been lost. Within the idea of soul loss, a traumatic event such as a car accident can leave survivors somewhat dis-spirited; their experiences would be, for example, shock, disorientation, and difficulty in healing. Lorin Smith experienced a major car accident years back. Through serious spiritual work, he feels that his soul was healed.

I really believe that when I turned healer, all that came back to me after a while—that's my belief for me. I don't know how others experience it, but I feel I have everything back now. And now I'm ready to go if I'm called to go.

It has been said that in dying, a loved one will come to help us pass over, and occasionally Lorin has seen his mother or father coming to him in this world.

My mother came last time I was sick to see how bad I was. Then somebody told her I wasn't ready, and I said I'm not ready to go yet. Then she left. She was standing there smiling; I guess I will always be a little boy to her. She didn't say one word—she just had a smile on her face. My dad came after me one time, too. I was lying north and south, and he came from more of east and south. He came walking in. I don't know what brought him in so far, but he walked in and looked at me and he knew when I started moving around that I wasn't ready to go. They watch me closely to see if—when I get sick, they think, maybe this is the day he's coming with us.

When that day comes, Lorin says, a book containing all the things he said and did in his life will be opened.

Yeah, there's a book—what they call the Book of Life. Everything you do is written in it, so when it comes your judgment day—I have been there, too. I came to a place first time when I "died." There were people walking around with gowns on, workers, you know, like not in an office, but they had records of all the people, how they lived, things they said to criticize people, and . . . of the knowledge they had of helping people with problems. They were showing me my book, but they didn't open it, because I wasn't dead.

They'll open it [when I die finally] and I'll see what else I did wrong. I imagine half of it would be filled up. It's real interesting. They say you can come and see this, but you're not going to stay that long. But this is where you come first time—everybody comes there, they say, and according to how you lived they send you up to where you're supposed to be. Like if you die, you'll go to a certain place, but you have to come there first. Where you'll go is according to how you lived here, your choices; that's the choice you have.

MICHAEL GROSSO

Fear of Life after Death

Michael Grosso, Ph.D., teaches philosophy and religion at Jersey City State College. He is the author of numerous articles and the book The Final Choice.

Talking about life after death with an educated person can be difficult. "Let's admit," I say, "that the prospect of death can be depressing—even, on occasion, a little terrifying." My friend, who may be a bright academic or a liberal-minded lawyer, nods in agreement.

"As it happens," I continue, "I've looked into certain facts suggestive of an afterlife."

"Facts?" my friend says.

I then say that there really is a significant literature dealing with evidence—not necessarily proof—of life after death. "Just think, if there *were* life after death," I suggest, "we could continue with the adventure of consciousness and evolution, the quest for more experience and more knowledge. Wouldn't it be worth our effort to look into these queer facts of apparitions, mediumistic phenomena, out-of-body experiences, reincarnation memories, and other things that point to the possibility of an afterlife?"

"Yes," remarks my friend, joylessly.

The next move is to offer Xeroxed articles, important books on the subject. "Read this," I say, "and let's discuss it."

The type of person I have in mind will come up with weak, if not irrational, excuses for not reading the book I place in his hand. In one case, the argument ran: "It's only words on paper; no reason to take any of it seriously." Another academic said he didn't have the time. "You mean you can't find a few hours to read a book that might change your basic outlook on life and death?" I asked.

How strange that these intelligent people should be not merely indifferent but resistant to the data. It's as if there were a conspiracy against this information, a need to make it harmless, irrelevant, or nonexistent. This resistance is an interesting phenomenon, and I suspect it is part of a deep-seated fear of the irrational—a fear, in Jungian lingo, of the Shadow.

Of course, that is not how the typical educated believer in modern scientific materialism sees it. Automatically, he will assume that people who believe in life after death are indulging in magical thinking or wishful fantasizing. I think, however, it can be shown that some people are as motivated to *disbelieve* in life after death as others are motivated to believe. Let us look at a few motives for this disbelief.

The Primordial Fear of the Dead

Sir James Frazer found that among native tribal people, "immortality has a certainty which the individual as little dreams of doubting as he doubts the reality of his conscious existence."[1] Early people spontaneously believed in life after death. How did they come to this admittedly rather odd belief? Scientific materialists invoke wishful thinking as the explanation. Freud, for instance, argued that beliefs in God and immortality are products of infantile wish fulfillment, symptoms of neurotic rebellion against the harsh tyranny of the reality principle. Otto Rank maintains similarly that the fear of death inspires us to invent the idea of a double—that shadowy replica of ourselves that is said to survive in a phantom "next" or "other" world. In Rank's view, doubling the image of the self is the work of a narcissistic denial of the idea of personal extinction.

Do these psychological explanations of belief in an afterlife tally with the evidence of anthropology? No. Quite to the contrary, the facts indicate that the first people feared not extinction, but life after death; they feared not death, but the dead.

Frazer, for example, collected accounts from missionaries and anthropologists attesting to this primal fear of the dead. Tribal peoples everywhere, in Melanesia, Polynesia, New Guinea, India, Asia, Africa, and North and South America, believe that the spirits of the dead are capable of inflicting all kinds of mischief on the living, close relatives being regarded as the most lethal.

While spirits are thought occasionally to give good counsel, for the most part native people view them with fear and apprehension.

The spirits are a constant but elusive source of harm before which such people are ever driven to cringe, to beg for favors, to deceive, or to coerce the powers of the unseen. But to say, as psychologists such as Rank would have it, that belief in these powers is the product of narcissistic wish fulfillment doesn't ring true. For if the unconscious were merely forging a dream world to placate the narcissistic ego, why not forge a more agreeable one?

Throughout the world, tribal people believe that during the time immediately after death, spirits hover about their former earthly abodes and do their greatest harm. For instance, among the Tarahumara Indians of Mexico, "a mother says to her dead infant, 'Now go away! Don't come back anymore, now that you are dead.' And the father says to the dead child, 'Don't come back to ask me to hold your hand. I shall not know you anymore.'"[2] Here the fear of the dead outweighs the usually strong bonds of parental love.

Frazer cites strategies for dealing with the dangers of departed souls. For example, native people often believe that a person's soul "sticks," as it were, to his or her personal belongings. Thus, one strategy is to destroy the dead man's house and personal effects. The Aracaunian, Puelche, and Patagonian Indians of South America go a step farther and wreck his entire village. The economic effects of fear of the dead are plainly ruinous. Therefore, to say that belief in survival is "consoling" seems facile; it would be a great deal more consoling *not* to believe in an afterlife. There would be far less to worry about; one could settle down and start to enjoy life.

The primordial fear of the dead, and the enormous paranoia it presupposes, is probably still part of the heritage of our collective psyche. If depth psychologists have demonstrated anything, it is that we humans are walking psychic museums. Each of us carries inside ourselves the psychic archaeology of the species. The nameless terrors that plagued our ancestors have been repressed but not uprooted.

From the standpoint of our psychic evolution, the invention of scientific materialism was a powerful fetish for banishing, at least from our conscious minds, the primordial fear of hostile spirits. The primal mind is hemmed in by a superstitious fear of the *other*. For instance, the age-old fear of the "evil eye" shows how disposed we are to project our dark impulses on the other agent of consciousness.[3] Sartre has given us a modern analysis of the "evil eye" in his discussion of "the look."[4] We seem to have an innate fear of the other. Behind the physical eye, there is an invisible subject of consciousness, which, like a Medusa, always threatens to turn us to stone and make us over into mere things.

One can understand the appeal of scientific materialism: It deanimates nature; it wipes out mind, soul, and consciousness by reducing them to mere by-products of biochemical reactions, doomed to annihilation with the death of the body. Science makes our fear of the other go away. There's nothing in the dark to frighten us, science reassures us. Nothing at all. There are no souls out there with uncanny powers to stare us down, enchant, glamorize, or overlook us. There are no spirits out there with the power to inflict mischief on us. And just in case there are, death will get rid of them. Extinction is the ultimate talisman against the evil eye—against the fear of the uncontrollable consciousness of the other.

The Pagan Fear of Life after Death

The pagan conception of life after death was rooted in the primal fear of the dead. There was, however, a shift from fear of the dead to fear of an unappetizing form of life after death. Ancient writings amply testify to this. The most famous example is from Homer's *Odyssey* (bk. 11, 488). During Odysseus's descent into Hades, Achilles says to Odysseus: "Better by far to remain on earth the thrall of another . . . rather than reign sole king in the realm of bodiless phantoms." The poet Anacreon wrote: "Death is too terrible. Frightening are the depths of Hades." The Greeks were at home in the daylight; nighttime made them sad and uneasy.

We might best picture Hades as a gloomy altered state of consciousness, a prolonged nightmare or aimless out-of-body wandering. Hades was, without question, the locale for a type of life after death, but an unpleasant "life" of servitude to dark, inscrutable powers—powers we know something about through the revelations of art, drugs, and psychosis.

With the philosophy of Plato and the mysteries of Eleusis, a more positive conception of the afterlife emerged among the ancient Greeks, although the fearsome ideas of Hades continued to dominate the popular mind.

The Greek philosopher who did much to fight the fear of life after death was Epicurus (341–270 B.C.). He used the materialism of Democritus to argue the case for the dissolution of the soul at death. Epicurus is instructive in our present discussion, because he, like the modern materialist, was *motivated* to *disbelieve* in a life after death. Seen as a benefactor of humankind, Epicurus espoused a philosophy that was one of the most popular in the ancient world. He was a healer among the ancients, professing an expressly therapeutic philosophy. And what did he heal? The fear of life after death.

According to Lucretius, Epicurus delivered the human race from the "dread of Acheron [the river of death] . . . troubling as it does the life of man from its innermost depths." Materialism and the denial of life after death in Epicurean philosophy freed people from a peculiar form of anxiety—the anxiety that comes from the thought of having to face the "innermost depths" of human life. I take these "innermost depths" to be the dark side of the unconscious, intu- itively felt by the ancients to be what awaits us in the afterlife.

The case of Epicureanism sheds some light on the motives be- hind the rise of classical materialism. Two main motives can be discerned in the rise of this worldview, and they seem to involve a contradiction. On the one hand, ancient materialism was a weapon for avoiding contact with the dark side of the afterlife—which I take to be Jung's Shadow. (Hades, of course, is the preeminent domain of shades and shadow.) On the other hand, ancient materialism was an attempt to found a new religion, which it did by focusing on the sacred and eternal character of matter. The atoms of Democritus, for instance, possess the defining feature of the gods, which is deathlessness.

The religiosity of classical materialism is clear from the origins of Greek natural philosophy. Starting with Thales, the early Greek thinkers concentrated on discovering the *arche*—the source, origin, or principle of all things. Whether this principle was thought to be water (Thales), air (Anaximenes), fire (Heraclitus), the boundless (Anaximander), or atoms (Democritus), the quest was for the same *arche* of immortal power once possessed by the gods. Greek natural philosophy—from which came modern physics—renounced per- sonal immortality in hopes of capturing the timeless principles of nature.

The origins of scientific materialism were thus rooted in a quest for the sacred. The *arche* of the physicists is a sublimation of *theos*— the divine and godlike. With Plato's *Ideas* we have a principle that mediates between the cosmic *arche* of physics and the *psyche* of animism. In modern times, Einstein is known for his appreciation of the cosmic mystery—the sacred dimension of the world studied by science.

By and large, however, modern science is phobic about lingering traces of the sacred, the uncanny, or the numinous. The progress of natural science has been identified with eliminating anything that hints of the shadowy "inner depths" that so frightened Lucretius. It would be sacrilege to destroy the unity of science by validating alien forces like "mind" and "soul," for one would then expose oneself to a Lucretian fear of the inner depths.

Fear of Psychic Terrorism and Uncanny Forces

The point, however, cannot be overstated: Our fears are historically conditioned. The idea of life after death underwent a positive transformation with the Christian good news of the resurrection. But this shift, while it opened the Western imagination to a vision of death's higher possibilities, also raised the specter of hell, guilt, and damnation. There are good historical reasons why educated people in Western culture associate the belief in a life after death with oppressive institutions and cruel practices.

Religion has retarded the evolution of Western science, as Andrew Dickson White's *A History of the Warfare of Science with Theology in Christendom* makes clear in great detail.[5] Eastern ideas of karma, caste, and reincarnation raise similar misgivings. To entertain the belief in life after death is to open a can of worms: hell, devils, witchcraft, witch-hunting, hags, incubi, elves, demons, and much more that educated people regard as superstitious, irrational, and socially reactionary.

A universe in which life after death is a fact would be a universe filled with unknown and possibly frightening entities and forces. Reports of demonic possession, hauntings, and other eerie phenomena could no longer be dismissed out of hand if there were reason to believe in an afterlife. Now, I do not doubt that fear of uncanny supernatural forces is alive and well in the unconscious minds of many superficially rational human beings. The study of dreams and the behavior of psychotics show how close the "shades" of the unconscious are to our normal mental life. The possibility of life after death could stir up fears of the uncanny in timid rationalists; hence, the appeal of a materialist paradigm that can be used as a rationalistic shield against such fears.

The spell of the materialist paradigm prevents many educated people from even considering the possibility of rational grounds for believing in a life after death. People invest themselves, emotionally as well as intellectually, in scientific materialism. Any hint of psychic anomaly might well awaken in some of us the Lucretian dread of Acheron. Groups like the Committee for the Scientific Investigation of Claims of the Paranormal (the infamous CSICOP) are as motivated to believe in materialism as any Bible-thumper is motivated to believe in the kingdom of God.

Other Reasons for Fearing Life after Death

Fear of judgment, guilt, and karmic retribution.   If we had reason to believe in a life after death, many of us might feel the fear of God, of hell, or of judgment. The prospect of an afterlife could awaken ideas of sin, guilt, pollution, defilement, punishment, purification, and other things we are bound to view as unsavory and disturbing. Like some new-agers, scientific rationalists are anxious to rid the world of these unpleasant ideas, especially the ideas of guilt and hell. It would thus serve our purpose to disbelieve in the afterlife.

Plato says in the *Phaedo* that a bad man would welcome death if it were extinction, for then he wouldn't have to worry about the consequences of his deeds. Nor, if there were no reincarnation, would he have to worry about striving for self-perfection from life to life. After all, not many of us relish forever struggling with our weaknesses. Thus, moral and spiritual laziness are good motives for disbelieving in an afterlife.

Fear of enlightenment.   According to the Tibetan Book of the Dead, as well as reports of those who have had near-death experiences, after death we meet a dazzling, awe-inspiring light. In the Tibetan tradition, this light is said to be profoundly disorienting and, in the case of the average human being, ultimately leads to reincarnation, because most of us are not spiritually ready to recognize the nature of this light, nor to merge with it and thus attain liberation from the realms of conditional existence.

Now, suppose that reincarnation were a fact. In that case, we might unconsciously remember past meetings with this light. The less we were prepared for enlightenment, for merging with the light, the more we would recoil from such meetings. The spiritually unready would thus be motivated to disbelieve in life after death; extinction would be preferable, just as dreamless sleep is preferable to nightmare.

Fear of helplessness in a strange environment.   The idea of having to carry on in a place where one's usual status, cognitive skills, and material possessions are useless is very unpleasant. In an after-world, totally different kinds of internal skills would be needed.

If Plato is right, we bring nothing with us to the next world but our *paidea*—our education. People uneasy about their spiritual education might fear life after death; overly rational types would be reluctant to find themselves in a place where they had to rely on nonrational skills to get around. The more rule bound the mentality, the less cordial one might be to the prospect of after-death.

Pessimism and the fear of life after death.   The philosopher C. D. Broad once remarked that he would be more annoyed than surprised if he found himself conscious after death. Life after death is not likely to be any better than life before death, says Broad. And it might even be worse. Broad knows that belief in an afterlife is logically independent of belief in God: If there is no God, there could still be an afterlife. Thus, we might find ourselves after death in a godless world where evil is as powerful as ever. Hence, a pessimist might fear life after death more than sheer extinction. Extinction has its virtues: We would at least not be conscious, and therefore not aware of moral or sensory pain.

The Preference for Meaning over Evidence

An intriguing phenomenon is the growing interest in "past lives." More and more people are talking about their past lives; yet this interest, in the great majority of cases, has nothing to do with trying to *prove* authentic memories of past lives. Past-life lovers do not pore over the learned tomes of Dr. Ian Stevenson. They do not search for a rational scientific foundation for their belief.

It appears, then, that something else is happening, that we are witnessing the spontaneous formation of a *myth* of reincarnation. The search for past lives seems to involve more a search for present meanings, closely connected with a search for split-off fragments of the psyche that need to be integrated. In other words, the "past lives" that people fancy they have lived may really be parts of themselves, the "subselves" that they need to bring to awareness in order to become whole. Hence, the search for evidence, for a rational analysis of the concept of reincarnation, would only interfere with their myth-making and soul-making process.

For this type of person, then, a disinclination to consider the evidence is not due to fear of life after death, but to the fact that they automatically take life after death for granted. Such people regard the scientific and philosophic investigation of life after death as secondary to the more urgent task of trying to make their present lives more meaningful and coherent. Indeed, talk of "proof" might be experienced as an annoyance, a threat to inner stability. From this I am tempted to conclude that what many people want is less the assurance of a life after death than the assurance that their present lives, especially their sufferings, are meaningful.

A New Survival Paradigm

We have examined some motives for disbelieving in life after death. But even believers may be motivated not to examine the question too critically. In both cases, we have hit on obstacles to getting at the truth about an afterlife.

I want now to turn to some constructive remarks on the problem of survival research. I suggest that we look at the "afterlife" question from an evolutionary perspective. The usual assumption is that we either survive or do not survive after death. If we are evolutionists, however—and it's hard to deny the general evolutionary outlook—we assume that life and human consciousness emerged in time. It follows that the fact of an afterlife must also either have emerged in the past or be presently emerging. My suggestion is that the conditions for an "afterlife" may be in the process of emerging.

One advantage of this hypothesis is that the ambiguity and incompleteness of the evidence would make more sense; the incompleteness of the evidence would merely reflect the uncompleted evolution of afterlife mechanisms.

Are we, in fact, only beginning to evolve the "organs" of immortality? We do not yet know the evolutionary implications of such things as mediumistic transports, near-death visions, out-of-body travels, anomalous time perceptions, apparitions, poltergeists, miracles of saints and avatars, and a good deal more. Such phenomena may be only the beginning of a vast evolution of the species mind. We can open the horizons of our thought by remembering that we inhabit an evolving universe and that we ourselves are evolutionary oddities. Historians of science have come to recognize that anomalies are crucial in the evolution of science itself. We should thus consider the possibility that anomalies in human behavior may be crucial to the evolution of the human species.

The human animal is a puzzle to itself. We need all the evidence we can find in order to assess the potential range of our being and our function. Our ordinary "consensus" view of reality is a human construct, a mere selection of data, a mere arrangement of ideas into a conceptual lens through which we view the world and ourselves. But we can always select new data, rearrange our ideas, readjust our conceptual lens in order to revision human reality. If we wish to do so, parapsychological research offers data of great interest.

Would-be builders of a new death paradigm can find an assortment of death-related psychic anomalies, from telekinetic displacement of physical objects at the moment of death to transcendental deathbed visions. There are quite a few puzzling things about death, but most scientists sweep them under the rug. Materialistic science, as we have already noted, is not comfortable with the strangeness of death, and survival research is a neglected branch of study, even among modern parapsychologists. In my view, we need a new approach, a new survival paradigm. Perhaps I can make this a little clearer if I say something about three *types* of afterlife research. The new paradigm, as I see it, needs to combine all three of these approaches.

To begin with, there is the *trace* model of survival research. In this model, reincarnation memories, apparitions, out-of-body experiences, mediumistic claims, electronic voice phenomena, spiritistic photographs, and so forth allow us to catch a trace of a deceased human being. From such traces, we are led to believe, for example, that our deceased Uncle Octavius is still a conscious subject of experience, somewhere, somehow.

But there are problems with the trace model. For instance, where does the trace come from? Is it actually from the deceased person, or is it, as some researchers have proposed, from a psi-mediated phantom, engineered by an all-cunning, self-deceiving subliminal mind? The trace model is fascinating, but so far has proven inconclusive. There is certainly enough material here to warrant further investigation. I myself have tangled with a few ghostly entities and respect their puzzling nature.

A more direct approach to survival research we can call *state-*

specific. The near-death experience is a perfect example. You have a certain kind of extraordinary experience that allows you to feel that you know something. (For now, bracket the epistemology of state-specific "knowledge.") The important thing is that the person becomes *subjectively* convinced of the reality of an afterlife. Such experiences can change us utterly, often in interesting ways. We can call this the "gnostic" model. After-death gnosis might come through near-death as well as other transformative experiences: deep meditation, ecstatic lovemaking, UFO encounters, great dreams, psychoactive drugs, trance-dancing, collective apparitions, channeling, and so forth.

But, by itself, the gnostic or state-specific model is not enough: It needs to be supplemented by the trace model. To avoid delusion and psychic inflation, our state-specific "knowledge" needs to be grounded in the realm of objective fact. But neither are the trace and state-specific models enough by themselves. They, too, need to be supplemented by yet a third approach, which I call the *resurrection* model.

According to this model, the ordinary living human body has a potential to transform into a higher type of spiritual body. The hypothesis here is that our bodies have been designed with many hidden potentials for transmutation. The Christian tradition, of course, thinks of this transmutation in religious terms. But the resurrection model, insofar as it stresses the potential to mutate, is also an evolutionary model. Religion here foreshadows evolutionary science.

What's the evidence for this approach? For Christians it's the resurrection of Jesus. Jesus in fact predicted that people would come after him and do even greater works. There would come in his place a Comforter—a Healing Spirit. And Jesus was right about the prodigies to come. The annals of the Catholic Church contain an impressive amount of documentation of exotic marvels of human potential. Catholic miracle data are evidence for the resurrection model. They tell us something about the possible evolution of the human species. Levitation, stigmata, healings, materializations, bodily incorruption, living without food, and other extraordinary phenomena have been documented.[6]

Why are these phenomena important for survival research? In the first place, they demonstrate the existence of agencies that seem to operate independently of the known laws of physics. They point to the existence of a different physics, a physics of the creative spirit.

The miracle data are evidence for partial and fleeting "resurrections," for a drastic elevation of human bodily function.

As mentioned, the new survival paradigm I propose would make use of all three models: trace, state-specific, and resurrection. All three have something to offer, and all are needed to complete one another.

The trace model has left us with a mass of puzzling facts whose main effect is to startle us into a sense of new possibilities.[7] The value of studying these elusive traces of deceased persons is to open our minds to possibilities of life we would never have dreamed of if we had not come in contact with the data in question. They give us a theoretical edge over disbelievers.

But theory is not enough. As human beings, we need to feel our truths, as well as think them. The state-specific model of survival research is a route to the subjective dimension of truth. (Some philosophers deny that there is such a thing as "subjective truth"; but this assumes only a very restricted concept of truth.)

My point is that we are fortunate if we have an experience that gives us a gut feeling about the afterlife. An out-of-body trip on the brink of death, an abduction through strange dimensions, a vision of a light goddess, or a meeting with mysterious men in black—such experiences may be telling us something about the afterlife. The region of the afterlife in any case must envelop, and at certain points intersect with, this life. Certain types of experiences might indeed be windows into the "other world" of the afterlife.

As people share their other-world experiences, they will build a new consensus. And the creation of this new consensus may, in turn, have implications for evolution. For if a need coalesces into a group dynamic, if a new "morphogenetic field" of intentions solidifies, it is possible that some of the habits or laws of nature could get "broken," or changed, thus making new forms of life possible. If a new consensus of state-specific believers agree that there is an afterlife, nature may modify itself and create a new form of life after life.[8]

The state-specific approach to survival, however, offers subjective truth only. But there are many sides to truth. *Verum et factum convertuntur* is Vico's formula for historical or evolutionary truth: What is true and what we make true are one and the same.[9] A Vichian model of truth allows us to look at the afterlife question in a new way. For the afterlife to *be true*, according to this model, we would have to *make it true*. This is an ancient model of truth—of creative truth—different from the propositional kind of truth that merely mirrors fact. For Vico, truth is always what we make it.

And here is where the resurrection model comes in. In this model, the "afterlife," or "next life," refers to certain extreme creative potentials latent in *present life*. The accent is not on the soul's immortality, but on resurrection, transformation of the body. The latter is a practical, experimental theory of the afterlife. The "afterlife" here becomes part of the evolutionary potential of this life, and the only way to know that it is true is to make it true.

But how? One way is to transcend basic limits of bodily existence. The phenomena of the saints—levitation, hyperthermia, materialization, bilocation, and the like—do transcend basic limits of bodily function; and, in doing so, they point to possible forms of function in future humanity.[10]

According to this third model of survival research, then, the embodied world becomes the new field for "afterlife" studies. It is here on earth that we see the first signs of the "afterlife." The most spectacular signs are the psychophysical anomalies we call "miracles." When Joseph of Copertino levitates, or Padre Pio produces the stigmata, or Therese Neumann stops eating and drinking (as well as eliminating) for thirty-five years,[11] we are watching material existence being transmuted into forms that increasingly resemble a spiritual "afterlife." Copertino's body is literally drawn upward toward heaven. Matter is gradually becoming transparent to the aspirations of spirit.

But that is only the first step in the resurrection model—the shaping of outward form. There is a great deal more. The resurrection of a whole person—of Jesus into Christ—is our archetype. As Jung said, Christ is the archetype of individuation. The Jungian revelation is that there is no Christianity. There is only the unique and unrepeatable struggle of each individual to embody the God image.

This third way to research survival therefore has to do with becoming an individual. The concrete "resurrection" and transformation of every individual on earth is part of the experiment. Every life saved, liberated, enhanced adds to the building of the new earth and the new heaven. It is here in the liberation and transformation of earthly existence that the "afterlife" is *proven*—but "proven" in the Italian sense of *provare*—"to experience."

Let me state my point as bluntly as I can: The best way to "prove" life after death is to bring paradise down to earth. For one thing, this would help to justify our desire for an afterlife. C. D. Broad did have a point: We need assurance that things are going to improve. The cure for Broad's pessimism is to taste paradise on earth.

The first step toward creating paradise on earth would be to heal the ecology of the planet. The word *paradise* is Persian; it means "garden." As we begin to transform the planet into a garden—into a paradise—we will begin to materialize the "afterlife." By restoring the beauty of the planet and liberating the splendor of individual life forms, we will move toward overcoming the dualism of heaven and earth, eternity and time, divine and human.

We should try to create paradise on earth, anyway, to make up for all the hells we've already made. Oddly, our diabolical genius for creating unnecessary pain and ugliness on earth gives grounds for hope in the resurrection mode. For the same extreme energies of destruction are in principle usable for creating paradise on earth. To restore paradise on earth calls for a healing revolution. Our ideas of God, truth, value, work, power, and human relations will have to be turned upside down and inside out.

Is there an afterlife? Let us make it so by creating paradise now.

DAVID FEINSTEIN

Personal Mythologies of Death and Their Evolution

David Feinstein, Ph.D., is a clinical and community psychologist and the director of Innersource in Ashland, Oregon. He is coauthor of Personal Mythology: The Psychology of Your Evolving Self *and* Rituals for Living and Dying *(in press).*

"If people understood that they return again and again as part of their soul's evolution," claims my father, who at the age of eighteen became a passionate disciple of Madame Blavatsky's teachings on reincarnation, "it would make *all* the difference in how they live their lives." My mother, in contrast—unpersuaded after nearly fifty years of hearing this argument—sees death as the frightfully dark ending of a life whose purpose is obscure and whose length seems to be cut too short. Their ongoing debate mirrors an enduring controversy in the mythology of the culture in which they live. Some version of this debate is also being waged deep in the psyche of every person reading this book.

In this essay, we will explore the way in which every one of us, more or less consciously, has formulated and takes guidance from a personal mythology regarding the nature of life and death. The term *personal mythology* as used here has a precise meaning.[1] It refers to the deep, largely unconscious, and often internally inconsistent complex of images, emotions, and concepts by which an individual interprets the past, understands the present, and finds guidance for the future. Myths in this sense are *not* falsehoods: They are the lens through which the human psyche perceives and organizes reality. Here we will focus particularly on the vital relationship between the position taken by this mythology on the issue that divides my parents—belief in the existence or nonexistence of an afterlife—and the values and choices that shape our lives.

Personal myths explain the world, guide individual development, provide social direction, and address spiritual longings in a manner analogous to the way that cultural myths carry out these functions for entire societies. Personal myths do for an individual what cultural myths do for a community. Myth making, at both the individual and collective level, is the fundamental (though often unperceived) psychological mechanism by which human beings order reality and navigate their way through life. With its compelling symbolism and narrative, mythology is the natural language of the psyche. As the human species evolved, mythological thinking—the ability to symbolically address large questions—replaced genetic mutation as the primary vehicle by which individual consciousness and societal innovations were carried forward.

I grew up in a world whose scientific secular mythology supported my mother's side of the debate about life after death. In school, I soon learned that to mention my father's beliefs was to risk being considered even stranger than I was already thought to be. Now, however, as this book documents, new evidence seems to be supporting my father's side of the argument. Reports of near-death experiences of a profoundly spiritual nature, followed by durable positive changes in the individual's attitudes, self-esteem, and sense of well-being, are no longer rare. Indeed, it is estimated that as much as 5 percent of the American population, or eight million people in the U.S. alone, have experienced such phenomena. There is also an accumulation of increasingly well-documented reports of past-life "memories" and of clinical breakthroughs after such memories.[2] Particularly impressive are the memories of children as young as two or three who, in describing a past life, are able to provide verifiable details about people and places to whom they could have had no exposure during their present life.[3]

Not surprisingly, the scientific community has not eagerly embraced such findings.[4] Prevailing myths and paradigms die hard. In discussing the reception of new evidence regarding life after death, Roger Woolger cites a remark made by the pioneering quantum physicist Max Planck: "A new scientific truth does not triumph by convincing its opponents and making them see the truth, but rather because its opponents eventually die and a new generation grows up that is familiar with it." Of those who summarily dismiss as fantasies the thousands of past-life reports now on record, Woolger says that they remind him of "flat-earthers who refuse to go too close to the edge and see for themselves because they might fall off."[5]

Raymond Moody, a physician who has done extensive research on the near-death experience (NDE), tells a story that illustrates how reports of phenomena that do not conform to existing models may be resisted:

> At the end of one of Dr. Michael Sabom's lectures, an irate cardiologist stood up and confronted the noted NDE researcher. He had been a doctor for thirty years, he declared, during which time he had brought hundreds of people back from the brink of death.
>
> "I've been in the middle of this stuff for years," he said angrily. "And I've never talked to a patient who had one of these near-death experiences."
>
> Before Sabom could respond, a man behind the doctor stood up. "I'm one of the people you saved, and I'll tell you right now, you're the last person I would ever tell about my near-death experience."[6]

However, alternative explanations for each of the basic phenomena reported in near-death experiences have also been proposed. The many reports of convincing visions, a sense of well-being, and a loss of critical judgment, for example, have been attributed to the hypoxia caused by a decrease in oxygen to the brain.[7] The reported sense of going down a tunnel and seeing brilliant light that does not hurt one's eyes has been explained as resulting directly from phosphenes stimulating the visual cortex. Some researchers have proposed that experiences of "intense joy, profound insight, and love may be caused by a flood of endorphins designed by evolution to blot out pain when pain's message is too frightening to be functional."[8] Similarly, others have posited temporal-lobe stimulation, carbon dioxide overload, and other biochemical explanations to explain the effects in question. According to Ronald Siegel,

> these phenomena arise from common structures in the brain and nervous system, common biological experiences, and common reactions of the nervous system to stimulation. The resultant experience can be interpreted as evidence that people survive death, but it may be more easily understood as a dissociative hallucinatory activity of the brain.[9]

The scientific jury is still out on the question of what the most coherent explanation of NDEs is, however, and the existence of an afterlife is far from having been proven or disproven by any rigorous objective standard. Thus, coming to terms with the survival debate remains an individual matter.

Understanding how our personal myths evolve can be immensely useful in pursuing this question and embracing its full personal and spiritual significance. At some level, you are continually dealing with the issues involved with your understanding of life and death. Making this process more conscious can ultimately lead you toward a more viable and empowering personal mythology of death.

Peg Elliott and I have elsewhere developed a system for mindfully engaging in this inner debate.[10] On the one hand, our certainty that we are mortal is fueled by our primal instinctive terror of death and supported by our materialistic worldview. On the other hand, our sense—or at least hope—that some essence survives physical death is fueled both by our inability to conceive of our own annihilation (Freud observed that the conscious ego cannot conceive of *not* existing) and by whatever we are taught or intuit about the existence of an afterlife. Although it is beyond the scope of this essay to describe thoroughly the series of personal rituals we use to help people engage their mythologies of death, the following overview of that program offers a framework for attuning yourself to the mythology you already have within you and a glimpse into the possibility of examining, evaluating, and altering it.

The program involves a five-stage process. Each stage has a specific purpose and corresponds with one of the natural phases by which we believe personal myths develop. In the preparatory phase of the program, participants first survey their mythology of death by writing a stream-of-consciousness "philosophy of death" report. They then examine their central concerns regarding death with techniques based on imagery and contemplation, using guided fantasy to take a journey back in time to some of their earliest memories regarding death, and also creating a "death shield" for symbolizing and keeping track of the discoveries they make about their relationship with death.

Having established this background, participants move into the first stage of the program, which is organized around the theme of "rattling" one's system of death denial. Work here is based on the assumption that some of the difficulties people have regarding death are closely related to repressed or unconscious fears. Thus, the personal rituals in this stage include "Opening Your Heart to Your Deeper Fears" (involving a visit to a person in a life-threatening circumstance), "The Fear of Death at Its Foundation" (involving an age regression to the source of some personal fears about death), and "Creating a Death Fable—'Death in the Shadow of Fear.'" The death fable depicts a poignant scene where the main character is dying and knows it. In this first death fable, the central figure, though perhaps of a different age, sex, or social standing, holds the same fears about death that the participant has identified in the earlier rituals. Set in another culture and not bound by the rules of ordinary logic, the death fable is a metaphorical device that is used to examine the fear of death and that speaks to both the particular and the universal, as well as to the conscious and the unconscious.

In the second stage of the program, participants search for counterforces to their fear of death, focusing particularly on the psyche's quest to find ways of transcending death—for example, attempts to achieve what Robert Jay Lifton has termed "symbolic immortality."[11] Lifton describes five modes for attempting to transcend death by achieving symbolic immortality. The first is "biological immortality," where one finds comfort in imagery of an endless genetic chain, linked to one's sons and daughters, their offspring, and on and on into eternity. Other modes of symbolic immortality include creative contributions that may live on in the world or through other people; identity with nature and comfort that one will merge again with the natural world after one's physical demise; comfort in specific concepts of life after death; and inner experiences that are "so intense and all-encompassing that time and space disappear [and there is] a sense of extraordinary psychic unity, and perceptual intensity, and of ineffable illumination and insight."

Personal rituals in this stage of the work include "Transcending the Fear of Death by Looking Fear in the Teeth" (in which participants examine the most troubling fears they identified earlier in the program, analyze them as components of their death anxiety, and devise steps they can take to approach them with understanding and a sense of mastery), "A View of 'Symbolic Mortality' through Sacred Time" (in which participants enter an altered state that brings them into sacred time—which is not of the clock but of the heart—as they examine and deepen their personal system of symbolic immortality), and "A Second Death Fable—'Death in the Light of Transcendence'" (in which the character depicted in the first death fable uses the same means for transcending the fear of death that the participant was exploring during the sacred-time ritual).

The third stage involves a confrontation between one's fear of death and one's images of death transcendence. Having examined in the first stage the mythology constructed around their instinctive fear of death, and having examined in the second stage the mythology that grew out of their natural impulse to find a way of transcending that fear, participants then bring these two mythic positions into a direct confrontation. The task at this stage, once the differences between both sides have been highlighted, is to facilitate a process of deep reconciliation in which the best of each mythology is integrated into the structure of the psyche and elevated into a new and more effective mythic image. Having embraced both sides of the conflict, images of integration become more possible. The individual is taught to recognize that facing deep inconsistencies in one's guiding mythology about death, without a retreat into one's fears of annihilation or a flight into one's hopes of transcendence, allows a richer mythology that is informed by the emotional and spiritual considerations on both sides of the issue.

In the fourth stage, "Toward a Renewed Mythology about Death," participants' newly synthesized mythologies are further articulated, expanded, and anchored. The mythic vision that was synthesized in the previous stage is now refined to the point where a commitment to that vision may be maturely entered. While it is sometimes necessary to allow the natural resolution of conflicting myths to simply take its course, consciously identifying with a judiciously cultivated mythic image can both shape and hasten the resolution.

The first personal ritual in this stage is called "Receiving Your Death Chant." Invoking the maximum sense of peace and integration that was associated with the resolution image attained in the previous stage of the program, participants enter an altered state in which they become receptive to a sound that symbolizes the feeling. Modeled after practices used by various Native American tribes, the death chant becomes a vehicle to transport participants to the deeper sources of awareness they have been developing about their eventual death. They are encouraged to use their death chant whenever they face threat, loss, or a need for healing.

In the next ritual, called "Personal Death Fable—Vision of a Good Death," unlike the previous death fables, the participants themselves are the main characters, and they formulate a vision of their own death. There is power in creating a thought form, and formulating a positive vision of death has a favorable effect on their anticipations and thus on their feelings about life as well. In the third ritual in this stage, "Your Philosophy of Death Revisited," participants review the philosophy of death written at the outset of the program and elaborate upon ways in which it has deepened or changed.

The task for participants during the fifth stage, "Bringing Your Renewed Mythology about Death into Life," is to realign the way they live in order to embody the wisdom of their new guiding mythology. This involves stepping out into the practical world and making changes at that level. The first ritual, "Attending to That Which Will Survive You," helps participants learn to be ready in an instant to let go of life in the physical world. Putting one's worldly affairs in order, from the perspective of a vital mythology about death, is a dynamic way of preparing for the inevitable, and attending to issues such as unfinished business, distributing personal belongings, preparing special messages for loved ones, and disposal of one's body determines the content of this ritual. The next ritual, "Creating Ceremony for the Final Hour and Beyond," involves a guided-imagery journey in which participants create a fantasy about their final hour, their funeral or memorial service, and their eulogy. Experiencing a positive fantasy of one's moment of death, along with vibrant guiding images, provides a sort of emotional inoculation against some of the irrational fears that attend thoughts of dying. The final ritual of the program, "Establishing a 'Right Relationship' with What You Do Between Now and Your Final Hour," is based on the way that living with the knowledge of one's mortality makes each moment more precious. Again, from an altered state of consciousness in which they open their hearts to the fact of death, participants consider the actions they might take that would establish a more fulfilling relationship with life and death.

In our work with personal mythologies, we have found that taking yourself on an inner journey in which you confront your deepest fears about death and excavate archetypal impulses toward death transcendence can have a number of benefits. "The dark background which death supplies," writes the philosopher George Santayana, "brings out the tender colors of life in all their purity." By squarely facing your mortality, you bring a new intensity to the life you have. A great irony, often observed by those who have had the privilege of knowing a person who has died well, involves the way in which the person came to participate fully in living. As death approaches, the dying person's attention often shifts and he or she begins to recognize and savor the preciousness of each breath, each color, each interaction. Often this involves opening to one's deeper nature and to qualities of existence that transcend individual identity. Whether or not traditional religious concepts are invoked as an explanation, people near death often experience a greater sense of purpose and connection with other people and the universe, and their highest emotions—love and the appreciation of beauty, truth, and justice—are stimulated. Those who have observed the peaceful and simple dignity that comes upon a person confronted with imminent death may wonder why we must wait until the final season to attain such grace.

Perhaps we do not. An impassioned exploration of one's mortality is a viable way of following the counsel of St. Thomas Aquinas: "Let death be thy teacher." The most powerful intentional way of exploring one's mortality is in deliberately induced psychological "death-rebirth" experiences. Stanislav and Christina Grof, in developing a new method of psychotherapy known as holotropic therapy, have described rites of passage throughout history and across cultures that provoke a sense of death and rebirth. Participants experience extremes of anguish, chaos, confusion, and liminality, emerging from the process of annihilation with a sense of rejuvenation and rebirth. The Grofs highlight the significance of such experiences in changing the individual's relationship with the certainty of death:

> The depth and intensity of the death-rebirth experience provide a dramatic framework for the termination of the old social role and the assumption of the new one. However, repeated encounters with annihilation followed by a sense of redefinition have another important function: They prepare the individual for eventual biological death by establishing a deep, almost cellular awareness that periods of destruction are those of transition rather than termination.[12]

Analogous experiences, often harking back to traditional rites of passage, are also available today through various "vision quest" outings and workshops on shamanic practices. A fervent exploration of one's mortality also often prompts a reexamination of one's beliefs regarding what happens following death. What, if anything, survives? For the first time, there is a growing body of data on how changing one's position on this question activates other changes in one's psychological life. For example, following a close brush with death, people often report having had so unmistakable an encounter with a "being of light" and with an afterlife that the existence of each is beyond question for them. This conclusion is independent of any prior religious or spiritual beliefs. They also frequently appreciate life and other people more, become less materialistic, less concerned with pleasing others, and more concerned with ultimate questions such as the meaning of life. These changes are often lasting. Perhaps most remarkably, they "enjoy an overwhelming increase in self-confidence, security, and self-esteem."[13]

In their critical review of the near-death experience, Gray Groth-Marnat and Jack F. Schumaker note: "Virtually all investigators agree that the NDE is likely to produce powerful short- and long-term changes in the person. One of the most frequently reported changes is a reduced fear of death and a more favorable view of life."[14] Raymond Moody states that in his twenty years of intense exposure to those who have had NDEs, "I have yet to find one who hasn't had a very deep and positive transformation as a result of [the experience]."[15] He goes on to note that "all of the scholars and clinicians I have talked to who have interviewed NDEers have come to the same conclusion: They are better people because of their experience." He claims that an NDE not only makes the individual more positive and pleasant to be around, it also "helps them grapple with the unpleasant aspects of reality in an unemotional and clear-thinking way." He lists the kinds of personal changes he has observed that contribute to "the luminous serenity present in so many NDEers": no fear of dying, sensing the importance of love, a sense of urgency about the shortness and fragility of life and about living in a world "where vast destructive powers are in the hands of mere humans," as well as a more highly developed spiritual side.

A principal consequence of NDEs, frequently reported, is that life takes on a different meaning when it is understood within the context of a larger story. One seeks to discover not only the local code for right action, but the code that is part of this bigger plan. The attitudinal changes that researchers have consistently identified following NDEs, discussed above, provide a phenomenological list of the emotional, cognitive, and spiritual changes associated with assuming an experience-based belief in an afterlife (as contrasted with either no such belief or a doctrine-based belief). This is perhaps the most intriguing data available pertaining to the question of the influence on one's life of a personal mythology regarding death.

In this essay, I have suggested that the mortality-immortality debate goes on within each of us; that one's conscious position on the question may conceal deeper conflict; that it is possible to bring this underlying dialectic into awareness and mindfully participate in it; and that there may be substantial psychological benefits in doing so.

Perhaps my parents' debate cannot ultimately be resolved from this side of mortality. Hamlet speaks of death as "the undiscovered country from whose bourn no traveler returns." But we are each compelled to address the issue, because our personal mythology of death provides the contour of our mythology of life, the purpose of life, and what is ultimately required of us.

GARY DOORE

Journeys to the Land of the Dead: Shamanism and Samadhi

Gary Doore, Ph.D., is a scholar of comparative philosophy and religion. He holds a doctorate from the University of Oxford and is the compiler and editor of Shaman's Path: Healing, Personal Growth, and Empowerment.

When Sri Ramana Maharshi, the legendary sage of South India, was sixteen years old, he had a visionary experience of death that changed his life. It happened one day in 1896 when he was sitting alone in an upstairs room in his uncle's house in Madurai. Although his health was excellent at the time, he suddenly experienced an overwhelming fear of death so intense that it began to produce the actual symptoms of death in his body. He describes the experience in this way:

> The shock of the fear of death drove my mind inwards and I said to myself mentally, without actually framing the words: "Now death has come; what does it mean? What is it that is dying? This body dies." And I at once dramatized the occurrence of death. I lay with my limbs stretched out stiff as though rigor mortis had set in and imitated a corpse so as to give greater reality to the enquiry. I held my breath and kept my lips tightly closed so that no sound could escape, so that neither the word "I" nor any other word could be uttered. "Well then," I said to myself, "this body is dead. It will be carried stiff to the burning ground and there burnt and reduced to ashes. But with the death of this body am I dead? Is the body "I"? It is silent and inert, but I feel the full force of my personality and even the voice of the "I" within me, apart from it. So I am Spirit transcending the body. The body dies, but the Spirit that transcends it cannot be touched by death.[1]

Of course, many people have felt from time to time that they are more than the body. But in Sri Ramana's case, the feeling was so intense that it propelled him into a state of deep *samadhi*, or yogic trance, in which he became directly aware of his fundamental identity with Universal Consciousness. Unlike most people who experience such an awareness, however, Sri Ramana remained in it for the rest of his life:

> All this was not dull thought; it flashed through me vividly as living truth which I perceived directly, almost without thought process. "I" was something very real, the only real thing about my present state, and all the conscious activity connected with my body was centered on that "I." From that moment onwards the "I" or Self focused attention on itself by a powerful fascination. Fear of death had vanished once and for all. Absorption in the Self continued unbroken from that time on. Other thoughts might come and go like the various notes of music, but the "I" continued. . . . Whether the body was engaged in talking, reading, or anything else, I was still centered on "I."[2]

Sri Ramana apparently knew intuitively that it is impossible to escape the fear of death by fleeing from it. Thus he decided to face the object of his dread squarely, accept it, and relax into it. And because the fear of death is the root of all other fears, by accepting death he acquired an unshakable fearlessness in all situations.

Probably everyone would like to be able to overcome the fear of death with the same apparent ease as Sri Ramana. Yet there is a practical problem here: It is very difficult to "accept" or "relax into" one's own inevitable death unless one can imagine very vividly what death will be like. Not everyone, however, has the ability of a Sri Ramana to conjure up a realistic vision of death. Even after reading or hearing about near-death experiences, altered states of consciousness, bardos, and so forth, we still find it impossible to visualize the experience of death in a convincing way. Why? Different schools of thought suggest different answers.

According to yoga, for example, we have all been incarnated in numerous bodies before this present one; hence, we have all undergone the experience of death many times in the past. But, say the yogis, death is so traumatic, and in many cases the visionary phenomena encountered in the bardos, or after-death states, are so terrifying, that we repress our memories of them very deeply, so that they are now virtually inaccessible without the use of certain special meditative methods. Yet, ironically, only by encountering this repressed knowledge and coming face-to-face with the experience of death—and our fear of it—can we be fully alive.

Yoga is not the only spiritual tradition in which initiates are forced into a confrontation with death. There is an even more ancient path—that of the shaman—in which visionary "death and rebirth" experiences are the key to spiritual awakening. In shamanic initiation, the initiate often has visions of his or her body being dismembered by wolves or other predatory animals, or in some other way experiences the dissolution of the physical frame. Yet even after the body is gone—pulverized or torn apart and scattered to the farthest limits of the universe—the shaman finds that the core of consciousness, the deepest sense of self (referred to by Sri Ramana as *the Self*), is still intact. Then the realization "My body is gone, but *I* still exist; therefore *I* am not the body" is brought home in the most forceful way. Detachment and victory over the fear of death are born. Thus the shaman earns the title "master of death."

Although the shamanic tradition has all but died out in the West, traces of the shamanic knowledge of death can be found in the Western philosophical tradition. When Socrates said, "The unexamined life is not worth living," he was referring, at least in part, to our unexamined fear of death. In dialogues such as the *Phaedo*, we find Socrates to be a man who has met and conquered his own fear of death and is acting as a "midwife" to help others give birth to their own fearlessness. But it is clear from the historical record that both Socrates and Plato were members of the Orphic-Pythagorean mystery schools, a shamanic secret society that apparently used a potent psychedelic to induce the death-rebirth experience.

Samadhi and the Shamanic Journey

From descriptions of the shamanic initiation journey and the stages of *samadhi* in yoga, it is clear that both shamans and yogis visit the same inner dimensions in their mystical "trances," but that they describe it in different terms. It is also apparent that both the shamanic journey and yogic *samadhi* are strikingly similar to reports of near-death experiences.

Whether through yogic meditation, shamanic drumming, or the

use of sacred mind-altering plants, the candidate for knowledge is brought face-to-face with the experience of death and the states of consciousness that appear immediately after death. Sometimes this experience may be an actual close encounter with death, as in those cases in which a man or woman becomes a shaman after a serious illness; in other cases, the initiatory experience may be controlled by an experienced elder shaman or guru who may use any of a variety of techniques to bring about a non–life-threatening visionary "simulation" of the death experience. In rare cases, such as that of Sri Ramana, the "close simulation" type of experience may occur spontaneously, without deliberate intent or supervision (although it is of course possible to speculate about "unseen guidance" from a spiritual dimension even in these instances).

In shamanism, the means to induce the visionary death experience may include fasting, isolation in the wilderness, power plants, or rhythmic percussive sound—shamanic drumming. In yoga, one also finds the use of rhythmic perceptual phenomena, such as mantras, chanting, visualization of pulsating or rotating inner lights, perception of subtle inner sounds, and so forth. In both cases, as consciousness is "entrained," or fixated, by these methods, the initiate sinks deeper and deeper into a trance and thereby discovers a new dimension of reality—an "other world" inhabited by spiritual entities where the distinction between the dead and the living becomes blurred.[3]

As the shamanic or yogic initiatory journey unfolds and the realm of death seems to be approaching closer and closer, inner experience becomes more intense and vibrant, as the life force of the body is withdrawn from all the lower organs and limbs and becomes concentrated in the brain, thus increasing one's powers of perception—especially the inner perception of psychophysical states. In tantric yoga, this experience is referred to as the ascent of the serpentine *kundalini* energy at the base of the spine, traveling up the center of the spinal column (the *sushumna*) to the "thousand-petaled lotus," or crown chakra, in the center of the brain. In shamanism, too, representations of serpentine forms within the shaman's body are common motifs, as are images of the "World Tree," or "Tree of Life," which is an apt representation of the spinal column and nervous system through which the life force ascends to "heaven," located above the top of the tree—that is, at the top of the brain. (Often, especially in Siberia, the shaman draws a Tree of Life on the front or back of his body, or on the clothing covering it, corresponding with the physical location of the spinal column.)

Eventually, the overwhelming current of life force into the brain triggers the mind's imaginative faculties, producing visionary phenomena that blot out external reality altogether and throw the initiate abruptly into a totally different reality. At this stage, external time seems to slow down, whereas internal time may seem to be vastly accelerating, often producing a "panoramic memory" of the events of one's life. As awareness expands still further, breathing slows down and may finally seem to stop altogether, thus mimicking the physical symptoms of death. The pulse may race wildly for a while, then slow down to a rate characteristic of deep sleep, or even become imperceptible, as in actual physical death. The neophyte may also have a sense of falling or of levitating toward a bright light, often through a dark tunnel and often accompanied by a feeling that the soul is separating from the entranced physical body. (It is interesting that both shamanism and yoga recognize "magical flight," referred to in yoga as the *siddhi,* or yogic power, of "skygoing.")

After passing through the lower stages of trance, in which one may encounter demonic or angelic forces or entities, the shamanic or yogic initiate finally reaches the deepest levels of trance, known in yoga as *nirbija samadhi,* a realm of pure interiority, or "nonobjective" awareness in which consciousness alone remains, beyond all distinctions of subject and object. In shamanism this stage may be symbolized as "dismemberment" by wolves or other predatory animals, symbolic of the destruction of ego and the dawning of nondual consciousness—the perception of the fundamental unity of all existence. In the Tibetan Book of the Dead (which, like much of Tibetan Buddhism, is heavily influenced by shamanism), such ego-death and entrance into nondual consciousness is referred to as merging with the clear-light void, the primal Nothingness from which the realms of conditional existence are said to be born.

This "undifferentiated" state of consciousness is the last stage prior to "rebirth." It is not the ultimate phase of the candidate's otherworldly journey, however, because it is still an *introvertive* trance in which there is no awareness of or ability to function in the external world of ordinary reality. "Rebirth," as the final stage, involves a putting back together, humpty-dumpty-like, of the initiate's worldly personality, forming a new arrangement capable of maintaining a connection between the worlds of ordinary and nonordinary reality.[4]

At this stage the shaman's psychic abilities and the higher *siddhis,* or spiritual faculties, of the yogi emerge—the magical powers that make the shamanic or yogic adept into a healer and holy person. Yet the greatest of these powers is said to be the firm establishment, in ordinary life, of nondual awareness—a continuous perception of the oneness and interconnectedness of all things, transcending all sense of separateness.

In this last, integrative phase, shamanic or yogic enlightenment is "brought down," as it were, from the inaccessible realms of nonobjective consciousness in "the beyond" and grounded in the mundane world of ordinary reality. It is the stage of "active *samadhi*" for the yogi, of realizing samsara in nirvana for the tantric Buddhist, and of becoming a true healer for the shaman. Because only when the shaman or yogi is healed of the most serious and fundamental illness—the illusion of separateness, which is the root of all other psychophysical diseases—is he or she capable of helping others to heal themselves.

Fear of Death and Global Healing

But what do these unusual states of consciousness have to do with the ordinary person who is not a shaman or yogi and who has never had a near-death or out-of-body experience? Just this: For millennia, most human beings have chosen *not* to confront and explore the realms of death and after-death experience, preferring to leave such frightening investigations to a small, secret elite of shamans, yogis, and other mystical specialists. But this strategy, while perhaps giving temporary comfort in the short run, has had one great drawback: By repressing a fear, one becomes driven unconsciously by its energy and is therefore prone to outbursts of irrational and uncontrollable behavior. When the majority of human beings in the world are subject to such unconscious drives, the result is an extremely dangerous situation—a global village of violent and aggressive individuals, which is poised on the brink of self-annihilation.

Thus it is appropriate that shamanism and yoga are today becoming "democratized" and made available not only to a small clique of specialists but to anyone who is willing to undertake the necessary training and discipline to partake of the previously secret knowledge. For it seems evident that the self-destructive tendency of modern Western society can be reversed only if large numbers of people somehow undergo a radical change of consciousness. Unless the average person gains access to the kind of direct spiritual knowledge and experience made possible through the methods of shamanism, yoga, and other mystical "technologies of consciousness," such a reversal will never occur and our race may be headed for extinction, along with millions of other species currently threatened by our destructive modern lifestyle.

Hence, it is no longer sufficient merely to hire a shaman or other specialist to "heal" us when we become ill, or to assist us when we are in the process of dying. Mother Earth herself appears to be edging closer to the brink of death, or perhaps to an initiatory near-death experience on a global scale, and each of us needs to acquire the knowledge necessary to assist her in this ordeal. To do so, we must learn to "die before we die," exploring the death and rebirth experience and confronting our own fear of death directly, thus practicing *philosophia* in the original Socratic sense of "preparation for death"—at least if we wish to do more than pay lip service to the ideal of global healing.

Perhaps the explosion of interest in psychedelics and altered states of consciousness in the 1960s was an indication of the planetary need for masses of people to investigate the realms of inner space. As became evident from the drug culture of that era, however, the path of chemically induced mystical experience is strewn with pitfalls. No doubt we need a new Western mystical tradition, with appropriate rites of passage and initiations allowing for the healing experiences of death and rebirth; but this tradition must be developed responsibly, so that such experiences can be induced and integrated in safe ways.

This points to a need for more research on the phenomena of shamanic drumming, meditation, altered states of consciousness, yogic breathing, visualization, and other mind-altering techniques ancient and modern. But, perhaps most of all, we need a new attitude toward things spiritual, toward those aspects of reality that pertain to consciousness and spirit—an attitude in which those who take an interest in such matters will not be relegated to a lunatic fringe beyond the pale of official science and polite society.

Epilogue:
What Should We Believe?

In the preceding pages we examined evidence from a number of different fields that *suggests* that consciousness, in some form or other, survives the death of the body. Although much of this evidence is impressive, most reasonable people, and certainly most scientists, would probably still agree that the case for survival cannot be considered "proven" according to strict scientific standards. Of course, this fact will not bother those readers who agree with Ken Wilber that the immortality of the soul is a *contemplative* hypothesis, to be tested with the "eye of contemplation," not a *scientific* hypothesis to be tested with the "eye of reason." Yet those who think that survival might be scientifically testable (as many parapsychologists believe) must be sobered by the fact that, as Arthur S. Berger pointed out, parapsychological researchers have been trying for years, without success, to produce a scientifically valid test of survival. The most that parapsychology has shown so far, as Charles T. Tart noted, is that, contrary to the materialists' claim, survival is *not impossible in principle.* But to prove that survival is not impossible is a long way from proving that it actually occurs.

The upshot of this exploration, therefore, seems to be that the issue between the survivalists and materialists is, from a scientific perspective, a standoff—that is, the evidence and arguments on both sides of the question must be regarded by a reasonable person as inconclusive.

Given this premise, an interesting question is whether we are justified in *believing* in an afterlife. In other words, are we being irrational if we still believe that we will have a life after death, even though there is no conclusive evidence that it exists? Or, on the contrary, is it more rational to remain agnostic—to suspend judgment and refrain from either believing or disbelieving?

An agnostic can make a strong case for his position at this point: If the evidence is in fact inconclusive, why should we jump to any conclusions, one way or the other? Why should we believe something until there is enough evidence to prove it? Indeed, some scientifically minded thinkers have gone so far as to suggest that it would be *morally wrong* to believe in a life after death—or, indeed, any other hypothesis—without sufficient evidence for its truth. For example, W. K. Clifford, a famous nineteenth-century rationalist, maintained that "it is wrong always, everywhere, and for everyone, to believe *anything* upon insufficient evidence."[1] If this view is correct, then agnosticism about life after death is not only justifiable, it is somehow morally necessary.

Proof or Consequences?

The principle that we should never believe anything without sufficient evidence for its truth (which I will refer to as the Rationalistic Principle) is extremely widespread among contemporary scientists and philosophers—a hallmark of the "tough-minded" attitude toward matters of belief on which scientific thinkers pride themselves. And no doubt it *is* a virtue for a scientist or scholar to refrain from being excessively credulous. But does the Rationalistic Principle apply to *all* kinds of beliefs? Should we *always* wait for sufficient evidence before we believe *anything*?

It seems not. Indeed, there are a large number of beliefs that we routinely hold—and rightly so—without sufficient evidence for their truth. Many of these beliefs fall in the category of "giving a person the benefit of the doubt." For instance, consider the belief that your spouse (lover) is being faithful to you. It seems clear that if you habitually refuse to hold this belief without "sufficient evidence" for its truth, your relationship is not going to last very long. In this case, as in other cases of giving a person the benefit of the doubt, it is *not* true that we should wait until all the evidence is in before we believe. In these types of cases, to demand "sufficient evidence"—proof "beyond reasonable doubt"—would lead to unnecessary tension, ill feelings, and broken relationships; hence, it is better to settle for *less* evidence than would prove the issue by scientific standards.

These kinds of cases point to the fact that "evidence" is not always the only thing we need to consider when deciding whether to believe or not believe something. Sometimes the *consequences* of believing need to be taken into account as well. Of course, when we are considering a purely "academic" or scientific question, where we can afford to wait for more evidence and where the consequences of believing are not likely to be of any moral or spiritual significance, then it is no doubt more prudent and wiser to remain agnostic. But not all questions in life are purely academic or scientific.

The Consequences of Worldviews

If we consider the matter carefully, we may well conclude that the issue of whether we should accept a materialistic worldview is *not* purely academic or scientific. Consider, for example, the following formulation of what we might call the Materialist's Creed, as expressed in a famous passage by the philosopher Bertrand Russell:

> That man is the product of causes which had no prevision of the end they were achieving; that his origin, his growth, his hopes and fears are but the outcome of accidental collocations of atoms; that no fire, no heroism, no intensity of thought and feeling can preserve an individual life beyond the grave; that all the labors of the ages, all the devotion, all the inspiration, all the noonday brightness of human genius are destined to extinction in the vast death of the solar system, and that the whole temple of man's achievement must inevitably be buried beneath the debris of a universe in ruins—all these things, if not quite beyond dispute, are yet so nearly certain, that no philosophy which rejects them can hope to stand. Only within the scaffolding of these truths, only on the firm foundation of unyielding despair, can the soul's habitation henceforth be safely built.[2]

Although I respect Russell's stature as a philosopher, I cannot help thinking that he is wrong here. As we have seen from the essays in this book, the case for the materialistic worldview he espouses in this (rather rhetorical) passage is not as "nearly certain" as he would have us believe. Indeed, I have argued that the issue seems to be at a standoff, with the case being far from conclusive on either side. Hence if we are to choose what worldview is most reasonable to hold, we must find some grounds *other than evidence* for our choice. I have suggested that we might look for such grounds in the consequences of holding the worldviews in question. How does the materialistic position fare according to this criterion?

It seems clear that the philosophy voiced above by Russell leads to despair, hopelessness, and a loss of meaning in life. In order to live our lives well, we need to believe in the sense and purposefulness of the universe. Even if we cannot find enough evidence to prove it "beyond reasonable doubt," we have a need to feel that the cosmos we inhabit is not merely a chance configuration of dead material particles that accidentally gave rise to life and mind, but that it is an arena for the evolution of consciousness and spirit—a place where our individual efforts can make a difference toward the realization of some kind of summum bonum, or highest good.

Some people conceive of a highest good in terms of a community of supremely happy, morally and spiritually perfected individuals, as in the Christian notion of heaven; others tend to think in terms of enlightenment, a state of supreme spiritual freedom characterized by an awareness of one's identity with the perfect being, consciousness, and bliss of the Absolute, as in Eastern spiritual traditions. (I have argued elsewhere that these two notions of a highest good are compatible.[3]) But however we conceive it, there is no doubt that the notion of a highest good, as a state of being toward which our own efforts can contribute, is a potent energizing force in the moral and spiritual dimensions of our lives.

For example, the ideal of a highest good in the perennial philosophy rests on the doctrines of reincarnation and spiritual evolution—and these doctrines are definitely energizing and uplifting factors in the lives of many people. One reason is that those who accept these ideas are inspired with an altruistic hope—namely, the hope of gradual spiritual development through the course of many lives, which in turn will allow them to become more spiritually beneficial to other people. Indeed, according to the doctrines in question, it is possible for a spiritual practitioner to eventually become a coworker of the great sages and seers who have contributed most to the enlightenment of the human race. Hence, believers tend to set themselves very high standards of personal conduct and aspiration, which in turn enables them to endure great hardships and suffering for the sake of the ideal—in short, to meet life's trials and temptations with much more patience, courage, and strength than would be possible if they were content merely to consider the hypotheses of reincarnation and spiritual evolution from an agnostic standpoint.

If we adopt the materialistic worldview, however, we are forced to the conclusion that all our ideas of a highest good are mere pipe dreams, nothing but products of wishful thinking, with no basis in reality. For if the soul perishes with the body, all our efforts to develop ourselves morally and spiritually must be regarded as ultimately in vain. Thereby we become dispirited and demoralized— that is, our moral and spiritual endeavors tend to lose much of their force and vitality and are robbed of their greatest potential transformative power. And this loss of vitality occurs even if we merely remain cooly agnostic, because the inner fires of spiritual inspiration and strength are fanned only by a positive, optimistic confidence in the ultimate purposefulness and goodness of the universe.

The Question of Self-Deception

"Yes, yes," the skeptic will say, "but without sufficient grounds for their 'uplifting' beliefs, aren't believers just being intellectually dishonest? Aren't they involved in a type of self-deception?"

Not necessarily. Clearly, belief in an afterlife does not imply self-deception in the sense of trying to conceal the truth from oneself. For, in these cases, we are supposing that *the truth is not known.* (Indeed, that is why the rationalist urges agnosticism.) If the truth were known, we should obviously believe what we know to be true.

"Very well," our skeptic may reply, "but self-deception doesn't necessarily involve straightforward lying to oneself. It might be instead more like a long campaign of subtle conditioning or brainwashing in which you ignore or discount all the evidence against your belief and concentrate only on finding evidence that will support it. And that's still a kind of intellectual dishonesty. Or, at least, it would tend to prejudice an objective inquiry into truth."

The answer to this objection is that, instead of ignoring or discounting whatever negative evidence may exist, a person can merely put it to one side, "bracket it" for the time being, still recognizing it for what it is, but persisting in his or her faith that there is some explanation that will eventually turn up to account for it. Is this unscientific? Not at all: It is precisely what a scientist does when testing a scientific hypothesis. In fact, virtually all scientists and scholars are "prejudiced" to some extent in favor of one or more theories or schools of thought on their subject. But this type of "prejudice" is actually a good thing for scientific and scholarly research. For if researchers were ready to drop their favored theories at the first sight of incompatible evidence, they would thereby lose the incentive to seek further for more confirming evidence, and thus many good theories would be abandoned and lost through "lack of faith." Hence, not only do scientists and scholars need and exhibit a kind of "faith," it is also quite reasonable for them to do so.[4]

We may conclude, then, that even if the evidence for survival is inconclusive by scientific standards, we are still acting rationally if we choose to believe in an afterlife for the purpose of "testing" that belief in our lives, and are also being reasonable to adhere to it with considerable determination, even in the face of negative evidence or personal doubts, just as a scientist is being reasonable when adhering to a favored theory while testing it in the laboratory.

The Experimental Approach to Spiritual Truth

The attitude we have been discussing might well be called the "experimental" approach to spiritual truth. (WIlliam James called it the "pragmatic" approach.) Note that calling it an "approach" implies that one does not yet *know* the truth, but is seeking to discover, or at least come closer to, the truth.

This standpoint is, of course, far removed from the dogmatic position often taken by institutionalized religions. Yet it is not entirely foreign to all of the world's great spiritual traditions. It can be found, for example, in the Yoga Sutras of Patanjali and in the scriptures of early Buddhism. Indeed, the Buddha insisted that his followers examine and *test* practically the doctrines that he taught, and that they reject any they might find to be unreasonable or personally useless. The Kalama Sutta makes this quite clear:

> Do not believe on the strength of traditions, even if they have been held in honor for many generations and in many places; do not believe anything because many people speak of it; do not believe on the strength of sages of old times; do not believe that which you have yourselves imagined, thinking that a god has inspired you. Believe nothing which depends only on the authority of your masters and priests. After investigation, believe that which you have yourselves tested and found reasonable and which is for your good and that of others.

In this statement we see a clear expression of the "experimental" attitude toward spiritual truth. Here the Buddha advises his followers to believe "after investigation" only that which they themselves have "tested" (that is, by personal experimentation), "found reasonable," and which is "for their good and that of others." Thus, he urges that they should not only consider the *evidence* for the truth of his doctrines (although that is certainly part of what they should consider), but also weigh the *practical consequences* of believing those doctrines.

This advice is equally valid when applied to the question of whether we are justified in believing in an afterlife. If the evidence both for and against the survival hypothesis is truly inconclusive; if we must therefore decide whether to believe or not believe on the basis of the consequences of our belief or nonbelief; and if believing makes us stronger, more courageous, more enduring for difficulties and setbacks, less prone to defeat and despair than would be the case if we adopted either agnosticism or materialism—then these are legitimate grounds for choosing to hold the belief as a working hypothesis on the basis of which to live and to pursue a spiritual discipline through which we may eventually acquire the type of direct "contemplative evidence" mentioned by Ken Wilber, which will give us final certainty.

As the philosopher William James pointed out in his essay "The Will to Believe," in order to establish a friendship with another person, we must first *trust* that person more than is warranted by any evidence we have about his or her trustworthiness. For without such a preliminary act of trust, the relationship can never get started, and we will therefore never have the opportunity to gather any evidence one way or the other. Similarly, in order to test the hypothesis of survival and see whether it is beneficial in our lives, we must first "trust the universe," so to speak, which means trusting that the universe is basically good; that it is indeed a purposeful arena for the unfoldment of consciousness and spirit; that it is a place where our moral and spiritual efforts are not in vain because the results of those efforts—the growth of our soul in virtue and wisdom—continue beyond the death of the soul's temporary physical habitation. Without such a preliminary trust, we will never have the incentive and energy to undertake the spiritual discipline necessary to contemplatively verify the soul's immortality in a personally convincing way.

Notes

Introduction
1. R. Moody, *Life after Life* (New York: Bantam, 1975).
2. See G. Doore, ed., *Shaman's Path: Healing, Personal Growth, and Empowerment* (Boston: Shambhala, 1988), part 1, for more detailed definitions and discussions of shamanism.

Grof/Survival after Death
1. This chapter is based on a longer essay, "Survival of Consciousness after Death: Myth and Science" in John S. Spong, ed., *Consciousness and Survival: An Interdisciplinary Inquiry into the Possibility of Life beyond Biological Death* (Sausalito, Calif.: Institute of Noetic Sciences, 1987).
2. See S. Grof, "The Shamanic Journey: Observations from Holotropic Therapy," in *Shaman's Path: Healing, Personal Growth, and Empowerment*, ed. G. Doore (Boston: Shambhala, 1988), pp. 161–75.
3. R. Moody, *Life after Life* (Atlanta: Mockingbird Books, 1975); *Reflections on Life after Life* (Atlanta: Mockingbird Books, 1977).
4. K. Ring, *Life at Death* (New York: Coward, McCann & Geoghegan, 1980); *Heading toward Omega* (New York: William Morrow, 1984).
5. M. Sabom, *Recollections of Death* (New York: Harper & Row, 1982).
6. E. Kübler-Ross, "Death: The Final Stage of Growth," presentation at the Ninth Annual Conference of the International Transpersonal Association (Kyoto, Japan, April 1985).
7. S. Grof, *Beyond the Brain: Birth, Death, and Transcendence in Psychotherapy* (Albany, N.Y.: SUNY Press, 1985).
8. C. T. Tart, "Out-of-the-Body Experiences," in *Psychic Explorations*, ed. E. Mitchell and J. White (New York: Putnam's, 1974).
9. See S. Grof, *Realms of the Human Unconscious: Observations from LSD Research* (New York: Dutton, 1976), pp. 57–60.

Almeder/On Reincarnation
1. I. Stevenson, *Twenty Cases Suggestive of Reincarnation*, 2nd ed. (Charlottesville: University of Virginia Press, 1974).
2. For the details of this case, see I. Stevenson, *Cases of the Reincarnation Type*, vol. 1: "The Case of Bishen Chand Kapoor" (Charlottesville: University of Virginia Press, 1976), pp. 176 ff.
3. For the details of this case, see Stevenson, *Twenty Cases*.
4. Ibid., pp. 80–83.
5. I. Stevenson, *Xenoglossy* (Charlottesville: University of Virginia Press, 1976).

6. Stevenson, *Twenty Cases.*
7. P. Edwards, "The Case Against Reincarnation," *Free Inquiry,* June 1987, p. 26. Emphasis added.
8. I. Wilson, *Mind Out of Time* (London: Victor Gollancz, 1981), pp. 58–60.
9. C. T. K. Chari, "Reincarnation Research: Method and Interpretation," in *Signet Handbook of Parapsychology,* ed. M. Ebom, (New York: New American Library, 1978), p. 319.

Berger/Tests for Communication with the Dead

1. A. Spraggett, with W. V. Rauscher, *Arthur Ford: The Man Who Talked with the Dead* (New York: New American Library, 1973).
2. A. S. Berger, *Lives and Letters in American Parapsychology: A Biographical History, 1850–1987* (Jefferson, N.C., and London: McFarland, 1988).
3. F. W. H. Myers, *Human Personality and Its Survival of Bodily Death* (London: Longmans, Green, 1903), vol. 2.
4. "Opening of an Envelope Containing a Posthumous Note Left by Mr. Myers," *Journal of the Society for Psychical Research* 12 (1905), pp. 11–13.
5. W. H. Salter, "F. W. H. Myers's Posthumous Message," *Proceedings of the Society for Psychical Research* 52, pp. 1–32.
6. R. H. Thouless, "A Test for Survival," *Proceedings of the Society for Psychical Research* 48, pp. 253–63.
7. A. S. Berger, "Foreword: A Tribute to Robert H. Thouless," in *Advances in Parapsychological Research* 4, ed. S. Krippner (Jefferson, N.C., and London: McFarland, 1984).
8. I. Stevenson, "The Combination Lock Test for Survival," *Journal of the American Society for Psychical Research* 62 (1968), pp. 246–54.
9. I. Stevenson, "Further Observations on the Combination Lock Test," *Journal of the American Society for Psychical Research* 70 (1976), pp. 219–29.
10. A. S. Berger, "Experiments with False Keys," *Journal of the American Society for Psychical Research* 78 (1984), p. 41.
11. Ibid.
12. A. Flew, "Foreword," in A. S. Berger, *Aristocracy of the Dead: New Findings in Postmortem Survival* (Jefferson, N.C., and London: McFarland, 1987).
13. Berger, *Lives and Letters.*
14. G. Murphy, "Body-Mind Theory as a Factor Guiding Survival Research," *Journal of the American Society for Psychical Research* 59 (1965), pp. 148–56.
15. A. S. Berger et al., "A Majority Vote to Open the Pratt Lock," in *Research in Parapsychology* 1980, ed. W. Roll and J. Beloff (Metuchen, N.J., and London: Scarecrow Press, 1981), p. 102.
16. R. Hodgson, "A Further Record of Observations of Certain Phenomena of Trance," *Proceedings of the Society for Psychical Research* 13 (1898), pp. 284–582.
17. Berger, *Aristocracy of the Dead.*
18. Ibid., p. 149.
19. Ibid.

Greene and Krippner/Panoramic Vision

1. R. Moody, *Life after Life* (New York: Bantam, 1975); "Notice of Rear-Admiral Sir Francis Beaufort," *London Daily News,* January 15, 1858; K. Ring, *Life at Death* (New York: Coward, McCann & Geoghegan, 1980); F. G. Green, "A Glimpse Behind the Life Review," *Journal of Religion and Psychical Research* 4, no. 2 (1981), pp. 113–30; F. G. Green, "Accelerated Cerebration: An Integrated View of Mysticism, Creativity, and ESP," *The Academy of Religion and Psychical Research 1984 Annual Conference Proceedings,* 1984, pp. 61–72; Nucgaek Sabinm, *Recollections of Death* (New York: Harper & Row, 1982).

2. S. K. Wilson, *Modern Problems in Neurology* (London: Arnold, 1928).
3. S. Grof and J. Halifax, *The Human Encounter with Death* (New York: E. P. Dutton, 1977).
4. W. Gerhard, *Resurrection* (London: Cassell, 1934).
5. R. Noyes, Jr., and R. Kletti, "Panoramic Memory: A Response to the Threat of Death," *Omega*, 1982, pp. 181–94.
6. Moody, *Life after Life*, pp. 64–65.
7. K. Ring, *Heading toward Omega* (New York: William Morrow, 1984), p. 186.
8. Johann Christop Hampe, *To Die Is Gain* (Atlanta: John Knox, 1979).
9. Ring, *Heading toward Omega*; Ring, "Prophetic Visions in 1988: A Critical Reappraisal," *Journal of Near-Death Studies* (formerly *Anabiosis*) 7, no. 1 (1988).
10. M. Sabom, *Recollections of Death* (New York: Harper & Row, 1982).
11. G. W. Gallup, Jr., and W. Proctor, *Adventures in Immortality* (New York: McGraw-Hill, 1982), p. 32.
12. Noyes and Kletti, "Panoramic Memory," pp. 181–94.
13. A. Heim, "Notizen über den Tod durch Absturz," *Jahrbuch des Schweizer Alpenklub*.
14. Wilson, *Modern Problems in Neurology*.
15. W. Penfield, *The Mystery of the Mind* (Princeton, N.J.: Princeton University Press, 1975).
16. D. Stacy, "Transcending Science," *Omni* 11, no. 3 (1988), pp. 54–56, 60, 114–16.
17. D. Carr, "Pathophysiology of Stress-induced Limbic Lobe Dysfunction: A Hypothesis Relevant to Near-Death Experiences," *Anabiosis* 2 (1982), pp. 75–89.
18. Hampe, *To Die Is Gain*.
19. Noyes and Kletti, "Panoramic Memory," pp. 181–94.
20. Ibid., p. 189.
21. Ibid., p. 190.
22. H. Hart, *The Enigma of Survival* (Springfield, Ill.: Charles C. Thomas, 1959).
23. Grof and Halifax, *The Human Encounter with Death*.
24. Ring, *Life at Death*.
25. M. Grosso, *The Final Choice* (Walpole, N.H.: Stillpoint Press, 1985).
26. S. F. G. Brandon, *The Judgment of the Dead* (London: Weidenfeld & Nicolson, 1967).
27. 1 Cor. 11–13.

Rogo/Spontaneous Contact with the Dead

1. UPI, May 30, 1970.
2. Reported in the *Proceedings of the Society for Psychical Research* 36 (1927), pp. 517–24.
3. C. Oyler, *Heading toward the Light* (New York: Harper & Row, 1988).
4. E. Gurney, F. W. H. Myers, and F. Podmore, *Phantasms of the Living* (London: Trubner's, 1886).
5. F. W. H. Myers, "On Indications of Continued Terrene Knowledge on the Part of Phantasms of the Dead," *Proceedings of the Society for Psychical Research* 8 (1892), pp. 170–252.
6. Prof. Sidgwick's Committee, "Report on the Census of Hallucinations," *Proceedings of the Society for Psychical Research* 10 (1894), pp. 25–422.
7. Bereavement counseling is short-term psychotherapy for people recovering from the loss of a friend or relative. It is designed to offer support during the first phases of bereavement and to help people who cannot resolve their grief.
8. P. Morris, *Widows and Their Families* (London: Routledge & Kegan Paul, 1958).
9. J. Yamamoto et al., "Mourning in Japan," *American Journal of Psychiatry* 125 (1969), pp. 1660–65.

14. H. Bergson, *Matter and Memory* (New York: Zone Books, 1988).
15. B. Russell, *The Analysis of Mind* (London: George Allen & Unwin, 1921).
16. C. D. Broad, *The Mind and Its Place in Nature* (London: Routledge & Kegan Paul, 1925).

Woodhouse/ Beyond Dualism and Materialism

1. I have been greatly inspired by Ken Wilber's extensive writing on the perennial philosophy, especially the principle of hierarchical interpenetration. See K. Wilber, *The Spectrum of Consciousness* (Wheaton, Ill.: Theosophical Publishing House, 1977), and K. Wilber, "Physics, Mysticism, and the New Holographic Paradigm," *ReVision* 2 (1979). Wilber, of course, would not necessarily agree with my reading or application of the perennial wisdom.

2. D. Bohm, "Of Matter and Meaning: The Super-Implicate Order" (interview with Renée Weber), *ReVision,* Spring 1983, p. 34.

3. Quoted in M. Capek, *The Philosophical Impact of Contemporary Physics* (New York: Van Nostrand, 1961), p. 319.

4. H. Weyl, *Philosophy of Mathematics and Natural Science* (Princeton, N.J.: Princeton University Press, 1949), p. 171.

5. N. Herbert, "How Large is Starlight? A Brief Look at Quantum Reality," *ReVision,* Summer 1987, p. 32.

6. E. Schroedinger, *Science, Theory, and Man* (New York: Dover Publications, 1967), p. 59.

7. For extensive examples of intelligent self-organization in nature, see L. Watson, *Lifetide* (New York: Simon & Schuster, 1979).

8. This emphasis appears to beg the issue against Buddhist forms of meditation, which stress the arising and ceasing of "event-moments." While I cannot argue the case here, I would suggest that the event-moments in fact do not arise from a vacuum and that the void is a plenitude that never becomes detached from the events to which it gives rise. Consequently, the emphasis upon discreteness, while powerfully effective from a transformational point of view, is nonetheless consistent with understanding such discreteness to be an abstraction from a deeper vibratory point of view—the tip of a larger wave form.

9. This argument is also developed in M. B. Woodhouse, "Near-Death Experiences and the Mind-Body Problem," *Anabiosis* 1, no. 1 (1981).

10. For a brief review of related attempts, see C. Alvarado, "The Physical Detection of the Astral Body," *Theta* 8 (1980).

11. For a useful review, see S. Krippner and D. Rubin, *The Kirlian Aura* (Garden City, N.Y.: Anchor Books, 1974). The weakness of the auric interpretation of Kirlian photographs is that it does not account for the many physical variables that affect the outcome (voltage, moisture, etc.) or for the fact that Kirlian images do not appear in a vacuum. The weakness of the coronal-discharge interpretation is that it does not account for the "phantom leaf" effect or for the correlation of distinctive images with various diseases and psychological states. Energy Monism avoids both of these shortcomings. By its interpretation, the Kirlian image is a gestalt that emerges from the *interaction* of electrical and auric fields. The image itself is neither just an aura nor just an electrical field; it is neither merely physical nor merely nonphysical. Should a clear picture of a spirit leaving a body ever be taken in some scientifically agreed-upon manner, precisely the same type of analysis would apply. Any fundamental cleavage in nature between the physical and the nonphysical is an artifact.

Tart/ Who Survives?

1. C. T. Tart, *Waking Up: Overcoming the Obstacles to Human Potential* (Boston: Shambhala, 1988).

2. C. T. Tart, *States of Consciousness* (El Cerrito, Calif.: Psychological Processes, 1983; originally published New York: Dutton, 1975).

3. P. Stafford, *Psychedelics Encyclopedia* (Los Angeles: Jeremy P. Tarcher, 1982).

Ring/Shamanic Initiation, Imaginal Worlds, and Light after Death

1. J. Neihardt, *Black Elk Speaks* (New York: Pocket Books, 1972).
2. H. Kalweit, *Dreamtime and the Inner Space* (Boston: Shambhala, 1988), p. 96.
3. B. Spencer and F. Gillen, *The Native Tribes of Central Australia* (New York: Dover, 1968).
4. Kalweit, *Dreamtime*, pp. 102–3.
5. M. Harner and G. Doore, "The Ancient Wisdom in Shamanic Cultures," in *Shamanism: An Alternate View of Reality*, ed. S. Nicholson (Wheaton, Ill.: Theosophical Publishing House, 1987), pp. 3–16; C. Zaleski, *Otherworld Journeys* (New York: Oxford University Press, 1987); Kalweit, *Dreamtime*.
6. K. Ring, "Near-Death and UFO Encounters as Shamanic Initiations," *ReVision*, in press.
7. A note of caution concerning these parallels is in order here. Specifically, by claiming that NDEers undergo a kind of shamanic initiation, I do *not* mean to imply that they are therefore fully realized shamans. *Au contraire*, they have simply received the *first* initiation; they have not "completed the course," which for a shaman-to-be in a traditional society often takes years of effort. Therefore, whereas NDEers may return with some shamanic skills and something of a shamanic orientation, it would be best to view them as shamans-in-training, still learning their craft.
8. Kalweit, *Dreamtime*, p. 12; my italics.
9. J. Hillman, *ReVisioning Psychology* (New York: Harper & Row, 1975); H. Corbin, *Mundus Imaginalis or the Imaginal and the Imaginary* (Ipswitch, England: Golgonooza Press, 1976; originally published in *Spring*, 1972); R. Avens, *Imagination Is Reality* (Dallas: Spring Publications, 1980); J. Achterberg, "The Shaman: Master Healer in the Imaginary Realm," M. Harner and G. Doore, "The Ancient Wisdom in Shamanic Cultures," J. Houston, "The Mind and Soul of Shamanism," and R. Noll, "The Presence of Spirits in Magic and Madness," in *Shamanism*, ed. Nicholson; C. Zaleski, *Otherworld Journeys* (New York: Oxford University Press, 1987); T. McKenna, "New Maps of Hyperspace," *Magical Blend*, April 1989, pp. 58–66; K. Ring, "Toward an Imaginal Interpretation of 'UFO Abductions,'" *MUFON UFO Journal*, in press.
10. Corbin, *Mundus Imaginalis*, p. 17; italics are Corbin's.
11. Ibid., p. 9.
12. Avens, *Imagination Is Reality*, p. 102.
13. Corbin, *Mundus Imaginalis*. p. 14; italics are Corbin's.
14. H. H. Price, in his justly famous article "Survival and the Idea of 'Another World,'" proposed an interpretation virtually identical to mine after having made a distinction equivalent to Corbin's between *imaginary* and *imagy*: "My suggestion is that the Next World, if there is one, might be a world of mental images. . . . The Next World, as I am trying to conceive of it, is an *imagy* world but not on that account an imaginary one" in J. R. Smythies (ed.), *Brain and Mind* (London: Routledge, 1965), pp. 4–5.
15. J. Whitton and J. Fisher, *Life between Life* (Garden City, N.Y.: Doubleday, 1986).
16. H. Kalweit, *Dreamtime*, pp. 66–67; my italics.
17. Blake's expression for Jesus Christ, it will be recalled, was "Jesus the Imagination."
18. McKenna, "New Maps of Hyperspace," pp. 58–66.
19. R. Bly, *The Kabir Book* (Boston: Beacon, 1977), pp. 24–25.

Mertz and Smith/Where Children Are Crying

1. M. Eliade, *Shamanism: Archaic Techniques of Ecstasy* (New York: Pantheon, 1964), p. 181.
2. Ibid., p. 88.

3. A. Hultkrantz, "Shamanism: A Religious Phenomenon?" in *Shaman's Path: Healing, Personal Growth, and Empowerment,* ed. G. Doore (Boston: Shambhala, 1988), pp. 33–42.
4. M. Harner, *The Way of the Shaman: A Guide to Power and Healing* (San Francisco: Harper & Row, 1980).

Grosso/Fear of Life after Death
1. J. Frazer, *The Belief in Immortality* (London: Macmillan, 1913), p. 468.
2. Ibid., p. 176.
3. F. T. Elsworthy, *The Evil Eye* (Secaucus, N.J.: University Books, 1895).
4. J. P. Sartre, *Being and Nothingness* (New York: Washington Square Press, 1966).
5. A. D. White, *A History of the Warfare of Science with Theology in Christendom* (Magnolia, Mass.: Peter Smith, 1965).
6. H. Thurston, *The Physical Phenomena of Mysticism* (London: Burns & Oates, 1953); R. Rogo, *Miracles* (New York: Dial Press, 1982).
7. A. Gauld, *Mediumship and Survival* (London: Heinemann, 1982).
8. R. Sheldrake, *A New Science of Life* (Los Angeles: J. P. Tarcher, 1981).
9. G. Vico, *Selected Writings,* ed. Leon Pompa (Cambridge: Cambridge University Press, 1982).
10. M. Grosso, "Padre Pio and Future Man," *Critique,* February 1989, pp. 26–34.
11. J. Steiner, *Therese Neumann* (New York: Washington Square Press, 1966).

Feinstein/Personal Mythologies of Death and Their Evolution
1. D. Feinstein and S. Krippner, *Personal Mythology: The Psychology of Your Evolving Self* (Los Angeles: J. P. Tarcher, 1988).
2. R. Woolger, *Other Lives, Other Selves: A Jungian Psychotherapist Discovers Past Lives* (New York: Doubleday, 1987).
3. I. Stevenson, *Children Who Remember Past Lives* (Charlottesville: University of Virginia Press, 1987).
4. R. K. Siegel, "The Psychology of Life after Death," *American Psychologist* 35 (1980), pp. 911–31.
5. Woolger, *Other Lives, Other Selves,* p. 43.
6. R. Moody, *The Light Beyond* (New York: Bantam, 1988), p. 85.
7. E. A. Rodin, "The Reality of Near-Death Experiences: A Personal Perspective," *Journal of Nervous and Mental Diseases* 168 (1980), pp. 259–63.
8. P. Shaver, "Consciousness without the Body" [review of *Flight of Mind: A Psychological Study of the Out-of-Body Experience* and *Heading toward Omega: In Search of the Meaning of the Near-Death Experience*], *Contemporary Psychology* 31 (1986), p. 647.
9. Siegel, "The Psychology of Life," p. 911.
10. D. Feinstein and P. Elliott Mayo, *Rituals for Living and Dying: A Guide to Spiritual Awakening* (San Francisco: Harper & Row, 1990).
11. R. J. Lifton, *The Broken Connection: On Death and the Continuity of Life* (New York: Basic Books, 1980).
12. S. Grof and C. Grof, *Beyond Death: The Gates of Consciousness* (New York: Thames & Hudson, 1980), p. 23.
13. Shaver, "Consciousness without the Body," p. 646.
14. G. Groth-Marnat and J. F. Schumaker, "The Near-Death Experience: A Review and Critique," *Journal of Humanistic Psychology* 29, no. 1 (1989), p. 118.
15. Moody, *The Light Beyond,* p. 27.

Doore/Journeys to the Land of the Dead
1. Quoted in A. Osborne, *Sri Ramana Maharshi and the Path of Self-Knowledge* (London: Rider, 1970).
2. Ibid.
3. See also G. Doore, "Shamans, Yogis, and Bodhisattvas," in *Shaman's Path: Healing, Personal Growth, and Empowerment*, ed. G. Doore (Boston: Shambhala, 1988).
4. See Doore, "Shamans, Yogis, and Bodhisattvas," p. 222.

Epilogue
1. In W. K. Clifford, *Lectures and Essays* (1879); reprinted in *Readings in the Philosophy of Religion*, ed. B. A. Brody (Englewood Cliffs, N.J.: Prentice-Hall, 1974), p. 246; italics added.
2. B. Russell, "A Free Man's Worship," in *Mysticism and Logic* (London: Allen & Unwin, 1917), pp. 47–48.
3. See G. Doore, "Religion within the Limits of the Quest for the Highest Good," *Religious Studies* 16 (1980).
4. See B. Mitchell, "Faith and Reason: A False Antithesis?" *Religious Studies* 16 (1980), p. 137; cf. T. S. Kuhn, *The Structure of Scientific Revolutions* (Chicago: University of Chicago Press, 1970).

New Consciousness Reader Series

Dreamtime and Dreamwork. The definitive book on the worldwide use of dreams as a special source of knowledge, dream interpretation, problem solving and healing through dreams, shared dreaming, lucid dreaming, forming dream groups, and new brain research. $12.95 Tradepaper, 272 pages

Healers on Healing. Reveals the common thread that unites healers from a wide range of approaches and techniques. Thirty-seven original essays by leading physicians, therapists, and writers in alternative and mainstream healthcare. Over 35,000 copies in print. $10.95 Tradepaper, 224 pages

Reclaiming the Inner Child. The best writing on the most current topic in psychology and recovery by the world's leading experts. Thirty-seven wide-ranging articles offer a comprehensive overview of the inner-child concept and its application to healing, creativity, and daily joy. Highlights many applications for people in all forms of recovery. $12.95 Tradepaper, 336 pages

Spiritual Emergency. Leading experts explore the relationship between spirituality, madness, and healing. Edited by Stan and Christina Grof, this ground-breaking work reveals that within the crisis of spiritual emergency lies the promise of spiritual emergence and renewal. $12.95 Tradepaper, 272 pages

To Be a Woman. A striking collection of original writing by the best-selling authorities in women's psychology. In twenty-three essays this book reveals the next stage of development in women's awareness: conscious femininity. For all women who long to feel strong, yet fully feminine. $12.95 Tradepaper, 288 pages

What Survives? This thought-provoking collection of twenty new essays examines emerging evidence and developments in the fields of parapsychology, near-death studies, consciousness research, new-paradigm biology, and physics, helping the reader to arrive at an optimistic, yet informed and rational, answer to the question "what survives the body after death?" $12.95 Tradepaper, 304 pages